100 Hikes in

NORTHWEST OREGON

William L. Sullivan

Navillus Press
Eugene

Suspension footbridge over Eagle Creek.

©1993 by William L. Sullivan; **revised and updated 1996**
Maps and photography by the author

Published by the Navillus Press
1958 Onyx Street
Eugene, Oregon 97403

Printed in USA on Envirotext, 100% recycled paper

Cover: Mt. Hood near McNeil Point, wild rose at Champoeg Park.
Spine: Punchbowl Falls. Back cover: Mt. St. Helens from Norway Pass.
Frontispiece: Fairy Falls.

SAFETY CONSIDERATIONS: Many of the trails in this book pass through Wilderness and remote country where hikers are exposed to unavoidable risks. On any hike, the weather may change suddenly. The fact that a hike is included in this book, or that it may be rated as easy, does not necessarily mean it will be safe or easy for you. Prepare yourself with proper equipment and outdoor skills, and you will be able to enjoy these hikes with confidence.

Every effort has been made to assure the accuracy of the information in this book. The author has hiked all 100 of the featured trails, and the trails' administrative agencies have reviewed the maps and text. Nonetheless, construction, logging, and storm damage may cause changes. Corrections and updates are welcome, and may be sent in care of the publisher.

Contents

Easy / Moderate / Difficult		Great for kids / Open all year / Backpackable*
	Introduction 7	
	PORTLAND AREA 12	
●	1. Warrior Rock 14	●●
●	2. Oak Island on Sauvie Island . . . 16	●
●●	3. Northern Forest Park 18	●
●●	4. Maple Trail 20	●
●●	5. Southern Forest Park 22	●
●●	6. Washington Park 24	●●
●	7. Council Crest 26	●
●	8. Oaks Bottom 28	●●
●	9. Tryon Creek Park 30	●●
●	10. Powell Butte 32	●●
●	11. Lacamas Park 34	●●
●	12. Oxbow Park 36	●●
●●	13. Champoeg Park 38	●●
●	14. Willamette Mission Park 40	●●
	SOUTHWEST WASHINGTON . . 42	
●	15. Silver Star Mountain 44	
●	16. Siouxon Creek 46	●●●
●	17. Mount Mitchell 48	
●	18. Sheep Canyon 50	●
●●	19. Ape Cave 52	●●
●●	20. Mount St Helens Rim 54	C
●	21. Ape Canyon 56	
●●	22. Lava Canyon 58	●
●●	23. Mount St Helens Crater . . . 60	
●●	24. Spirit Lake 62	●
●	25. Lewis River Falls 64	●●
●	26. Cultus Lake 66	●
●●	27. Junction Lake 68	● ●
●●	28. Thomas Lake 70	● ●
●●	29. Trapper Creek 72	●●
●	30. Three Corner Rock 74	
● ●	31. Beacon Rock Park 76	●●
●●	32. Gillette Lake 78	●●●
● ●	33. Grassy Knoll 80	
●●	34. Dog Mountain 82	●
●	35. Catherine Creek 84	●●
	COLUMBIA GORGE 86	
●	36. Larch Mountain Crater 88	
●	37. Latourell Falls 90	●●

*C – Crowded or restricted backpacking area

3

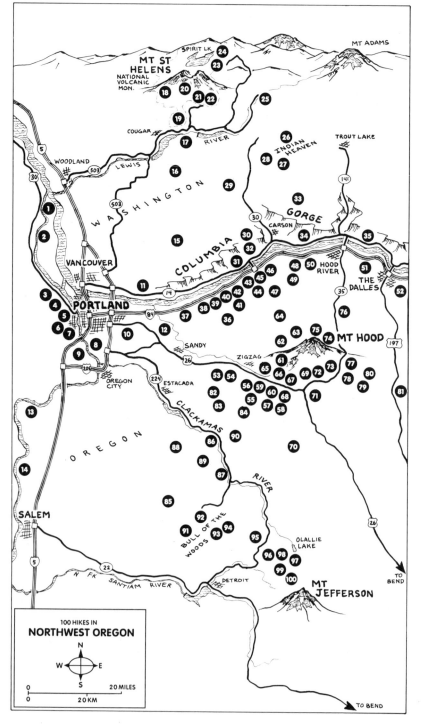

100 HIKES IN
NORTHWEST OREGON

N
W E
S

0   20 MILES

0   20 KM

Easy	Moderate	Difficult			Great for kids	Open all year	Backpackable*
	●		38. Angels Rest	92	●		
	●		39. Multnomah and Wahkeena Falls	94	●		
●			40. Oneonta and Horsetail Falls	96	●	●	
		●	41. Nesmith Point	98			
●			42. Wahclella and Elowah Falls	100	●	●	
●	●	●	43. Wauna Point	102		●	●
●	●	●	44. Eagle Creek	104		●	● c
		●	45. Ruckel Creek	106			
●	●	●	46. Herman Creek	108		●	●
●			47. Wahtum Lake	110			c
●		●	48. Mount Defiance North	112		●	●
●	●		49. Mount Defiance South	114			●
●	●		50. Wygant Trail	116			
●	●		51. Tom McCall Preserve	118	●	●	
●	●		52. Lower Deschutes River	120	●	●	●
			MOUNT HOOD - WEST	122			
	●		53. Wildcat Mountain	124			
		●	54. Huckleberry Mountain	126			
		●	55. Salmon Butte	128			
●			56. Lower Salmon River	130	●	●	
●	●		57. Central Salmon River	132	●	●	c
		●	58. Upper Salmon River	134			●
	●	●	59. Hunchback Mountain	136			
●		●	60. Devils Peak Lookout	138			
●	●	●	61. Ramona Falls	140	●		c
●	●		62. McNeil Point	142			c
●	●		63. Cairn Basin	144			c
●	●		64. Lost Lake	146	●		
●		●	65. West Zigzag Mountain	148		●	
	●	●	66. East Zigzag Mountain	150			c
●			67. Laurel Hill	152			
●	●		68. Mirror Lake	154	●		c
●	●	●	69. Timberline Lodge Trails	156	●		c
●		●	70. Timothy Lake	158	●		●
			MOUNT HOOD - EAST	160			
●	●		71. Twin Lakes	162	●		c
	●	●	72. Elk Meadows	164			c
●	●		73. Tamanawas Falls	166	●		
	●	●	74. Cooper Spur	168			
●	●		75. Elk Cove	170	●		c
		●	76. Bald Butte	172			
●	●		77. Lookout Mountain	174			●
		●	78. Badger Lake	176			●

*C – Crowded or restricted backpacking area

Easy / Moderate / Difficult				Great for kids / Open all year / Backpackable*		
●●			79. Badger Creek 178	●●		●
	●		80. Ball Point 180			●
●			81. Tygh Valley Falls 182	●●		
			CLACKAMAS FOOTHILLS . . . 184			
	●		82. Eagle Creek 186	●●		
	●		83. Old Baldy 188			
●		●	84. Sheepshead Rock 190			
●●			85. Table Rock 192			
	●		86. Clackamas River Trail 194	●●		
●			87. Riverside Trail 196	●●		●
●●			88. Memaloose Lake 198	●	C	
	●		89. Fish Creek Mountain 200			●
●●			90. Rock Lakes 202	●		●
	●		91. Whetstone Mountain 204			
●			92. Bagby Hot Springs 206	●●	C	
●●			93. Pansy Lake 208	●	C	
	●●		94. Dickey Creek 210			●
	●		95. Hawk Mountain 212			
●●			96. Red Lake 214			●
●			97. Monon Lake 216	●		●
●●			98. Top Lake 218	●		●
	●		99. Ruddy Hill 220	●		
●●●			100. Jefferson Park Ridge 222		C	
			All-Accessible Trails in NW Oregon 224			
			100 More Hikes in NW Oregon . . 226			
			Index 235			
			About the Author 240			

*C — Crowded or restricted backpacking area

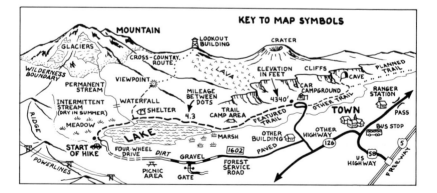

KEY TO MAP SYMBOLS

Introduction

Where else but in Northwest Oregon could hikers have so many great options within a 2-hour drive? This guide covers more than just the well-known trails of the Portland area, Columbia Gorge, and Mt. Hood. You'll discover a path to a free Willamette River ferry, a historic cabin overlooking Mt. Jefferson, and a natural rock arch near Hood River. Forty-one of the trips are open even in winter. And because some of the area's newest trails are just north of the Columbia, there's comprehensive coverage of Mt. St. Helens National Volcanic Monument and the Indian Heaven Wilderness, too.

This guide book features several difficulty levels. Hikers with children will find 46 hikes carefully chosen for them. As a parent of 2 pre-teens, I understand how enthused children become about splashing creeks and how curiously uninspired they seem by steep trails. On the other hand, a quarter of the hikes included are unabashedly difficult. Nearly half of the trails are rated as suitable for backpackers as well as day hikers. At the back of the book you'll find a list of 21 all-accessible trails suitable for strollers and wheelchairs. And if you really want to get away from it all, there's an appendix describing 100 *more* hikes in Northwest Oregon — little-known but interesting trails for adventurous spirits.

HOW TO USE THIS BOOK

It's Easy to Choose a Trip

The featured hikes are divided into 6 regions, from the Clackamas Foothills to Southwest Washington. To choose a trip, simply turn to the area that interests you and look for the following symbols in the upper right-hand corner of each hike's heading. Whether you're hiking with children, backpacking, or looking for a snow-free winter trail, you'll quickly find an outing to match your tastes.

 Children's favorites — walks popular with the 4- to 12-year-old crowd, but fun for hikers of all ages.

 All-year trails, hikable most or all of winter.

 Hikes suitable for backpackers as well as day hikers. Crowds unlikely.

 Crowded or restricted backpacking areas. Expect competition for campsites, especially on summer weekends.

The Information Blocks

Each hike is rated by difficulty. **Easy** hikes are between 2 and 7 miles round-trip and gain less than 1000 feet in elevation. Never very steep nor particularly remote, they make good warm-up trips for experienced hikers or first-time trips for novices.

Trips rated as **Moderate** range from 4 to 11 miles round-trip. The longer hikes in this category are not steep, but shorter trails may gain up to 2300 feet of elevation — or they may require some pathfinding skills. Hikers must be in good condition and will need to take several rest stops.

Difficult trails demand top physical condition, with a strong heart and strong knees. These challenging hikes are 8 to 15 miles round-trip and may gain 4000 feet or more.

Distances are given in round-trip mileage, except for those trails where a car or bicycle shuttle is so convenient that the suggested hike is one-way only, and is listed as such.

Elevation gains tell much about the difficulty of a hike. Those who puff climbing a few flights of stairs may consider even 500 feet of elevation a strenuous climb, and should watch this listing carefully. Note that the figures are for each hike's *cumulative* elevation gain, adding all the uphill portions, even those on the return trip.

The **hiking season** of any trail varies with the weather. In a cold year, a trail described as "Open May through October" may not yet be clear of snow by May 1, and may be socked in by a blizzard before October 31. Similarly, a trail that is "Open all year" may close due to storms.

All hikers should carry a topographic **map,** with contour lines to show elevation. Maps listed as "USFS" are available from U.S. Forest Service offices for a dollar or two. Those tagged "USGS," published by the U.S. Geological Survey, can be found at many outdoor stores. The slightly more expensive Green Trails and Geo-Graphics maps are available at most outdoors stores and at some bookstores. In addition, it pays to pick up a Mt. Hood National Forest Visitor Map (for the south side of the Columbia) or a Gifford Pinchot National Forest Map (for the north) at a ranger station.

WILDERNESS RESTRICTIONS

Certain restrictions apply to designated Wilderness Areas, and affect 41 of the hikes featured in this guide:

- Groups must be no larger than 12.
- Campfires are banned within 100 feet of any water source or maintained trail.
- No one may enter areas posted as closed for rehabilitation.
- Bicycles and other wheeled vehicles (except wheelchairs) are banned.
- Horses and pack stock cannot be tethered within 200 feet of any water source or shelter.
- Motorized equipment and fireworks are banned.
- Live trees and shrubs must not be cut or damaged.

In addition, some rules apply to all federal lands:

- Collecting arrowheads or other cultural artifacts is a federal crime.
- Permits are required to dig up plants.

SAFETY ON THE TRAIL

Wild Animals

Part of the fun of hiking is watching for wildlife. Lovers of wildness rue the demise of our most impressive species. Wolves and grizzly bears are extinct in

Mt. Jefferson from Olallie Lake (Hike #97).

Oregon. The little black bears that remain are so profoundly shy you probably won't see one in 1000 miles of hiking. In this portion of Oregon, the only reason for backpackers to hang their food from a tree at night is to protect it from ground squirrels. Likewise, our rattlesnakes are genuinely rare and shy — and they never were as venomous as the Southwest's famous rattlers.

Ticks have received some publicity as carriers of Lyme disease, which begins with flu-like symptoms and an often circular rash. While this is a problem in the Eastern states, only a couple of cases have been reported in Oregon. Nonetheless, brush off your clothes and check your collar and cuffs after walking through dry grass or brush.

Mosquitoes can be a nuisance on hikes in the High Cascades, particularly in the Olallie Lake and Indian Heaven areas. To avoid these insects, remember that they hatch about 10 days after the snow melts from the trails and that they remain in force 3 or 4 weeks. Thus, if a given trail in the High Cascades is listed as "Open mid-June," expect mosquitoes there most of July.

Drinking Water

Day hikers should bring all the water they will need — roughly a quart per person. A microscopic paramecium, *Giardia,* has forever changed the old custom of dipping a drink from every brook. The symptoms of "beaver fever," debilitating nausea and diarrhea, commence a week or 2 after ingesting *Giardia.*

If you love fresh water and are willing to gamble, consider that the paramecium is spread only by mammals, enters the water by defecation, and moves only downstream. As a result, gushing springs and runoff immediately below snowfields are less dangerous. If you're backpacking, bring an approved water filter or purification tablet, or boil your water 5 minutes.

Proper Equipment

Even on the tamest hike a surprise storm or a wrong turn can suddenly make the gear you carry very important. Always bring a pack with the 10 essentials:

1. Warm, water-repellent coat (or parka and extra shirt)
2. Drinking water
3. Extra food
4. Knife
5. Matches in waterproof container
6. Fire starter (butane lighter or candle)
7. First aid kit
8. Flashlight
9. Map (topographic, if possible)
10. Compass

Before leaving on a hike, tell someone where you are going so they can alert the county sheriff to begin a search if you do not return on time. If you're lost, stay put and keep warm. The number one killer in the woods is *hypothermia* — being cold and wet too long.

COURTESY ON THE TRAIL

As our trails become more heavily used, rules of trail etiquette become stricter. Please:

- Pick no flowers.
- Leave no litter. Eggshells and orange peels can last for decades.
- Do not bring pets into wilderness areas. Dogs can frighten wildlife and disturb other hikers.
- Step off the trail on the downhill side to let horses pass. Speak to them quietly to help keep them from spooking.
- Do not shortcut switchbacks.

For backpackers, low-impact camping was once merely a courtesy, but is on the verge of becoming a requirement, both to protect the landscape and to preserve a sense of solitude for others. The most important rules:

- Camp out of sight of lakes and trails.
- Build no campfire. Cook on a backpacking stove.
- Wash 100 feet from any lake or stream.
- Camp on duff, rock, or sand — never on meadow vegetation.
- Pack out garbage — don't burn or bury it.

GROUPS TO HIKE WITH

If you enjoy the camaraderie of hiking with a group, contact one of the organizations that leads trips to the trails in this book. None of the groups requires that you be a member to join scheduled hikes, and when trip fees are charged they're usually just a dollar. Hikers generally carpool from a preset meeting place. If you have no car, expect to chip in about 5 cents a mile.

Chemeketans. Three to 10 hikes a week. Cabin near Mt. Jefferson, meetings at 360½ State St., Salem. Founded 1927. Write P.O. Box 864, Salem, OR 97308.

Lake Oswego Recreation Department. Thursday hikes carpool from Lake Oswego. Call (503) 636-9673.

Mazamas. Three to 10 hikes a week. Cabin at Mt. Hood, office and meetings at 909 NW 19th Ave., Portland, OR 97209. Founded 1894. Call (503) 227-2345.

Portland Park Bureau. Saturday hikes in Forest Park for $2 fee. Wednesday "Tot Walks" in Portland area for $3 fee. Call (503) 796-5132.

Ptarmigan Mountaineering Club. Weekly hikes. Meetings at Vancouver First Presbyterian Church. Founded 1960. Write P.O. Box 1821, Vancouver, WA 98668.

Sierra Club Columbia Group. Weekly hikes except in winter. Meetings at 1413 SE Hawthorne Blvd., Portland, OR 97214. Call (503) 231-0507.

Trails Club of Oregon. Hikes on Saturdays and Sundays. Cabins at Mt. Hood and Columbia Gorge. Founded 1915. Write P.O. Box 1243, Portland, OR 97207.

Tryon Creek Day Trippers. Weekly hikes except in winter. Carpool from Tryon Cr. Park, 11321 SW Terwilliger Blvd., Portland, OR 97219; (503) 636-4398.

FOR MORE INFORMATION

All major Forest Service offices in the area collect reports of trail conditions in TRIS, a computerized trail information system available to the public. By typing a trail's name or number into a computer terminal at a Forest Service office, you can theoretically access updated information on snow levels, trail maintenance, and new construction. Unfortunately, the information is often sketchy or out of date. Nonetheless, it's a promising beginning, with the laudable goal of eventually cataloguing every trail on public land in the state.

If you'd like to check on a trail, and if TRIS is inconvenient for you, call directly to the trail's administrative agency. These agencies are listed below, along with the hikes in this book for which they manage trails.

Hike	Managing Agency
77-80	Barlow Ranger District — (541) 467-2291
70, 71	Bear Springs Ranger District — (541) 328-6211
53, 85	BLM Salem District — (503) 375-5646
11	Clark County Parks.— (206) 699-2467
34-36, 39-49	Columbia Gorge Nat'l. Scenic Area — (541) 386-2333
83, 86-100	Estacada Ranger District — (503) 630-6861
63, 64, 72-76	Hood River Ranger District — (541) 352-6002
26-28	Mt. Adams Ranger District — (509) 395-2501
18-25	Mt. St. Helens Nat'l. Vol. Mon. — (206) 247-5472
12	Multnomah County Parks — (503) 248-5050
1, 2	Oregon Dept. of Fish and Wildlife — (503) 229-5403
9, 13, 14, 37, 38, 41, 42, 50, 52, 81	Oregon State Parks — (503) 378-6829
3-8, 10	Portland Park Bureau — (503) 796-5193
51	The Nature Conservancy — (503) 228-9561
15, 17, 30, 32	Wash. Dept. of Natural Resources — (800) 527-3305
31	Washington State Parks — (206) 753-5755
15, 16, 29, 33	Wind River Ranger District — (509) 427-5645
53-62, 65-69, 82, 84	Zigzag Ranger District — (503) 622-7674

Portland
Area

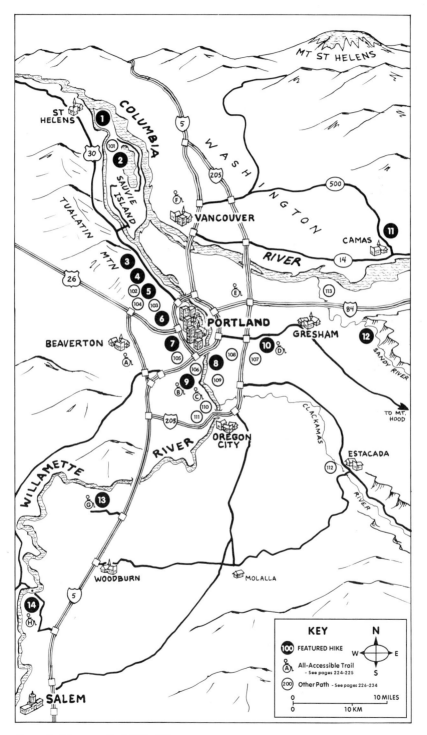

Opposite: Marquam Trail (Hike #7).

1   Warrior Rock

Easy
7 miles round-trip
No elevation gain
Open all year
Map: St. Helens (USGS)

At the tip of Oregon's largest Island, this woodsy hike along the Columbia River leads to a miniature lighthouse and a secluded, sandy beach. Because the route is within the Sauvie Island Wildlife Area, you can expect to spot great blue herons, geese, or even a bald eagle — particularly in winter. It's also fun to watch ocean-going freighters steam past, and at the end of the island there's a view across to the picturesque old town of St. Helens.

Sauvie Island was once the winter home of the Multnomah Indians, who subsisted mainly on fish and on the potato-like roots of the water-loving wapato (arrowhead plant) — a staple they shared with Lewis and Clark in 1805. In the 1830s a French-Canadian named Laurent Sauve converted much of the island to a dairy farm to supply Fort Vancouver. The southern end of the island was diked against floods in 1941 and now produces an enormous variety of vegetable and berry crops. The northern part of Sauvie Island is managed for wildlife and recreation. Overnight camping and unleashed dogs are prohibited.

To reach the starting point of the hike, drive north of downtown Portland on Highway 30 toward St. Helens. After about 10 miles, turn right across the Sauvie Island Bridge and head north along Sauvie Island Road toward Sam's Grocery. You can stop here to get a Sauvie Island Wildlife Area parking permit (cost: $2.50 a day or $10 a year). Permits are also available at many outdoor stores and at the Oregon Department of Fish and Wildlife in Portland. Equipped with a permit, drive 1.8 miles past the store on Sauvie Island Road, turn right onto Reeder Road, and follow this road for 12.6 miles to its end at a turnaround with a parking area and an outhouse. The final 2.2 miles of Reeder Road are gravel.

Climb over the parking lot fence at the stile and walk cross-country across a cow pasture to the beach. Sharp eyes will already be able to spot the lighthouse 3 miles ahead. The main hiking route to that goal is an old dirt service road that begins at the far end of the pasture and follows the shore. However, it's pleasant to start out walking along the beach itself for half a mile or so. When the sand narrows, climb up to the road and continue.

Tennis shoes will suffice in summer on this road, but other seasons call for boots, since cows share the road and trammel portions of it to mud in wet weather. Tall cottonwood trees and August-ripening wild blackberries line the route. Further on, the forest shifts to ash trees with licorice ferns sprouting from the mossy branches.

After 2.8 miles the road fades in a meadow and forks. Keep right to find the road leading 0.2 mile through the woods to a small rocky headland. The lighthouse here is private, but the white-sand beach beside it makes an ideal lunch spot. To find the hidden viewpoint of the town of St. Helens, hike to the end of the beach and follow a trail 200 yards across the tip of Sauvie Island.

Other Hiking Options

Hikers who wish to return on a slightly different route can follow a branch of the dirt road back from the viewpoint. Further toward the car, explorers may also want to try several unmarked side trails veering off to the right. These cow paths lead to lakes replete with geese, ducks, and many other birds — but beware of stinging nettles along the way.

Trail along the Columbia River.   Opposite: Pilings at the tip of Sauvie Island.

Oak Island and Sturgeon Lake.   Opposite: Teasels.

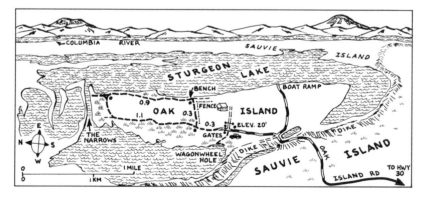

2   Oak Island on Sauvie Island

Easy
2.9-mile loop
No elevation gain
Open mid-January to mid-October
Map: Sauvie Island (USGS)

This walk explores an island on an island: an unusually wildlife-rich oak grassland in the middle of Sauvie Island's Sturgeon Lake. Over 250 species of birds visit this portion of the Sauvie Island Wildlife Area, including huge flocks of geese, ducks, and sandhill cranes during the spring and fall migrations. At any time of year it's pleasant to stroll beneath the huge, gnarled white oaks and look across the lake to the pale outlines of Mt. St. Helens and Mt. Adams.

From downtown Portland take Highway 30 toward the town of St. Helens, but after 10 miles turn right across the Sauvie Island Bridge. Head north along Sauvie Island Road past a small grocery store. If you don't have a Sauvie Island Wildlife Area parking permit, stop at the store to get one. Permits are $2.50 a day or $10 a year; they're also available at many outdoor stores and at the Oregon Department of Fish and Wildlife in Portland. Continue driving 1.8 miles past the store on Sauvie Island Road, turn right onto Reeder Road for 1.2 miles, and turn left onto Oak Island Road. After 2.7 miles cross a dike. Ignore a right-hand fork to a boat ramp and continue straight 0.4 mile to a parking area where the road is closed. Overnight camping and unleashed dogs are prohibited.

Start by walking along the abandoned road through oak woods. Wild roses bloom here in early summer. Look for squirrels and listen for pheasants' squawks. After 0.3 mile the road-like path forks at a broad meadow with a view of the Tualatin Mountains. Go straight across the field.

In another 1.1 miles the trail forks again at the beachless, somewhat brushy edge of Sturgeon Lake, with Mt. St. Helens seemingly just across the water. The left-hand fork (blocked by high water in rainy months) leads 200 yards to The Narrows, a neck of Sturgeon Lake edged with picnickably grassy banks. Expect to spot a stilt-legged great blue heron patrolling these shores for frogs and fish.

To continue the loop hike, return to the junction and take the path paralleling the lakeshore. After 0.9 mile watch for a faint fork in a small, grassy opening. Turn right here and head uphill past a bench, a memorial plaque, and a fenceline for 0.3 mile to return to the path leading to your car.

Other Hiking Options

Children will enjoy spotting wildlife on Oak Island, but they might be disappointed by the shortage of good places to get right down by the lake. If so, point them to the little gate at the parking area; a trail here leads 300 yards to Wagonwheel Hole and an accessible, grassy lakeshore ideal for exploring.

The Wildwood Trail in northern Forest Park.   Below: Trail sign.

3   Northern Forest Park

Easy (to Springville Rd)
4.6-mile loop
300 feet elevation gain
Open all year
Map: Forest Park (Portland Parks & Rec.)

Moderate (to Gas Line Rd)
8.3-mile loop
400 feet elevation gain

Forest Park is Portland's wilderness secret, with 4800 acres of soothing woodlands draped along a scenic ridge above the Willamette River. The nearly level loop hikes suggested here explore one of the quietest parts of the park. The hikes start on the famous Wildwood Trail, contour along steep hillsides, and return along Leif Erikson Drive, an old road closed to motorized vehicles.

From Interstate 5, take the Lombard Street exit (#305) in North Portland, drive west until you cross the St. Johns Bridge, turn right for 0.3 mile, and then turn left onto NW Germantown Road. Drive 1.5 miles up this road to a gravel parking lot on the left with a small sign: "Wildwood Trail, Pedestrians Only." If you're driving here from the west (Washington County), look for the trailhead half a mile past Germantown Road's intersection with Skyline Boulevard.

The Wildwood Trail sets out through a Douglas fir forest full of woodland flowers. April brings yellow violets and white, three-petaled trilliums. May adds stalks of fringecups and paired, white fairy bells. Pink salmonberries, red thimbleberries, and blue Oregon grape ripen as the summer progresses. The dense forest precludes any wide-ranging views, but then you won't see any buildings or automobiles on this hike either. The only evidence you're in a metropolis are occasional clangs and toots from the river docks far below.

Because your return route, Leif Erikson Drive, runs parallel to the Wildwood Trail but about a quarter mile downhill, you can cut over to it on a number of different cross-trails to make the loop hike as short or long as you wish. Your first option comes after just 0.6 mile, when you cross the Water Line Trail. Turning left here makes a 2.3-mile loop, but then you'd miss the best part of the Wildwood Trail, where it dips into shady canyons to cross creeklets amidst masses of trilliums and maidenhair ferns. So continue on the Wildwood Trail at least to Springville Road, a woodsy path closed to vehicles. To make a 4.6-mile loop, turn left here for 0.4 mile, then turn left onto Leif Erikson Drive for 1.7 miles, and finally walk up Germantown road 600 yards to your car.

If you're still going strong when you reach Springville Road, cross it and continue on the Wildwood Trail. To make a 5.6-mile loop, turn left at the Hardesty Trail junction; if, however, you're interested in an 8.3-mile loop, wait to turn off the Wildwood Trail until you reach the Gas Line Road, a marked trail running down the end of a ridge. Follow this old, grassy roadbed 200 yards downhill; just before it gets steep, look for a small path to the left that switchbacks through the woods to Leif Erikson Drive. Then head left on this rustic forest lane to return to Germantown Road.

Other Hiking Options

With a car shuttle you can hike longer sections of the Wildwood Trail one way. From Germantown Road, it's 10 miles to the Saltzman Road trailhead via the Maple Trail (see Hike #4), 18 miles to the Thurman Road Trailhead (see Hike #5), and 24.6 miles to the Vietnam Veteran Memorial by the zoo (see Hike #6).

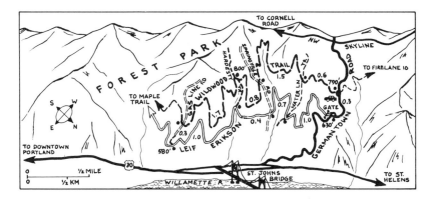

4   Maple Trail

Easy (to Leif Erikson)
4 miles round-trip
350 feet elevation gain
Open all year
Map: Forest Park (Portland Parks & Rec.)

Moderate (to Wildwood Trail)
7.7-mile loop
500 feet elevation gain

In the middle of Portland's vast Forest Park, the surprisingly quiet Maple Trail passes a viewpoint of Cascade peaks and explores grotto-like canyons where mossy bigleaf maples arch above delicate woodland wildflowers. For an easy hike, turn back where the Maple Trail crosses Leif Erikson Drive. For a longer loop hike, continue up to the Wildwood Trail and follow this almost level path as it contours around densely forested ridges back to the start of the Maple Trail.

Drive north of downtown Portland on Highway 30 toward St. Helens. A little past the 5-mile marker — and immediately after the "DEQ Test Center" sign — turn left onto NW Saltzman Road. Drive 0.8 mile to a gate closing the road. Parking space is tight, but don't block the gate.

Start the hike by walking 0.4 mile up the wide, paved road to a small "Maple Trail" sign on the left. Turn left onto this path, climbing through a forest of bigleaf maples, sword ferns, and western hemlock.

Two kinds of triple-leaved, white wildflowers thrive here: trilliums and vanilla leaf. It's easy to tell the difference in spring when they bloom, since trilliums have a dramatic, three-petaled flower while vanilla leaf puts up a modest, fuzzy stalk. By summer, however, the plants are best distinguished by their three big leaves: teardrop-shaped for trilliums but butterfly-wing-shaped for vanilla leaf. Forest Park's ban on flower picking is particularly important for trilliums, as they require 7 years to bloom again once cut.

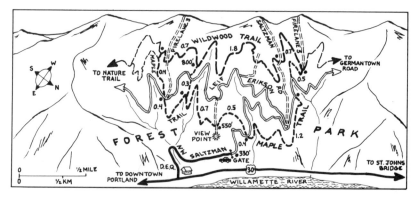

After half a mile, the trail crosses under powerlines on an open ridgetop. At this point, sidetrack left 150 yards to a viewpoint on the powerline's grassy service road. The vista extends across the Willamette River shipyards and the Fremont Bridge to East Portland, the Columbia River, Mt. Adams, and Mt. Hood.

Returning to the Maple Trail, the path now zigs and zags into mossy canyons with footbridges over little creeks. After 1.1 mile, reach Leif Erikson Drive — an old road closed to motor vehicles. Turn back here if you're tired. If you're interested in a longer loop, however, cross Leif Erikson and continue up the Maple Trail, avoiding the road marked "Firelane 3". After 0.4 mile turn right at a junction, and 150 yards later turn right again onto the Wildwood Trail. Follow this nearly level trail a total of 3.2 miles, crossing a couple of abandoned roads, several small creeks, and a few sets of powerlines. Mile markers on trailside trees measure the distance from the start of the Wildwood Trail in Washington Park. Just before reaching the "16-1/2" marker, come to a ridge end with a sign indicating Firelane 5 uphill to the left. At this junction *take an unmarked trail downhill to the right*. This path leads 0.3 mile down to Leif Erikson Drive.

Head right on Leif Erikson for 300 yards. At the road's first curve, cross a grassy flat on the left to a sign marking the Maple Trail. Follow the Maple Trail 1.2 miles back to Saltzman Road and turn left for 0.4 mile to your car.

Other Hiking Options

The Wildwood Trail continues in either direction from the Maple Trail, so you can hike one-way to a different trailhead by arranging a shuttle. The hike north to the trailhead at Germantown Road is 10 miles (see Hike #3), while it's 8.9 miles south to Thurman Street (see Hike #5) and 15.9 miles south to the Vietnam Veteran Memorial by the zoo (see Hike #6).

Maple Trail. Opposite: Maidenhair fern.

5   Southern Forest Park

Easy (to Alder Trail)
4.7-mile loop
400 feet elevation gain
Open all year
Map: Forest Park (Portland Parks & Rec.)

Moderate (to Nature Trail)
8.6-mile loop
700 feet elevation gain

This convenient portion of Portland's 4800-acre wilderness park is just a few minutes from skyscrapers, but a world apart. The hiking loops suggested here start by climbing to the Wildwood Trail and return via Leif Erikson Drive, a forest lane closed to motor vehicles. Because the Wildwood Trail and Leif Erikson parallel each other along these forested hillsides, the length of your hiking loop depends on which cross trail you choose between them. The 8.6-mile circuit via the Nature Trail is particularly tempting because it passes a secluded picnic shelter, scenic Rockingchair Creek, and a viewpoint of the mountains.

Preservation of Forest Park was originally proposed by the Olmsteads, a visionary New York landscape architect team hired to help Portland prepare for the grandiose Lewis and Clark Exposition of 1905. But most Portlanders of that day had seen more than their fill of forests. The city opened a woodcutting camp in the area to help the unemployed, and developers built the 11-mile Leif Erikson Drive in 1915 as part of a plan to subdivide and conquer the wilds. Fires, landslides, and the Depression finally defeated the realtors' schemes. In 1946 the Mazamas hiking club began planting trees and building trails in a campaign to revive the Olmsteads' plan. Forest Park was dedicated in 1948 — not merely as another manicured garden, but as a refreshing swath of wilderness in the city.

To reach this hike's trailhead from downtown, take Highway 30 toward St. Helens and promptly take the Vaughn Street exit. Turn left on 25th Avenue for

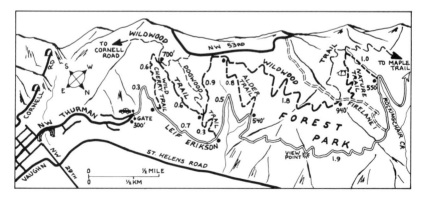

Nature Trail shelter.   Opposite: Fringecup.

two blocks, and then turn right on Thurman Street for 1.1 miles. At a switchback to the left, go straight 100 yards to a parking area and a gate blocking the start of Leif Erikson. If you're driving here from Washington County, take Cornell Road to 25th Avenue, turn left 8 blocks, and turn left on Thurman for 1.1 miles.

Start by walking along Leif Erikson 0.3 mile before turning uphill onto the well-marked Wild Cherry Trail on the left. Here the whitewater-like roar of the city below finally begins to fade. Douglas firs and maples form a canopy above bold clumps of sword ferns, spiny-leaved Oregon grape, and spring wildflowers: trillium, fairy bells, and candyflower.

Turn right at the junction with the Wildwood Trail. If you only have time for an hour's walk, it's possible to follow the Wildwood Trail just 0.6 mile, turn right onto the Dogwood Trail, descend a ridge to Leif Erikson, and walk back to your car for a 2.8-mile loop. If you're in for a longer hike, however, continue north along the Wildwood Trail. After briefly approaching NW 53rd Drive, you'll reach the Alder Trail junction and face another choice. Either you can descend on the Alder Trail and return to your car via Leif Erikson for a 4.7-mile loop, or you can hike further on the Wildwood Trail.

Let's assume you've got plenty of energy and march on. The Wildwood Trail contours along the hillside, zigging in to little canyons and zagging out to little ridges. After 1.8 mile, turn right on Firelane 1 for 150 yards and then fork left onto the Nature Trail. After passing a shelter with several picnic tables, the Nature Trail turns right at a trail junction and descends along Rockingchair Creek. At trail's end turn right onto Leif Erikson Drive — a 3.4-mile promenade with occasional views across the Willamette River to the shipyards, the University of Portland campus, Mt. St. Helens, Mt. Adams, and Mt. Hood.

6 Washington Park

Easy (to Hoyt Arboretum)
3.6-mile loop
500 feet elevation gain
Open all year
Map: Forest Park (Portland Parks & Rec.)

Moderate (to Pittock Mansion)
7-mile loop
800 feet elevation gain

The walk through Washington Park is a reminder of what's so wonderful about Portland. What other city would have a forest path leading from a world-class zoo, past a Japanese garden, to a mansion with a mountain view?

This first portion of the famous, 27-mile Wildwood Trail begins at the Vietnam Veteran Memorial. To get there, either take the Washington Park Tri-Met bus (#63) to the end of the line, or else drive west from Portland on Highway 26 toward Beaverton. If you're driving, take the zoo exit and continue beyond the zoo's huge parking area to a smaller lot on the right for the memorial.

The beginning of the Wildwood Trail is directly across the road from this parking lot. But it's much more dramatic — and not much longer — to start by walking under the white footbridge of the Vietnam Veteran Memorial. The memorial's path spirals before launching you upward onto the Wildwood Trail. From here on, expect signed trail junctions every few hundred yards; just keep an eye out for the Wildwood Trail signs. Within 0.4 mile you'll cross a paved road and pass a huge green water tank to a viewpoint of Mt. St. Helens and Mt. Rainier. Even if the weather hides these distant peaks, you'll still be able to spot a potential goal of your hike: the Pittock Mansion, atop a forested ridge.

After 1.7 miles on the Wildwood Trail you'll get a glimpse down through the forest to the Oriental bridges and manicured greenery of the Japanese Garden. Shortly afterward, a side trail switchbacks down to the right. If you've time, it's

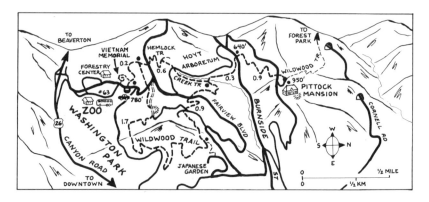

The Wildwood Trail in Washington Park.   Opposite: The Pittock mansion.

tempting to detour here to visit this acclaimed, 6.5-acre garden, complete with Japanese pavilion and a Portland panorama. Otherwise continue on the Wildwood Trail, which now climbs, crossing several paved roads and a ridgecrest before descending into the Hoyt Arboretum.

Arboretum means "tree museum," and in fact this entire valley is filled with native and exotic trees. You'll switchback down through ponderosa pines reminiscent of Central Oregon and then traverse an impressive grove of coastal redwoods and giant sequoias. Finally you'll reach a footbridge over a creek. If you're tired or if you're hiking with children, turn left onto the Creek Trail here to complete the shorter, 3.6-mile loop. In this case, follow the Creek Trail across a paved road, turn left onto the Hemlock Trail, and take that path over the ridge (crossing Fairview Boulevard) back to the Vietnam Veteran Memorial.

If, however, you've got enough energy for a 7-mile hike, continue on the Wildwood Trail through the Hoyt Arboretum. Soon the path crosses Burnside Street — a busy, fairly frightening highway you'll have to cross at a run. Then the trail climbs 0.9 mile through a Douglas fir forest, crosses a paved road, and reaches the Pittock Mansion parking lot. Walk through the portico on the left side of the mansion to the spacious front lawn where there's a magnificent view of downtown Portland and the mountains.

The 16,000-square-foot palace was built in 1909-14 by banker, real estate magnate, and *Oregonian* editor Henry L. Pittock. For its day, the mansion was astonishingly modern, with an elevator, intercom, and central vacuum cleaning. Tours are available daily between 1pm and 5pm (adults $3, children $1).

To complete your hike, go back on the Wildwood Trail to the Hoyt Arboretum footbridge, turn right onto the Creek Trail until it hits the Hemlock Trail, and then follow this path left, over the ridge to the Vietnam Veteran Memorial. At the end of your hike you might want to visit the nearby World Forestry Center, a museum with a 50-foot talking tree and exhibits about firefighting and tree products.

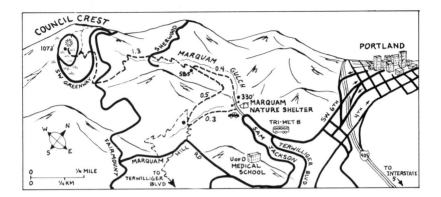

7   Council Crest

Easy
3.8-mile loop
700 feet elevation gain
Open all year
Map: Portland street map

Just a few blocks from downtown Portland, the path through Marquam Nature Park climbs a remarkably unspoiled forest canyon to Council Crest, a historic viewpoint of 5 Cascade peaks. The highest point in the City of Portland, Council Crest was named in 1898 by a gathering of church council picnickers. By 1904 the hilltop was converted to an amusement park, complete with roller coaster, observation tower, and landlocked riverboat. An electric streetcar brought excursionists up from the city in style. The carnival was gone by 1942 when a huge water tank was built here. But picnickers still love this grassy crest.

The easiest way to find the trailhead is to walk here; it's only a half-hour stroll from City Hall. Walk south on SW 6th Avenue until it turns into Terwilliger Boulevard. A long block later, keep right onto Sam Jackson Drive for 0.2 mile to a hairpin curve. Here turn right on gravel Marquam Road to a large, pyramidal shelter at the trailhead. It's also easy to arrive by Tri-Met, since the #8 Jackson Park bus stops at the corner of Terwilliger Boulevard and Sam Jackson Drive.

Car access is a bit more confusing due to the concrete spaghetti of off-ramps at the intersection of I-5 and I-405. Take an exit for the Ross Island Bridge and follow blue "H" hospital signs toward the University of Oregon Health Sciences Center. This will get you heading south on Terwilliger Boulevard. Then go straight onto Sam Jackson Drive, following a Shriners' Hospital sign. At the first hairpin curve turn right onto graveled Marquam Road and the parking area.

Marquam Nature Park's steep canyon was originally saved from development because of the unstable geology that makes Portland's west hills such a tricky place to build. Although Ice Age glaciers never reached Portland, their outwash plains repeatedly filled the flatlands with dusty silt. During arid interglacial periods, huge dust storms blew this silt onto the hills, leaving a layer of slippery topsoil up to 30 feet thick. Prolonged rains can launch landslides, especially where this layer is disturbed by houses or roads. Despite the danger, a trio of dentists proposed building 200 apartments in this canyon in 1968. Instead of merely protesting, a scrappy group of volunteers raised over $1 million in a citywide campaign and bought the land for the public.

To start the hike, follow the gravel road up the canyon to the right. The road soon becomes a well-graded path, steadily climbing amid ferns and maples. In spring, expect two kinds of white wildflowers with sprays of tiny blossoms: large smilacina (alias false Solomon's seal) and star-flowered smilacina. In summer, look for the delicate fronds of black-stalked maidenhair ferns along the trail. In autumn, the leaves of vine maple paint the woods scarlet.

By following signs to Council Crest, you'll go straight at a trail junction and cross 4 paved roads as you climb. After 1.6 miles, reach an unmarked trail junction at the edge of a park lawn. Go left across the lawn to the brick observation patio on the summit, where plaques identify sights from Mt. Rainier to Mt. Jefferson. Even in less-than-perfect weather, views still extend from Beaverton to the Fremont Bridge.

When you're ready to hike back, retrace your steps 1.3 miles to a trail junction. Go straight here, following the "Shelter Loop" sign. This path contours 0.5 mile around a ridge to a couple of trail junctions near a creek crossing. Keep left both times, following an abandoned road down the creek to the trailhead.

Trail in Marquam Nature Park.   Opposite: Mt. Hood from Council Crest.

8   Oaks Bottom

Easy
2.9-mile loop
100 feet elevation gain
Open all year
Map: Lake Oswego (USGS)

In the midst of the city but shielded by a 100-foot cliff, the animals in this riverside wildlife refuge don't seem to realize they're in a metropolis. As you hike the trail around these wetlands you're almost certain to see ducks, beaver-gnawed trees, and great blue herons calmly fishing for frogs. But wildlife watching isn't the only reason this trip is a hit with families. At the far end of the loop you can visit Oaks Park, an old-timey carnival midway complete with kiddy rides, refreshment stands, and even a roller-skating rink.

To find the trailhead, drive south from the Ross Island Bridge on McLoughlin Boulevard (US Highway 99E). After 1 mile take the Milwaukie Avenue exit and immediately pull into an unmarked gravel parking area on the right. You can get here easily by bus, too, since the #19 Woodstock bus stops by the trailhead.

The broad, graveled trail starts beside a sign reminding visitors that camping, fishing, hunting, and motorized vehicles are banned in the wildlife refuge and that dogs must be leashed. After 0.3 mile the trail forks. Veer left on a smaller path through shady bigleaf maples and soon cross a footbridge with your first view across the refuge's extensive swamplands. Waterfowl thrive in this Everglades-like sea of reeds and willows.

After another half mile pass beneath the 7-story fortress of the Portland Memorial Funeral Home and reach a couple of small gravelly beaches — the trail's only access to the refuge's large central lake. Look here for freshly-gnawed beaver wood in the swampy forest ringing the shore.

At the end of the lake go straight at a trail junction and switchback up to a viewpoint of the lake and the downtown Portland skyscrapers. At this point a left fork of the trail leads 50 yards to the lawns of Sellwood Park, with picnic tables and restrooms. By continuing straight at the viewpoint you'll reach a service road paralleling a rarely-used railroad track. Turn right along the tracks 0.2 mile to a steam locomotive displayed on a siding at the main entrance of the Oaks Park amusement park.

Oaks Park opened in 1905 just 2 days before tourists descended on Portland for the city's grand Lewis and Clark Exposition. In those days Portland had a second amusement park at Council Crest (see Hike #7), also located at the end of a trolley line to entice excursionists. The decline of trolleys and the opening of a newer amusement park at Jantzen Beach killed the Council Crest carnival and nearly bankrupted Oaks Park. In 1985 the owner donated the park to a non-profit

Footbridge at Oaks Bottom Wildlife Refuge.   Opposite: Oaks Park amusement park.

group dedicated to restoring the amusement park to its former splendor. Today admission is free and tickets to the 28 rides cost about $1 apiece. From mid-June to early October the park is open Tuesday through Sunday, noon to 10pm. From spring vacation to June it's only open weekends.

To complete the hiking loop, continue on the gravel service road beside the railroad tracks. Yellow Scotch broom blooms here in spring and blackberries ripen in late summer. After half a mile there's a view across the Willamette to East Island and Ross Island — active rookeries for Portland's symbol, the great blue heron. In another 0.2 mile turn right onto a major, 6-foot-wide path that cuts across a field, returning you to the trail to the parking area.

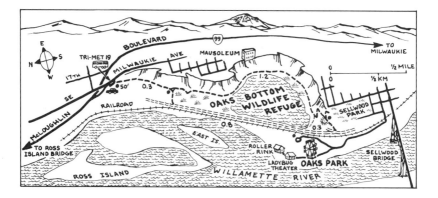

9 Tryon Creek Park

Easy
2-mile loop
200 feet elevation gain
Open all year
Map: Tryon Cr Trail Guide (State Parks)

Quiet paths and scenic footbridges highlight this densely forested canyon, a pocket wilderness tucked between Portland and Lake Oswego. The woods here are particularly beckoning in spring when the trilliums bloom, but any season is fine for a morning stroll or an afternoon outing with the kids.

Take the Terwilliger exit (#297) of Interstate 5 and drive south on Terwilliger Boulevard through numerous twists and intersections, following "Tryon Creek State Park" signs. After 2.2 miles, turn right onto the entrance road and park at the end of the loop. Dogs are allowed only on 6-foot or shorter leashes.

Start with a visit to Nature Center, an interpretive center with exhibits and a staff naturalist to help identify plants and explain forest ecology. If you wish, you can also pick up a brochure for the Trillium Trail, an all-accessible 0.3-mile self-guiding nature path.

Now walk back out the front door of the Nature Center and turn right at the signboard. In 100 feet the paved Trillium Trail veers off to the left. Detour briefly left to visit this pair of paved nature loops if you like, or else simply continue straight, following a "Red Fox Trail" sign 0.3 mile to Red Fox Bridge over Tryon Creek. Along the way, look for big white trilliums, yellow wood violets, stalks of white fringecups, and stands of stinging nettles. Also notice the little licorice ferns sprouting from the mossy branches of bigleaf maple trees.

After crossing the Red Fox Bridge it's worth detouring 0.3 mile downstream

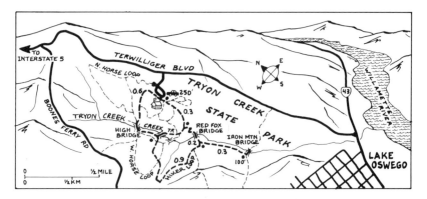

Red Fox Bridge over Tryon Creek.   Opposite: Trillium.

along the South Creek Trail to the Iron Mountain Bridge, just to see the creek grow wider and lazier in this lower end of the park. Then return to a trail junction near the Red Fox Bridge.

If the weather's dry enough that the paths aren't slick, follow the "Hiker Loop" pointer onto the Cedar Trail and a tour of a side canyon. The forest floor here is carpeted with waterleaf — a wildflower with large, dramatically lobed leaves. After 0.7 mile the Hiker Loop path twice crosses a confusing horse trail, but simply head for Tryon Creek and follow it upstream to reach High Bridge. (In wet weather this portion of the Hiker Loop is so slippery it's safer to shortcut on the Middle Creek Trail from Red Fox Bridge to High Bridge.) Then cross High Bridge, turn right, and follow "Nature Center" pointers back to the car.

A non-profit group, the Friends of Tryon Creek State Park, sponsors a number of activities at the park, including school class tours, a "Sunday at Two" lecture series, a photography club, a library of nature-oriented books, and organized hikes in the Portland area. In addition, the Trillium Festival on the first weekend in April brings wildflower exhibits, house plant sales, and a photo contest to the park. Call 636-4398 for more information about these programs or about the Friends of Tryon Creek.

Picnic area at Powell Butte's summit.   Opposite: Pathfinder plant, with bent leaf.

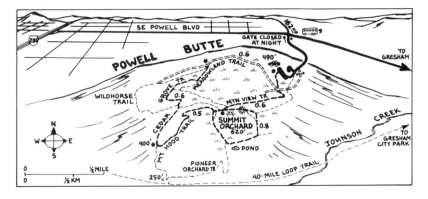

10 Powell Butte

Easy
3.1-mile loop
300 feet elevation gain
Open all year
Map: Brochure at trailhead

Perfect for a spring picnic or a quick winter walk, this convenient loop explores Powell Butte's broad summit meadow — with views across East Portland to 3 snowpeaks — and then winds through a quiet woodland glen.

Like Mt. Tabor and some 72 other hills between Portland and Sandy, Powell Butte is a volcanic cone less than 10 million years old. The butte earned its name when 3 pioneers by the name of J. Powell, all of them unrelated, took up homesteads near its base in 1852-53. The small orchard of walnut, apple, and pear trees on the butte's top was planted in the late 1800s. Today the delightfully wild 570-acre Powell Butte Nature Park coexists peacefully with a 50-million-gallon reservoir buried beneath the summit meadow. The unseen tank is the hub of Portland's water supply, receiving 152,000 gallons a minute from the Bull Run Watershed.

To reach the park, take exit 19 of Interstate 205, follow SE Powell Boulevard eastward 3.5 miles, turn right at 162nd Avenue, and drive up to the main parking area (at the restrooms). Alternatively, you can ride Tri-Met's #9 bus to the corner of Powell and 162nd.

Start up the paved Mountain View Trail through a meadow of buttercups and clover. Birds sing from hawthorn shrubs. The view of Mt. Hood is quite good, with flat-topped Mt. St. Helens to the north and Mt. Adams' white tip emerging above the foothills as you climb.

Pavement ends and the trail splits when you reach the butte's broad summit in 0.6 mile. Here there are picnic tables in an old walnut orchard and ripe blackberries in August. If you're hiking with children, you might take a shortcut by going straight at this trail junction. Otherwise, turn left onto the Orchard Loop Trail for a 0.8-mile summit loop. To follow the loop, keep right at all junctions until you return to the summit crest. Then go straight onto the signed Mt. Hood Trail.

The Mt. Hood Trail dives into a lush forest of Douglas fir, bigleaf maple, and droopy red cedar, with white wildflowers in spring: candyflower, fringecup, and smilacina. Beware of trailside nettles and expect a bit of mud in wet weather. After half a mile turn right on the Cedar Grove Trail and follow signs for this path 0.6 mile until it returns to the meadow. Finally turn left on the Meadowland Trail and follow it 0.6 mile back to the parking area.

11   Lacamas Park

Easy
3.4-mile loop
200 feet elevation gain
Open all year
Map: Camas (USGS)

Who would have guessed that Camas — the Washington mill town on the Columbia River — is hiding a miniature wilderness with a scenic lake, waterfalls, and a forest canyon? In fact this convenient park is just the right kind of quiet, woodsy place for a winter stroll or an easy hike with the kids.

Take Interstate 5 or 205 north across the Columbia, immediately turn right onto Highway 14, and drive east to Camas exit 12. Follow the exit road 1.4 miles to town, continue straight on 6th Avenue for 6 blocks, turn left on Garfield Street, and follow "Hwy 500 West" signs for 1.1 zigzagging miles to the Lacamas Park parking lot on your right. On summer weekends the lot may be full, but you can drive 100 yards up the highway and turn right on Leonard Road to an overflow parking area. The C-Tran #33 Camas bus also stops at Leonard Road. Camping and unleashed pets are prohibited in the park.

Start at the inlet of Round Lake in a picnic area with barbecues, restrooms, and a playground. Take the lakeshore path to the right 0.3 mile through a Douglas fir forest, cross a footbridge beside a humming generator, and then cross a 50-foot-tall concrete dam built early in the 20th century to provide power and water for the Camas mill.

Beyond the dam is a confusion of paths. Stick to the lakeshore for 300 yards to a large signboard with a park map. At this point it's possible to opt for a very short, 1.6-mile loop by simply keeping left around the lake. For the longer loop,

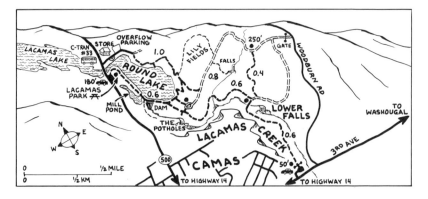

Footbridge and small waterfall at Lower Falls.   Opposite: Dam at Round Lake.

however, turn right for 100 yards to the turnaround of a gravel road. Here turn right again on an unmarked path 50 feet to a wire fence at an overlook of The Potholes, a pair of circular green pools separated by a 20-foot waterfall and weirdly pockmarked bedrock. The pockmarks were created when floodwaters swirled small rocks in depressions in the soft rock.

At The Potholes, turn left along the fence and follow Lacamas Creek 0.6 mile downstream to a 150-foot metal footbridge above Lower Falls. The creek bank here, polished into chutes and pools, makes a nice lunch stop.

To continue the loop don't cross the footbridge, but instead walk left up an old gravel road 100 yards and take an unmarked path uphill to the left. After 0.4 mile turn left on another old gravel road to return 0.8 mile to Round Lake. Along the way, optional, marked side paths lead to a patch of April-blooming blue camas lilies (on the right) and a very small waterfall (on the left).

Back at the lake, follow the shore path 0.7 mile to the right and continue briefly on a paved road around to your car.

Other Hiking Options

If you're not hiking with kids you might prefer a slightly longer loop beginning at the much quieter 3rd Avenue trailhead. To find it from Highway 14, take exit 12 for 1.4 miles into Camas, turn right on Adams Street for 3 blocks, turn left on 3rd Avenue for 0.8 mile to the American Legion Hall at East First Street, and turn left to a locked gate. Lower Falls is 0.6 mile up a wide graveled path through the woods.

12 Oxbow Park

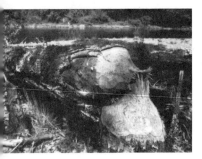

Easy
3.5-mile loop
100 feet elevation gain
Open all year
Map: Brochure at park entrance

Just 7 miles east of Gresham the whitewater Sandy River winds through a gorge where patches of old-growth forest still remain. The trails in popular Oxbow Park are never far from the swift, 200-foot-wide river, with its brushy islands and log jams. Hikers can picnic on pebble beaches, look for great blue herons, discover beaver sign, and watch drift boats negotiate the riffles. The park charges a $2-per-car fee ($3 on summer weekends), allows no pets, and closes at legal sunset except for the campground.

From Interstate 205, take exit 19 and head east on Division Street, which crosses Burnside Street in Gresham and eventually becomes the Oxbow Parkway. After 13 miles reach a 4-way junction, turn left following a park sign, and descend 1.6 miles to an entrance toll booth. Then continue 2.2 miles along the river past numerous pullouts, picnic areas, and hiking signs. After passing Group Area D, park at an unmarked boat ramp parking area on the left.

Walk down to the boat ramp and a small sandy beach with fishermen and chilly bathers. Then turn right along the river trail through a mossy forest of red cedars, Douglas firs, sword ferns, and cottonwoods. A lack of signs makes the park's trail network a little confusing. Turn left after 0.2 mile, avoiding log steps up to the right. In another 0.2 mile cross a trail in a gully. Then watch for a fork to the left leading to a long pebble beach. Hike along the beach to the dramatic tip of the river's 180-degree oxbow bend, where deep green eddies swirl against

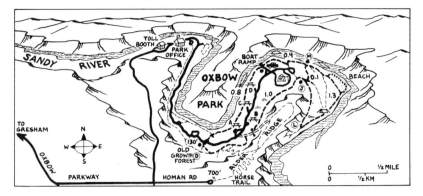

rock banks.

Return to the trail at the beach's edge and continue upriver half a mile to a trail junction in the forest at a post marked "L." The river trail peters out beyond this junction, so turn right for 0.2 mile to join a wide graveled path at a post marked "J." From this junction it's possible to shorten the hike by turning briefly right and then turning left on a gully-bottom trail back to the river. But if you're not yet tired, turn left at "J" and keep left at all junctions for 0.6 mile. When you reach an old gated road, turn right for 150 yards. Here the loop trail leaves the road, climbing to the left up steep steps overhung with maidenhair fern and bleeding hearts.

After climbing the steps, keep right at trail junctions to traverse a lush old-growth forest and reach the paved park road in 0.4 mile. The trail continues from a pullout on the far side of the road and leads to the riverbank. Follow the river trail to the right, passing several picnic lawns, to return to your car.

Other Hiking Options

For a longer hike, add a 1.6-mile loop atop Alder Ridge, a plateau with treetop osprey nests and a clifftop river overlook. Start the loop by walking up the old gated road across from Group Picnic Area A.

You can avoid the park's entrance fee by starting at the equestrian trailhead at the end of Homan Road, but parking's tight and your hike then ends with an uphill climb.

The Sandy River at Oxbow Park.   Opposite: Tree felled by beaver.

13 Champoeg Park

Easy (to pageant site)
3.2-mile loop
No elevation gain
Open all year
Map: Champoeg Park (State Parks)

Moderate (to Butteville)
8-mile loop
No elevation gain

In 1843, when the Oregon Country didn't officially belong to any nation, pioneers met at Champoeg, the earliest white settlement on the Willamette River, to discuss setting up a provisional government. At first it seemed the 100 white men at that meeting might reject the idea of government altogether. British traders and French-Canadian trappers feared the new American settlers would take control. When a line was drawn in the sand and sides were taken, the vote stood deadlocked, 50 to 50. Then a pair of late-arriving French-Canadians threw in their lot with the Americans and Oregon has belonged to the US ever since.

The town of Champoeg was virtually erased by monumental floods in 1861 and 1892. Today this scenic stretch of riverbank is a state park with museums, monuments, picnic areas, and trails. A 3.2-mile hiking loop visits the most important sites, but it's tempting to extend the loop to 8 miles by hiking the paved bike path to the quaint old town of Butteville.

Take the Donald exit of Interstate 5 (exit #278, at the Leather's gas station) and drive west following signs for Champoeg Park. After 3.5 miles you'll turn right at a crossroads and after another 2.2 miles turn right into the park entrance. Stop at the visitor's center to see the well-designed historical displays there. Then get back in your car and drive on, keeping left to the Riverside Day Use Area.

Park at the end of the Riverside loop, and follow the "Pavilion" trail sign to a monument and shelter built on the site of the famous 1843 meeting. Walk through the pavilion to the Willamette — a broad, lazy river reflecting clouds, a few geese, and perhaps a great blue heron. Turn left here to explore a paved but scenic 0.4-mile loop path through a stand of 4-foot-thick cottonwoods. In spring look for wildflowers: fringecup, star-flowered smilacina, and wild rose.

When this little loop returns to the pavilion, continue east along the riverbank. The trail ends at a paved road in front of a log cabin museum where an exhibit of pioneer artifacts is open Wednesday through Sunday from noon to 5pm.

Next continue 200 yards up the road to a curve where a paved bike path begins. Turn left here onto a dirt road, following the "Willamette River Trail" sign. In another 200 yards veer left onto the unmarked bark dust river path.

After 0.6 mile the river path traverses an outdoor amphitheater. The Champoeg Historical Pageant, a colorful musical drama, is performed here at 7:30pm every Thursday through Sunday in July; for ticket information, call 245-3922. Next the path skirts the Oak Grove Day Use Area lawns and ends at a wide,

The Willamette River at Champoeg State Park.   Opposite: Pioneer Cabin Museum.

paved bike path beside a road.

To complete the 3.2-mile hiking loop, turn right on the bike path. After 0.4 mile, detour briefly left toward the Visitor Center to see the pioneer campsite exhibit by the creek. Then continue on the bike path across the fields to return to the log cabin museum and your car.

If, however, you'd like to walk the bike path toward Butteville, turn left when you reach the bike path, cross Champoeg Creek on the road bridge, and head left again. After 100 yards, be sure to detour left onto the lovely, 0.4-mile nature loop to the mouth of Champoeg Creek. A short spur trail of this graveled path passes an 1845 grave and deadends at the site of a pioneer gristmill. Then continue on the wide, paved bike path 1.5 miles along the river's edge to Schuller Road; rustic Butteville is a half-mile roadside walk beyond.

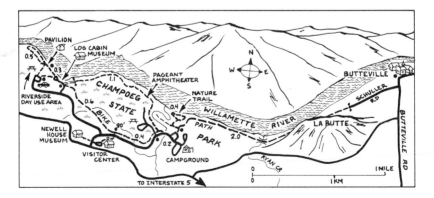

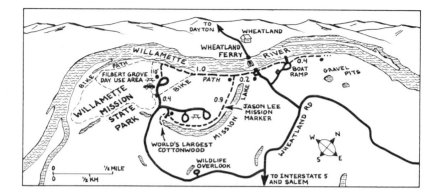

14   Willamette Mission Park

Easy
2.7 mile-loop
No elevation gain
Open all year
Map: Mission Bottom (USGS)

This riverside loop through Willamette Mission State Park not only visits the world's largest cottonwood tree and the site of a historic 1834 settlement, it also includes a free ferry ride across the Willamette River and back.

To find the park from Interstate 5, take the Brooks exit (#263) at the Bingo gas station 9 miles north of Salem. Drive 1.7 miles west on Brooklake Road, turn right onto Wheatland Road for 2.4 miles, and turn left at the Willamette Mission State Park sign. Follow the entrance road 1.8 miles, keeping left at all junctions, and park at the Filbert Grove Day Use Area — a picnic area set in an old hazelnut orchard. Some years the trees still produce a bumper crop of free, gatherable nuts in autumn.

The trail starts beside the restrooms at the far end of the parking loop. Walk 0.2 mile to the riverbank and turn right, either on a lower path through the cottonwood trees or on a higher, paved bike path skirting a grassy field. The two paths soon merge and continue as a paved promenade to the Wheatland Ferry landing.

This is the oldest ferry landing in Oregon, dating to 1844 when mules winched a log barge across the river with ropes. The present steel vessel uses an overhead cable and electric engines. Pedestrians ride free, but car drivers pay 50 cents. The ferry runs from 6am to 9:45pm every day except Christmas, Thanksgiving

— and about 30 or 40 days in winter when it closes for high water or repairs (call 588-7979 for schedule information).

The gravelly shore beside the landing is perfect for skipping rocks and watching the river. Children delight in finding tadpoles, frogs, and crawdads here. Look in the wet sand for the palm-sized tracks of great blue herons and the little hand-shaped tracks of raccoons. It's also fun to explore the riverbank beyond the landing; a path continues 0.4 mile before petering out.

To return to the loop, hike 300 yards back from the landing on the bike path and turn left onto a grassy, road-like trail. This path follows the shore of marshy Mission Lake. Before a flood changed the course of the Willamette River in 1861, this oxbow lake was the main channel. A trailside monument describes the mission built on this old riverbank by Methodist minister Jason Lee in 1834. In 1840, weary of the river's floods and the swampy environment, Lee moved operations to Chemeketa (now Salem), where he founded the Oregon Institute, which later became Willamette University. At the same time Lee gave up on teaching Indians and turned his attention to the children of white settlers instead.

After passing the monument, the trail enters a developed picnic area in an old walnut orchard. Keep left at all junctions for half a mile to the trail's end at a road. A sign here points out the world's largest black cottonwood — 155 feet tall and over 26 feet in circumference. Walk along the road to return to your car, turning left at the first stop sign and right at the next.

The Wheatland Ferry.   Opposite: Cottonwoods along the Willamette River.

Southwest
Washington

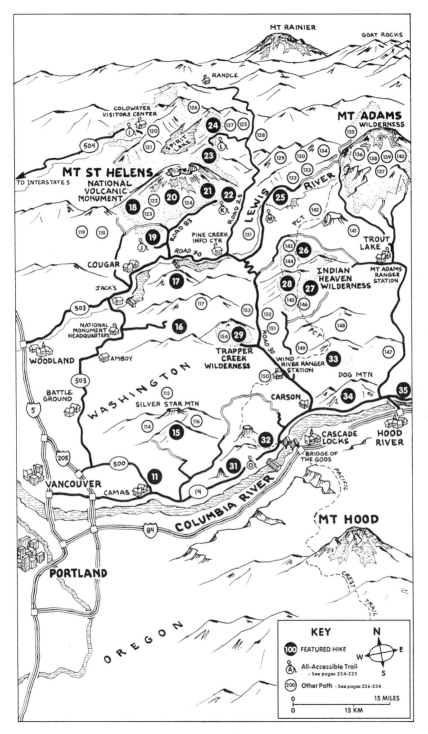

Opposite: Mt. Adams from Mt. St. Helens rim (Hike #20).

15 Silver Star Mountain

Difficult
9.7-mile loop
2400 feet elevation gain
Open May to mid-November
Maps: Larch Mtn, Bobs Mtn
(Washington, USGS)

From Portland, Silver Star Mountain appears as a humble brown ridge. From the mountain's wildflower-spangled meadows, however, the view is proud indeed, encompassing 4 snowpeaks and a long, silver ribbon of Columbia River.

In 1902 the mountain was overswept by the Yacolt Burn, largest forest fire in Washington history. Today, beargrass meadows thrive on the ridges where trees failed to reseed. Many of the trails in the area are abandoned, rock-strewn roads shared with horses and sometimes even motorcycles. If you walk straight to the summit and back the hike's only 6.6 miles, but for 3.1 extra miles you get a loop past a hidden waterfall and a side trip to a mysterious collection of Indian pits.

Take the freeway north over the Columbia River and immediately turn right toward Camas on Highway 14. When you reach milepost 16, turn left at the Washougal exit and go straight for 6.9 miles on what becomes Washougal River Road. Turn left at a sign for Bear Prairie, climb 3.2 miles to an "Entering Skamania County" sign, and turn left onto Skamania Mines Road for 2.7 miles. Then turn left on gravel 1200 Road and keep left on this rough, rocky road for 5.7 miles to Grouse Creek Vista, a pass with a trail sign on the right, "Tarbell Campground 10½ Miles."

This trailhead can also be reached by car from the north. To try this route, take Highway 503 north from Vancouver. Beyond Battle Ground 6.5 miles, turn right on Rock Creek Road (which becomes Lucia Falls Road) for 8.8 miles, turn right on County Road 12 for 1.9 miles, turn right onto paved Dole Valley Road (which becomes gravel Road L1000) for 5.1 miles, and then veer left onto Road L1200 for 4.5 miles to Grouse Creek Vista's pass.

Hike past the trail sign up a blocked, abandoned road. After 200 yards ignore the Tarbell Trail angling off to the left — the loop's return route. Continue up the rocky road a mile to meadows and views. At first the fields are thick with huckleberry bushes, fireweed, and pearly everlasting. As you climb past Pyramid Rock the flowers shift to beargrass, blue lupine, and red Indian paintbrush.

Keep left for 2.9 miles until you reach a 4-way junction. The road straight ahead leads to the summit, but it's worth it to turn right on the signed trail to the Indian pits. This path goes up and down along a fabulous alpine ridgecrest for 0.9 mile and ends at a rockslide with a sweeping view. The ancient stone walls and 6-foot pits here are thought to be vision quest sites where young Indian men fasted until they saw a guiding spirit. Do not move any rocks.

Silver Star Mountain.   Opposite: Indian pit.

As you walk back from the pits watch for a trail on the right that scrambles up to Silver Star Mountain's twin summits, one of which still has foundations of a lookout tower. Soak in the view, and then hike 0.4 mile down the road back to the 4-way junction.

If you have time for a longer, woodsier return path, turn downhill to the right from the 4-way junction. This steep, rubbly road soon forks, but keep left for 1.4 miles, passing beneath the columnar basalt cliffs of Sturgeon Rock. Then turn left onto the well-marked Tarbell Trail. This path switchbacks gently down to a footbridge over Rock Creek, To see the hidden waterfall downstream, look back as you hike on. The trail contours through second-growth woods to your car.

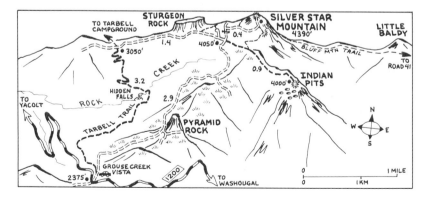

16 Siouxon Creek

Moderate
7.6-mile loop
700 feet cumulative elevation gain
Open all year
Map: Lookout Mtn (Green Trails)

Ancient forest frames Siouxon Creek's green pools and waterfalls. A newly rerouted trail follows the creek 3.7 miles to a footbridge in a mossy grotto ideal for a picnic. If you don't mind a bridgeless creek crossing you can return on a loop past 2 tall waterfalls in side canyons.

The drive to Siouxon Creek is entirely paved. Take Interstate 205 north across the Columbia River to the Orchards exit (#30). Go right on Highway 500, which becomes Highway 503 through Battle Ground and makes 3 right-hand corners in Amboy. A total of 26.2 miles from the freeway — just past the Mt. St. Helens National Monument Headquarters — turn right on NE Healy Road. Follow this road 9.2 miles to a fork, veer uphill to the left on unmarked Road 57 for 1.2 miles to a pass, and then turn left onto signed Road 5701 for 3.8 miles to a path on the left, 100 feet before road's end.

Hike down the path and turn right on the Siouxon Creek Trail. This trail descends 0.2 mile to a footbridge over West Creek, passes 3 campsites, and then follows Siouxon Creek amid big Douglas firs and red cedars. After 1.4 miles the path bridges Horseshoe Creek between a pair of charming little waterfalls. Side trails to the left end at brushy viewpoints. Continue on the main trail 0.3 mile to Siouxon Falls, a 40-foot, S-shaped slide that sloshes into a huge green pool.

At the 3-mile mark the path to Wildcat Falls joins from the left — the return route of the loop. For now, go straight another 0.7 mile and turn left across a

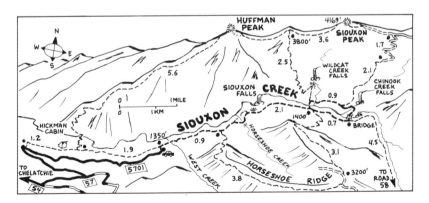

Bridge over Siouxon Creek.   Opposite: Siouxon Falls.

footbridge over a deep-pooled gorge with mossy rock ledges suitable for use as lunch tables. After resting here, continue 1/4 mile to a creek crossing below lacy, 50-foot Chinook Falls.

To complete the little loop, continue past Chinook Falls to the trail's first switchback and go straight onto an unmarked trail. This narrower tread leads 0.7 mile to the Wildcat Trail. If you have the energy, turn right for a steep 0.3-mile climb to a viewpoint of Wildcat Falls' 100-foot ribbon. Otherwise turn left to a ford of Siouxon Creek and the trail back to the car. In summer it's possible to make this creek crossing dry footed, but plan on a cold wade during winter high water. And incidentally — the name Siouxon rhymes with Tucson.

Other Hiking Options

Backpackers or rugged day hikers can choose among 3 more difficult loops. For a sweeping view from Siouxon Peak's former lookout site, take the Chinook Trail up from Chinook Falls to a jeep track, keep left to the peak, and return via the Wildcat Trail — a 16.6-mile trip gaining 3700 feet. For a 10.8-mile loop that gains 2600 feet, take the well-marked Horseshoe Ridge Trail up a steep, viewless crest, across a logging road, and back to Siouxon Creek. Finally, a 13-mile loop up Wildcat Creek passes within a cross-country scramble of Huffman Peak's scenic summit and follows a long, wooded ridge west to a lower portion of the Siouxon Creek Trail, gaining 3900 feet in all.

Swift Reservoir and Mt. St. Helens from Mt. Mitchell.   Opposite: Crags near summit.

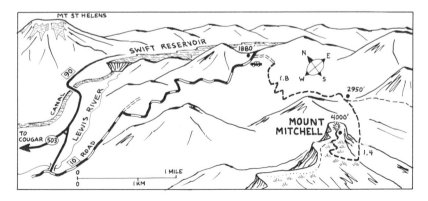

17   Mount Mitchell

Moderate
6.4 miles round-trip
2100 feet elevation gain
Open April through November
Map: Mt. Mitchell (Wash. USGS)

The best viewpoint of Mt. St. Helens' truncated south flank isn't in the National Monument at all — it's from this little-known peak above Swift Reservoir. The unmarked but easy-to-follow Mount Mitchell Trail leads through a high meadow of beargrass and blue gentian to an old lookout site amidst scenic crags.

To find Mt. Mitchell from Portland, drive 25 miles north on Interstate 5 to Woodland exit 21 and turn right onto Highway 503 for 31.6 miles, following signs for Mt. St. Helens. Beyond the town of Cougar 3.2 miles — immediately before Highway 503-Spur becomes Forest Road 90 — turn right onto an unmarked paved road for 0.3 mile, cross a bridge, and turn left on gravel 10 Road. After 1.6 miles, 10 Road turns sharply right at a junction. Follow 10 Road another 2.4 miles uphill and park on the shoulder where a dirt road veers off to the right through a 1990 clearcut. You'll know you've driven too far if 10 Road starts heading downhill.

Hike the unmarked dirt spur road across the clearcut and into a mossy second-growth forest of alder, cedar, sword fern, and Oregon grape. After 0.3 mile the road turns right and begins narrowing to a rocky trail that switchbacks steeply up through the woods. At the 1-mile mark the path straightens out on a pleasanter, less steep traverse around the mountain's slopes. At 1.8 miles ignore an unmarked side trail to the left.

The path's final mile ambles through ever grander beargrass meadows before climbing past the summit crags to the old lookout site, marked today only by foundations, glass, and a toppled outhouse. In addition to brilliant blue gentians, look for cushions of white phlox, delicate bluebells, purple penstemons, and spiny gooseberry plants. The view across Swift Reservoir shows Mt. St. Helens' relatively intact southern face. But the old lava flows and recent lahars (mudflows) snaking down from the long gray rim prove this topless volcano is no heavy sleeper.

For an adventurous side trip on the way back, hike a few hundred yards down the trail to the second switchback and go straight on a faint path that heads through the woods. to a broad, meadowed ridge, where you can easily bushwhack 0.8 mile west to another clifftop viewpoint.

18   Sheep Canyon

Moderate
7-mile loop
1700 feet elevation gain
Open mid-June through October
Map: Mt. St. Helens Nat'l. Mon. (USFS)

On the western edge of Mt. St. Helens' 1980 blast zone, this loop has a little of everything: intact old-growth forests, desolated canyons, wildflower-strewn timberline meadows, and a truly astonishing view of the mountain from the South Fork Toutle River's moonscape gorge. The river is still struggling to cut a chasm into a half-mile-wide mudflow unleashed by the flash melting of the Toutle and Tallus Glaciers.

Take Interstate 5 to Woodland exit 21 (north of Portland 25 miles) and turn right onto Highway 503 for 30.5 miles, following signs for Mt. St. Helens. Half a mile before the town of Cougar turn left onto Road 8100 at a sign for Merrill Lake. Follow this paved road 11.5 miles and then continue straight on gravel Road 8123 for 6.5 miles to a big parking lot at road's end.

Don't take the trail marked "Viewpoint ¼" — you'll see better views later. Instead go up an unmarked trail on the right-hand side of the parking lot. After briefly crossing a 1976 clearcut, this path ducks into old-growth woods with 5-foot-thick hemlocks and firs. Look for the hand-sized triple leaves of vanilla leaf, a humble white wildflower that gives off a sweet smell as it wilts.

After 0.6 mile the trail forks just before a dramatic 40-foot bridge across Sheep Canyon's mudflow-scoured gorge. Cross the bridge and continue 1.5 miles over a ridge to the more impressive desolation of the South Fork Toutle River's canyon. Your path meets the round-the-mountain Loowit Trail here, at the rim

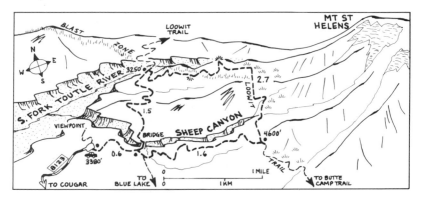

of the river's mudflow. The route of the loop hike heads to the right here, but first detour a few hundred yards to the left for a view up the river's tiered canyon to Mt. St. Helens. The raging, bouldery river is milky with pulverized rock from the grinding glaciers above.

Then turn around and follow the Loowit Trail up a ridge that marks the edge of the blast zone, with eruption-killed trees on one side. After climbing 1.5 miles the path levels out amid alpine meadows of bluebells, red Indian paintbrush, blue lupine, and huckleberries. Contour 1.2 miles through these heavenly timberline fields, turn right on the Sheep Canyon Trail, and descend through old-growth woods 2.2 miles to your car.

South Fork Toutle River.   Opposite: Bluebells.

19 Ape Cave

Easy (Lower cave)
2 miles round-trip
200 feet elevation gain
Open all year
Map: Mt. St. Helens Nat'l. Mon. (USFS)

Moderate (Upper cave)
2.7-mile loop
400 feet elevation gain

Longest lava tube in the western hemisphere, Ape Cave features a 0.8-mile lower section that's easy to hike and a rugged, 1.4-mile upper section that's fun for adventurers. The lower section, with a smooth, sandy floor, leads to The Meatball, a lava boulder wedged halfway to the cave's 30-foot ceiling. The rugged upper section of the cave offers a skylight, 2 frozen lava "waterfalls," and an above-ground return trail, but the upper cave's roof is drippy in wet weather and a jumble of rocks litter the floor.

Bring *at least* one lantern or flashlight for each person and be sure to dress warmly. Even on hot summer days the drafty cave remains a constant, chilly 42 degrees Fahrenheit. Pets, smoking, food, and beverages are banned.

Ape Cave formed 1900 years ago when Mt. St. Helens erupted a runny kind of basalt lava known as pahoehoe. As the flow's crust hardened, the liquid lava underneath drained out along the course of a buried stream gully, leaving a 11,334-foot-long tube. In places the tube was so tall it pinched into two separate levels, one above the other. Watch for stripes along the walls — "high-water marks" left by the ebbing lava. Also look for ripple patterns in the floor's rock — remnants of flowing lava that hardened in place.

As the lava ebbed, superheated gases blasted through the tube, remelting the walls' surface and leaving tiny, fragile stalactites known as "lava drips." Since then, earthquakes have shaken loose portions of the upper cave's ceiling. An

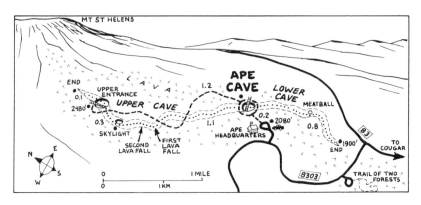

Ape Cave's main entrance.   Opposite: Mt. St. Helens from upper entrance.

eruption of Mt. St. Helens 450 years ago loosed a mudflow that spilled into the cave's main entrance and paved the lower cave with sand. Remarkably, the 1980 eruption had almost no effect here.

Discovered in 1946, Ape Cave was named for the Mt. St. Helens Apes, a group of Boy Scout cavers who took their tongue-in-cheek name from an alleged 1924 sighting of Sasquatch on the mountain's east flank at an otherwise unrelated valley, Ape Canyon (Hike #21). To find the cave, drive Interstate 5 to Woodland exit 21 (north of Portland 25 miles), turn right, and follow signs for Mt. St. Helens for 35 miles. Beyond the town of Cougar 6.5 miles, at a sign for Ape Cave, turn left onto paved Road 83 for 1.7 miles. Then turn left on Road 8303 for 0.9 mile to a parking lot at "Ape's Headquarters," a staffed information cabin.

Take a short path to the cave's main entrance, go down the stone stairs, and a few hundred feet later descend a metal stairway to the cave's main floor. No signs point the way here, but the route behind you (under the stairway) leads to the rugged upper cave while the route ahead of you goes to the easier lower cave. It's best to explore the popular, 0.8-mile lower cave first and then, if you'd like to get away from the crowds, return to the stairway and continue to the rougher upper cave.

The upper cave begins with a 40-foot-tall room, but the route then arduously clambers over the first of 10 major rockfalls. At the 0.8-mile and 0.9-mile marks you'll have to climb up 8-foot lava falls using whatever handholds and footholds you can find. The skylight opening after 1.1 mile is too high to use as an exit, but continue 0.3 mile and you'll reach a metal ladder to the upper entrance, just before the cave ends. The above-ground trail back to the main entrance crosses a sparsely forested lava bed and mudflow.

Mount St Helens Rim

Moderate (to Dryer Creek Meadows)
8 miles round-trip
1100 feet elevation gain
Open mid-June through October
Map: Mt. St. Helens NW (Green Trails)

Difficult (to summit)
9.4 miles round-trip
4500 feet elevation gain
Open mid-July to mid-October

From Mt. St. Helens' summit rim, the new crater gapes like the broken edge of a shattered planet. Rock avalanches rumble in slow motion down 2000-foot cliffs to the steaming lava dome. On the horizon, the snowpeaks of Washington and Oregon float above the clouds.

Now that the volcano has calmed, the Forest Service issues permits for 100 people a day to hike to the rim either by way of Butte Camp (Hike #122) or up the shorter Monitor Ridge route described here. The climb requires no technical climbing skills — only stamina and strong knees. Hikers start out on a well-graded forest path to timberline, then follow poles marking the way up a ridge of lava boulders, and finally trudge up a dune-like slope of ash.

If you're unsure about attempting the climb — or if you can't get a permit — consider taking the round-the-mountain Loowit Trail to the wildflowers at Dryer Creek Meadows instead. This alternative skips the steep climbing, yet still visits Monitor Ridge's interesting lava fields and offers views to Mt. Hood.

Climbing permits, required for travel above the 4800-foot level, are best reserved at least 3 weeks in advance by mail. For forms, call (206) 247-5800 or write the National Monument Headquarters at 42218 NE Yale Bridge Road, Amboy, WA 98601. Otherwise you'll have to wait in line for the 40 permits issued on a first-come first-served basis each day at Jack's Restaurant, 6 miles west of Cougar. Each person can get a permit for a party of up to 12. The sign-up list at

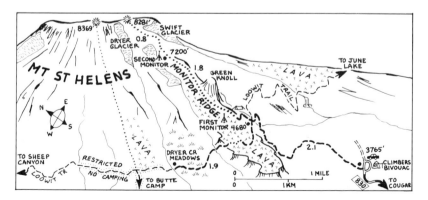

View from Mt. St. Helens' summit rim.   Opposite: Dryer Creek Meadows.

Jack's opens at 11am (come earlier on weekends!), but the permits aren't actually distributed until 6pm and are valid for the *following* day.

To find the trailhead, drive Interstate 5 to Woodland exit 21 (north of Portland 25 miles), turn right, and follow signs for Mt. St. Helens for 35 miles. Then, following signs to "Climbers Bivouac," turn left on paved Road 83 for 3.1 miles, turn left on Road 8100 for 1.7 miles, and turn right on gravel Road 830 for 2.7 miles to a turnaround. Climbers determined to get an early morning start can either pitch their tents in the bleak 1976 clearcut here or backpack to a small, crowded, often waterless dale at timberline.

Start on the Ptarmigan Trail and climb steadily 2.1 miles to a junction with the Loowit Trail amid the pink heather and snow-bent firs of timberline. If you're headed for Dryer Creek Meadows, turn left, follow the sometimes-faint Loowit Trail 0.9 mile across a rugged lava ridge, and continue another level mile through lovely August lupine fields to the mudflow gorge of the Dryer Glacier's outwash creek — a suitable turnaround point.

If you're climbing the mountain, cross the Loowit Trail to the signed climbers' route. The tread soon ends atop a rugged lava flow near one of the 2 tripod monitors that gave this ridge its name. The tripods' mirrors reflected laser beams to gauge the swelling of the mountain and thus predict eruptions.

Continue on a braided path marked by posts and then scramble up a ridge of boulders to the second monitor tripod. Shortly beyond this point the boulders end and the route ascends an ash slope between the Swift Glacier and a snowfield. Winds here often whip up gritty clouds of dust. When you reach the rim, don't venture too close to the unstable edge. Hiking is barred along the cliff to the right, but you can explore left as far as the Dryer Glacier headwall, which blocks safe access to what is technically the mountain's highest point.

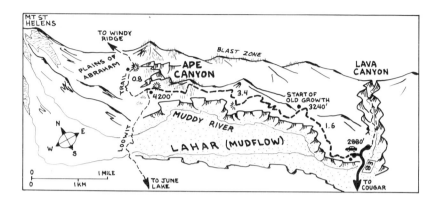

21 Ape Canyon

Difficult
11.6 miles round-trip
1300 feet elevation gain
Open July through October
Map: Mt. St. Helens Nat'l. Mon. (USFS)

One of the National Monument's new trails, this path climbs an old-growth forest ridge beside an awesome, mile-wide mudflow with views up to Mt. St. Helens' decapitated rim. The hike's goal is Ape Canyon's eerie, 300-foot-tall rock slot at the edge of the 1980 blast zone, but it's tempting to continue another 0.8 mile into the other-worldly desolation of the Plains of Abraham.

Ape Canyon won its name in 1924 when an ape-like creature threw rocks at 2 miners in a cabin here. In 1982 an old-timer confessed that he and another boy had staged the entire incident. But in the meantime the Sasquatch tale inspired a local Boy Scout group to name Ape Cave (see Hike #19), a lava tube 8 miles away on the mountain's south flank. Today, visitors are often confused that the canyon and cave are otherwise unrelated and are located so far apart.

Drive Interstate 5 to Woodland exit 21 (north of Portland 25 miles), turn right, and follow signs for Mt. St. Helens for 35 miles. Beyond the town of Cougar 6.5 miles, at a sign for Lava Canyon, turn left on Road 83 for 11.2 paved miles to the well-marked Ape Canyon Trailhead on the left.

The path starts out on a cliff edge overlooking the Muddy River's vast lahar — a flow of mud, rock, and ash unleashed when the volcano's 1980 eruption melted much of the Shoestring Glacier. The forest beside the moonscape lahar was unscathed by the blast. However, the first 1.6 miles of the trail's route are still recovering from a 1968 clearcut. Deer and elk frequently browse the vine maples and alder here. Look for red Indian paintbrush, dwarf blue lupine, and purple asters, too. Then the path dives into an impressive old-growth stand of 6-foot-thick hemlocks and Douglas firs hung with gray-green old-man's-beard lichen. White June wildflowers here include delicate inside-out flower and vanilla leaf.

At the 4.5-mile mark the trail enters the blast zone of trees killed by super-heated air. Ahead, the lahar's mudflow plain snakes up toward the gray volcano, serrated by ash gullies. To the right, Ape Canyon's still-green valley gradually narrows to a slot-like chasm framing a view of snowy Mt. Adams.

The path joins the round-the-mountain Loowit Trail in a pumice plain with an "Ape Canyon" sign. Unless you're bushed, it's worth turning right here to hike the Loowit Trail 0.8 mile to the Plains of Abraham, a rock-strewn desert backed by the mountain like a wall. Overhead hang the Shoestring, Ape, and Nelson Glaciers, slowly dwindling for lack of a summit.

Old-growth forest along the Ape Canyon Trail.   Opposite: Pearly everlasting.

22   Lava Canyon

Easy (to suspension bridge)
1.3-mile loop
300 feet elevation gain
Open mid-April to mid-November
Map: Mt. St. Helens Nat'l. Mon. (USFS)

Moderate (to Smith Creek)
5.9 miles round-trip
1400 feet elevation gain

This spectacular new trail follows a mudflow-scoured chasm past waterfalls and ancient lava cliffs. An easy loop circles the upper gorge, crossing the canyon twice on scenic footbridges. More adventurous hikers can continue downstream on a narrower tread that descends a dizzying 40-foot ladder before leveling out in the vast mudflow flats of raging Smith Creek.

The recently-exposed rock formations in Lava Canyon are remnants of a Mt. St. Helens lava flow that coursed down the Muddy River's valley 3500 years ago. The basalt lava fractured into a honeycomb of pillar-like columns as it cooled. When the river then cut down through the flow it carved waterfall chutes and left free-standing lava towers such as The Ship. Later stream debris buried the formations until the 1980 eruption, when the melting Shoestring Glacier loosed a gigantic lahar (mudflow) that washed Lava Canyon clean.

To find the trailhead, drive Interstate 5 to Woodland exit 21 (north of Portland 25 miles), turn right, and follow signs for Mt. St. Helens for 35 miles. Beyond the town of Cougar 6.5 miles, turn left on paved Road 83 and follow signs for Lava Canyon 11.3 miles to a turnaround at road's end.

The path's first 0.4 mile is a wheelchair-accessible promenade with viewpoint decks and interpretive nature trail signs. Turn right at a sign for the Lava Canyon Loop Trail and cross a metal footbridge above a series of churning river cauldrons separated by frothing falls. Hang tight to small children beyond this point,

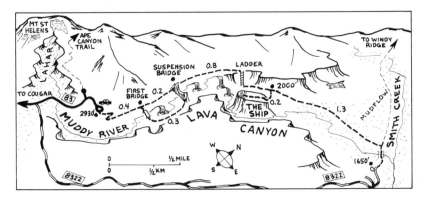

Lava Canyon from The Ship.   Opposite: Upper footbridge.

as the path downstream follows the long rim of a basalt cliff and then recrosses the gorge on a high suspension bridge.

For the short loop, turn left after crossing the second bridge and return to the car. For a more rugged hike (not suitable for children), turn right and continue downstream past a string of colossal waterfalls. The steep trail crosses cliffy slopes with no railings, and the tread can be slippery in wet weather, so be sure to wear boots with good soles. Climb down a 40-foot metal ladder and a few hundred yards later turn right on a side trail that scrambles 0.2 mile to a viewpoint atop The Ship, a 100-foot-tall lava block in mid-canyon. Then return to the main trail and continue downstream.

The trail's final mile cross a 1980 mudflow plain that's slowly regrowing with dwarf lupine wildflowers and scattered fir trees. An elk herd commonly ranges here. When you reach the road-like Smith Creek Trail, turn right to a 150-foot-long footbridge. This is a good turnaround point if you've left your car back at the Lava Canyon Trailhead.

With a short car shuttle you can hike the Lava Canyon Trail one way, all downhill. To leave a car at the lower trailhead, turn off Road 83 just 0.7 mile before the Lava Canyon Trailhead and follow gravel Road 8322 downhill for 4.8 miles to its end at the Smith Creek Trailhead.

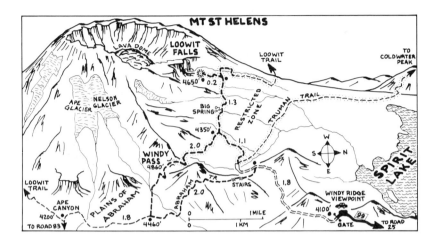

23   Mt. St. Helens Crater

Moderate (to Loowit Falls)
8.8 miles round-trip
800 feet elevation gain
Open late June through October
Map: Mt. St. Helens NW (Green Trails)

Difficult (to Plains of Abraham)
11.7-mile loop
1400 feet elevation gain

Now that Mt. St. Helens has quieted, the National Monument has opened a trail to the ragged mouth of the new crater, where steaming, 200-foot Loowit Falls tumbles through a badlands chasm. Pioneer wildflowers struggle from the ash at oasis-like springs. Log-jammed Spirit Lake stretches to the north.

Because this route crosses a restricted zone under scientific study, hikers must stay within 10 feet of the trail and camping is banned. If you'd like to return on a slightly longer loop, however, you can hike beyond the restricted zone to the breathtakingly desolate Plains of Abraham and a view-packed ridge ablaze with wildflowers. No trails access the lava dome inside the volcano's crater because of rockfall and eruption danger.

To find the Windy Ridge trailhead, drive Interstate 5 to Woodland exit 21 (north of Portland 25 miles), turn right, and follow signs for Mt. St. Helens for a total of 88 paved miles. Along the way, you'll follow Highway 503 through the town of Cougar, continue straight on what becomes Road 90 to the Pine Creek Information Station, go straight on Road 25 for 25 miles, and turn left on Road 99 for 16 miles to its end.

Park at the Windy Ridge Viewpoint and walk up the gated gravel road ahead.

Spirit Lake from the Loowit Falls Trail.   Opposite: Pumice.

Since the 1980 blast, only scattered trees have taken root on this ridge, but wildflowers have flourished. Look for tall red fireweed, pearly everlasting, purple daisy-shaped asters, and clumps of big purple penstemons. National Monument rules forbid disturbing plants or rocks, so don't take samples of the pumice littering the road.

After 1.8 miles the Abraham Trail joins on the left — return route of the optional loop. Continue to road's end and take the Windy Trail, which follows big cairns across a barren pumice plain and climbs to a mile to the round-the-mountain Loowit Trail. Turn right across a creek gully, contour 1.3 miles to the crater's mouth, and take a 0.2-mile side path up to the Loowit Falls viewpoint. While this ridgecrest is dramatic, it's a bit bleak for lunch. So go back down to the Loowit Trail and go left a few hundred yards to a cozier canyon where the path crosses the crater's outlet creek between several smaller cascades. The steaming lava dome, out of sight in the crater above, heats this creek to 96 degrees Fahrenheit.

If you'd like to make a loop on your return trip, hike back along the Loowit Trail and continue straight, climbing over Windy Pass to the eerily barren Plains of Abraham. The mountain rises like a wall from this rock-strewn desert. Camping is permitted, but the only water is a weird creek of what looks like chocolate milk oozing from the decapitated Nelson Glacier. Turn left at a well-marked junction, recross the sludgy creek, and traverse a glorious ridge packed with July wildflowers and views of Mt. Adams before descending 2 sets of steps to join the road back to the car.

24 Spirit Lake

Easy (to Harmony Falls)
2.2 miles round-trip
700 feet elevation loss
Open late June through October
Map: Mt. St. Helens Nat'l. Mon. (USFS)

Moderate (to Norway Pass)
7 miles round-trip
1000 feet elevation gain

When Mt. St. Helens' north flank slid into Spirit Lake in 1980 it not only buried Harry Truman's famous lodge under 200 feet of rubble, it launched a gigantic wave that sloshed 800 feet up the lake's far shore, obliterating 3 youth camps and denuding the slopes. Today wildflowers and small trees are gradually returning to this landscape purged by fire and water, but hikers can still see the pale high-water mark left by the wave and the square-mile jumble of driftwood it washed into the lake.

Choose either (or both) of 2 dramatic trails: the short, heavily-used Harmony Falls Trail that descends to the actual lake shore, or the nearby, slightly longer path to Norway Pass that offers even more picturesque views across the lake to the crater's smoldering lava dome.

Start by driving Interstate 5 to Woodland exit 21 (north of Portland 25 miles). Turn right and follow signs for Mt. St. Helens for a total of 85 paved miles. Along the way, you'll follow Highway 503 through the town of Cougar, continue straight on what becomes Road 90 to the Pine Creek Information Station, go straight on Road 25 for 25 miles, and turn left on Road 99 for 13.3 miles to the Harmony Viewpoint.

The 1.1-mile Harmony Trail descends from the viewpoint amid blast-killed

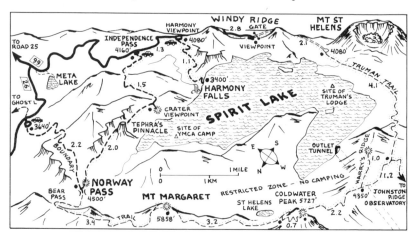

Mt. St. Helens from Norway Pass.   Opposite: Spirit Lake from Harmony Falls.

snags, young alders, and hopeful firs. Huge, bright red fireweed dominates these slopes, but also look for pearly everlasting, blue huckleberries, salmon-berries, and inside-out flower. The path passes below a cliff and then crosses a dusty plain with flotsam logs left from the tidal wave. Finally descend along Harmony Creek's stairstep falls to the shore, 200 feet above Spirit Lake's old level. Because this is a sensitive research area, off-trail hiking, camping, and venturing out on the driftwood logs are banned.

To hike to Norway Pass, drive 1.3 miles back on Road 99 to the Independence Pass Viewpoint. The path from this small parking area climbs a ridge ablaze with red fireweed. Look for Mt. Adams to the east and Mt. Hood to the north. After 1.5 miles a short side trail to the left descends to Crater Viewpoint, a knoll almost 800 feet above Spirit Lake's log-jammed shore. The trail contours 2 more glorious miles, passing Tephra's Pinnacle (a 100-foot spire of welded ash) on the way to the picture-postcard view of Mt. St. Helens from Norway Pass.

If you couldn't get a parking spot at the Independence Pass Trailhead, consider hiking to Norway Pass along the Boundary Trail instead. This 2.2-mile route has fewer views but is slightly shorter. Ideally, you could plan a car shuttle and hike both trails. To find this other trailhead, drive back 3 miles on Road 99 and turn left on Road 26 for a mile.

Other Hiking Options

For even more spectacular views, continue 3.4 miles past Norway Pass to Mt. Margaret's bald summit. Or hike 19.7 miles around the lake from Independence Pass to the Windy Ridge Viewpoint on Highway 99 — but finish in a single day, as camping is banned along the way.

Upper Lewis River Falls.   Opposite: Lower Lewis River Falls.

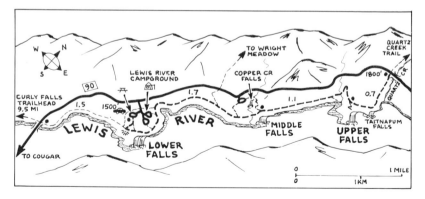

25   Lewis River Falls

Easy
7 miles round-trip
500 feet elevation gain
Open all year
Map: Lone Butte (Green Trails)

The Lewis River thunders over 3 colossal falls along this newly finished riverbank path. Because a paved road parallels the route, it's easy to plan a car (or bicycle) shuttle and hike the 3.5-mile trail one way — but the path's pretty enough you probably won't mind hiking it twice.

Drive Interstate 5 to Woodland exit 21 (north of Portland 25 miles), turn right and follow signs for Mt. St. Helens for 46.7 miles. Along the way, you'll follow Highway 503, go through the town of Cougar, and continue straight on what becomes Road 90. Just beyond the Pine Creek Information Station, turn right toward Carson on what is still Road 90 and follow this paved road for 14.2 miles to the Lower Falls Recreation Area on your right. Keep right to the picnic area loop and park by the restrooms.

A graveled trail sets off through Douglas fir woods with lots of pointy-leaved Oregon grape, dark-berried salal, and vine maple. After 100 yards take a right-hand fork of the trail that leads to an overlook of Lower Falls, where the Lewis River takes a magnificent Niagara-like plunge into a huge green pool.

Several trails from the nearby campground confuse things a bit here, but if you simply turn left, follow the riverbank upstream, and ignore all left-hand forks you can't go wrong. After half a mile the graveled path turns to duff. In another mile you'll cross a footbridge above Copper Creek's 200-foot, double-humped waterslide into the Lewis River. You can visit another of Copper Creek's waterfalls by taking a half-mile loop to the left on well-marked side trails — but save this detour for the return trip.

Continue along the Lewis River past Middle Falls, a 100-foot-long, milky-looking slide. The river trail soon ducks below a huge, overhanging cliff and enters a grove of massive old-growth Douglas firs and red cedars up to 10 feet thick. About 0.8 mile past Middle Falls you'll pass a trailside campsite with a bouldery beach and a glimpse ahead to Upper Falls. This is the only beach on the hike where kids can safely play by the river.

Next the trail bridges Alec Creek and climbs above Upper Falls, where a side trail leads to the 80-foot cascade's lip. The final 0.7 mile of the Lewis River Trail passes humble Taitnapum Falls and follows Quartz Creek to a bridge on Road 90, just 2.7 miles by road from your car.

Moderate (to Cultus Lake)
4.4 miles round-trip
1100 feet elevation gain
Open July to mid-October
Map: Indian Heaven Wilderness (USFS)

Moderate (to Lake Wapiki overlook)
6.8 miles round-trip
1600 feet elevation gain

The Indian Heaven country features alpine meadows, sparkling lakes, and world-famous huckleberry fields — but because this Wilderness lacks a major Cascade mountain it seldom draws crowds. The trail to Cultus Lake makes up for this by sneaking views of not-so-distant Mt. Adams. And if you hike an extra 1.2 miles through the heather you'll get even better views from craggy Lemei Rock, an ancient volcano that cups Lake Wapiki within its crater.

Until the 1920s Indians came to this high country each August to pick berries, hunt, and race horses. Natural and set wildfires maintained the berry fields and meadows. Even today the non-Wilderness huckleberry fields northeast of Highway 24 are reserved for Indians. Then as now, mosquitoes are a problem in July.

Drive Interstate 84 to Cascade Locks exit 44, pay a 75-cent toll to cross the Bridge of the Gods, turn right on Highway 14 for 5.9 miles, and turn left through Carson on Highway 30. Stick to this paved highway for 30.3 miles (be sure to keep right at a fork at the 14.5-mile mark). Finally turn right onto gravel Lone Butte Road (Road 30) for 7.9 miles and then turn right on gravel Road 24 for 4.2 miles to the Cultus Creek Campground. Park at the far end of the campground loop by a sign for the Indian Heaven Trail.

The trail climbs steeply through Douglas fir woods for a mile to a view (from

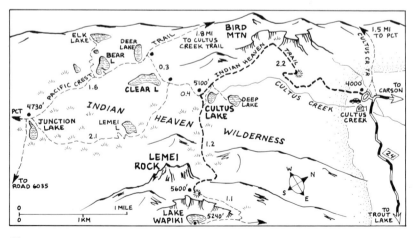

Lemei Rock from Cultus Lake.   Opposite: Lemei Rock from its base.

left to right) of Sawtooth Mountain, Mt. Rainier, the Goat Rocks, and Mt. Adams. Then the path continues uphill to a small meadow below Bird Mountain's cliffs before leveling off for a mile to an unmarked junction at your first glimpse of Cultus Lake. Explore to the left if you wish — the path deadends in 0.3 mile at Deep Lake. Otherwise keep right around beautiful, alpine Cultus Lake to a junction with the Lemei Trail. In Chinook jargon, the old trade language of Northwest tribes, *Lemei* means "old woman" and *Cultus*, oddly enough, means "worthless."

For a longer hike, take the Lemei Trail up through a mile of gorgeous heather meadows, switchback up to the base of Lemei Rock's summit crags, and continue a few hundred yards to the red cinder rim of the old crater overlooking lovely Lake Wapiki, Mt. Adams, and Mt. Hood. If you're eager for a swim, it's 1.1 miles further down to the meadows and sandy beach at Lake Wapiki, but remember to save energy for the return climb.

Other Hiking Options

Two moderate loop trips also begin with the hike to Cultus Lake. For a 9.2-mile meadow tour of 6 lakes, continue straight on the Indian Heaven Trail to the Pacific Crest Trail, turn left to Junction Lake (also accessible via Hike #27), and turn left on the Lemei Lake Trail. For a woodsy 6.2-mile loop around Bird Mountain, take the Indian Heaven Trail to the PCT, turn right for 1.8 level miles, and turn right on the Cultus Creek Trail over a low pass for the steep descent to your car.

Junction Lake. Opposite: Bear Lake.

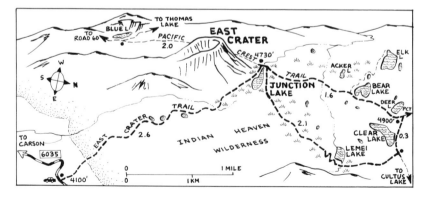

27   Junction Lake

Easy (to Junction Lake)
5.2 miles round-trip
700 feet elevation gain
Open mid-June to mid-October
Map: Indian Heaven Wildns. (USFS)

Moderate (to Lemei Lake)
9.2-mile loop
900 feet elevation gain

The East Crater Trail provides the easiest route to the famous alpine meadows of the Indian Heaven Wilderness. And once you reach huckleberry-rimmed Junction Lake, it's tempting to make an additional 4-mile loop on the Pacific Crest Trail past 4 other large lakes and vast fields of heather.

Drive Interstate 84 to Cascade Locks exit 44, pay 75 cents to cross the Bridge of the Gods, turn right on Highway 14 for 5.9 miles, and turn left through Carson on Highway 30 for 11.7 miles. Following signs for Panther Creek Campground, turn briefly right and then jog left on what becomes Road 65. Follow this curvy paved road for 11 miles, turn right on gravel Road 60 for 8.6 miles, and then follow an "East Crater Trail" pointer left onto Road 6030 (which becomes Road 6035) for 4.1 miles to a trailhead sign on the left.

The path's first 1.4 miles climb gradually through unremarkable mountain hemlock woods — a long stretch for hikers with small children. But then you pass 3 tadpole-filled ponds and the meadowed openings become larger and larger, leading over a low pass to Junction Lake. The heather blooms here in July — a month when mosquitoes are a real problem. In August the huckleberries ripen, while the crisp nights of September turn the huckleberry leaves gold and red. If you're backpacking, be sure to camp in the woods and not in the fragile meadows.

To continue on the loop, go to the Pacific Crest Trail junction at the far end of the lake, turn right across the outlet creek's bridge, and promptly turn right on the Lemei Lake Trail. This path ambles through heather and past grassy-banked Lemei Lake. After 2.1 miles turn left on the Indian Heaven Trail, which leads between a huge rockslide and Clear Lake. Then turn left on the PCT to complete the loop. Short side trails to the right of the PCT lead down to forest-rimmed Deer and Bear Lakes, as well as to unseen Elk Lake.

Other Hiking Options

To explore more of this high country, either take the Indian Heaven Trail north to Cultus Lake (see Hike #26) or take the PCT south to Blue Lake (see Hike #28). Adventurers who are careful to use compass can also bushwhack due south a mile from Junction Lake up the steep, forested flank of East Crater to a viewpoint on the volcano's east rim. In the middle of the crater is an eerie, hidden meadow with a rarely visited pond.

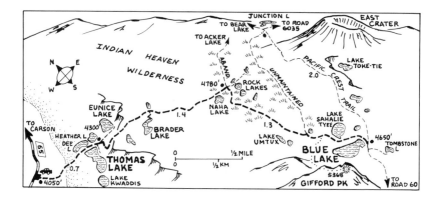

28   Thomas Lake

Easy (to Thomas Lake)
1.4 miles round-trip
300 feet elevation gain
Open mid-June to mid-October
Map: Indian Heaven Wilderness (USFS)

Moderate (to Blue Lake)
6.8 miles round-trip
900 feet elevation gain

Children and lake-lovers of all ages enjoy exploring the 5 lakes clustered in the forest within the first mile of the Thomas Lake Trail. For a longer hike, cross Indian Heaven's glorious heather-and-huckleberry meadows to sapphire Blue Lake, backed by the cliffs of Gifford Peak.

To find the trailhead, take Interstate 84 to Cascade Locks exit 44, pay 75 cents to cross the Bridge of the Gods, turn right on Highway 14 for 5.9 miles, and turn left through Carson on Highway 30 for 11.7 miles. Following signs for Panther Creek Campground, turn briefly right and then jog left on what becomes Road 65. After 12.9 paved miles, fork to the right on a gravel continuation of Road 65 for 6.7 miles to the signed Thomas Lake Trail parking area on the right.

The trail begins in a partially logged area with a view of Mt. St. Helens, but soon climbs into uncut woods of lichen-draped mountain hemlock and Pacific silver fir. Blue huckleberries ripen here in August. Mosquitoes can be thick in July.

After 0.7 mile the path squeezes between 3 lakes. Just beyond a little foot-bridge, explorers might want to try a side trail to the right leads that leads past several heavily used campsites and continues faintly 0.5 mile around Thomas Lake. Otherwise continue on the main trail 100 yards to a major, unmarked fork.

The left-hand fork deadends in 0.2 mile at Eunice Lake. If you've set a more distant goal, keep right and climb up a steep, rough switchback to a wooded plateau. After another half mile you'll pass a pond on the left. Immediately opposite this pond, on the right-hand side of the trail, a faint side path leads 100 yards over a small ridge to hidden, rarely-visited Brader Lake.

Beyond this point the main trail has a few more steep, rocky pitches before leveling off amid heavenly alpine meadows. Turn right at a 4-way junction, ramble 0.8 miles to a T-shaped junction at a pond, and turn right for a final half mile through the woods to the Pacific Crest Trail at the end of Blue Lake.

Other Hiking Options

The lake-dotted high meadows invite exploration. For a loop along an abandoned trail, turn left at the T-shaped junction 0.5 mile before Blue Lake, pass a "Trail Not Maintained" sign, and take the easily followed path 1.7 miles through the meadows to Junction Lake (also accessible via Hike #27). Then turn right on the PCT for 2 woodsy miles to Blue Lake.

Adventurers with compass in hand can also bushwhack to a rare viewpoint atop Gifford Peak. From Blue Lake, hike back past Sahalie Tyee Lake to the Thomas Lake Trail's highest point in the forest and strike off to the left up a wooded ridge, gaining 700 feet in 0.8 mile.

Blue Lake. Opposite: Gomphus *mushroom.*

29 Trapper Creek

Moderate (to Deer Cutoff loop)
7.2 miles round-trip
1000 feet elevation gain
Open all year
Map: Trapper Creek Wilderness (USFS)

Difficult (to Observation Peak)
14.6-mile loop
3200 feet elevation gain
Open June to mid-November

Just 15 miles north of the Columbia Gorge, the densely forested Trapper Creek Wilderness features a well-marked network of hiking paths. For a moderate trip, explore the valley's jungly old-growth groves on rugged trails built by Portland Mazama club volunteers. For a challenging loop with plenty of elevation gain, continue on smoother Forest Service trails to Observation Peak, a former lookout site with views from Mt. Rainier to Mt. Jefferson.

Metallic-tasting bubbly soda springs attracted health-conscious tourists to Trapper Creek in the early 1900s. A 3-story spa hotel burned in 1934, but Government Mineral Springs Day Use Area remains beside the springs at the lower edge of the Wilderness.

Drive Interstate 84 to Cascade Locks exit 44, pay a 75-cent toll to cross the Bridge of the Gods, turn right on Highway 14 for 5.9 miles, and turn left through Carson on Highway 30 for 14.5 miles to a junction. Go straight onto Mineral Springs Road for 0.4 mile and then turn right onto gravel Road 5401 for 0.4 mile to the trailhead parking lot.

Hike a few feet up the path and turn left on the Trapper Creek Trail, which contours 0.9 mile through second-growth Douglas fir woods to a 4-way trail junction. To the right is the return route of the loop to Observation Peak, but for now keep straight. Follow the narrowing Trapper Creek Trail another 1.9 miles and then go straight on the Deer Cutoff Trail 0.6 mile to a junction.

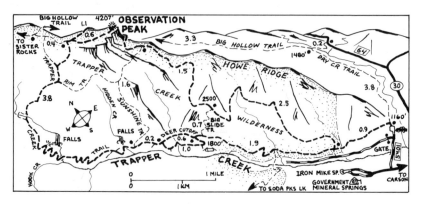

For the moderate hike, turn left here and descend a steep, rooty path to a mossy grove of huge, 7-foot-thick Douglas firs in the canyon bottom. Here you'll gain your first views of rushing Trapper Creek, though access to the brushy bank amidst this jungle still requires some scrambling. The 1-mile path passes a small campsite and climbs steeply back to the route to your car.

For the longer loop, continue straight from the Deer Cutoff Trail onto the upper continuation of the Trapper Creek Trail. The path is narrow and rooty for 1.4 miles. Then the path crosses Trapper Creek on a single-log footbridge and switchbacks steeply up a 1000-foot ridge, passing a viewpoint of 100-foot Trapper Creek Falls. Follow the path across a forested plateau, recross Trapper Creek, and 0.8 mile later ignore a junction for the Rim Trail on the right. In another 0.1 mile, however, turn right at a fork for the Observation Cutoff Trail. Ceramic insulators and wire along this route show it follows the old telephone line for the peak's long-gone fire lookout tower.

When you reach a larger trail at a saddle, turn right a few feet to another T-shaped junction. To the right is the 0.6-mile path to the summit viewpoint amid clusters of big blue gentians and delicate bluebells. To the left is the loop's return path — an amazingly well-graded 6-mile route down Howe Ridge.

Other Hiking Options

The well-maintained Big Hollow Trail provides an easier route to Observation Peak, gaining 2700 feet in just 4.5 miles. Drive as to the Trapper Creek Trailhead, but stick to Highway 30 for an additional 4.5 miles (following signs for Mt. St. Helens) to the trailhead on the left. The trail crosses Big Hollow Creek and climbs 3.8 miles up a ridge to a saddle junction. Here you can either turn left for 1 mile to Observation Peak or turn right for 0.5 mile and bushwhack left 0.5 mile up through huckleberry meadows to a similar view atop Sisters Rocks.

Trapper Creek.   Opposite: Mt. St. Helens from Observation Peak.

30   Three Corner Rock   ⋀

Easy
4.4 miles round-trip
800 feet elevation gain
Open May to mid-November
Maps: Beacon Rock, Lookout Mountain
(Washington, USGS)

Hike a rarely-visited portion of the Pacific Crest Trail to a landmark lookout site with a view of 5 snowpeaks and portions of the Columbia Gorge. Then explore a strange shelter built from a length of corrugated pipe in a beargrass meadow beside the summit.

Drive Interstate 84 to Cascade Locks exit 44, pay 75 cents to cross the Bridge of the Gods, and turn right on Highway 14 for 1.5 miles. At milepost 43, turn left onto Rock Creek Drive for 0.3 mile. Then turn left for 0.9 mile on Foster Creek Road (which becomes Ryan Allen Road), turn left again onto paved Red Bluff Road for 0.3 mile, and then veer right onto gravel Road CG 2000. Stick to this winding, uphill road for a total of 9.5 miles, taking care to watch for posts identifying Road CG 2000 at intersections. When the road finally crests at Rock Creek Pass, don't follow the main road to the right. Instead go straight on less-used Road CG 2090 for 0.3 mile up to another pass and park at a pullout on the right.

The Pacific Crest Trail crosses the road here, but the path is marked only by a small triangular PCT symbol on a tree. Start hiking up to the right amid mountain hemlocks and Pacific silver firs. White June wildflowers here include 4-petaled bunchberry and delicate sprays of star-flowered smilacina. The well-graded path switchbacks up past views of snowy Mt. Adams and the tops of Mt. Rainier and Mt. St. Helens.

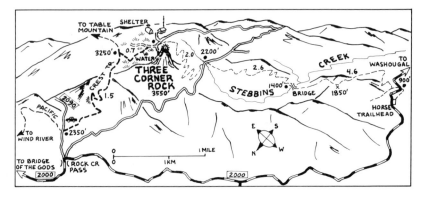

Stebbins Creek Valley from Three Corner Rock.   *Opposite: Shelter near the summit.*

After 1.5 miles a large fallen sign marks a junction for the Three Corner Rock Trail. Turn right and cross a high meadow filled in some years with the dramatic white plumes of blooming beargrass. A short, marked side trail leads to a drinkable, piped spring. When you reach a dirt road, turn right for a few hundred yards to a 4-way junction at a saddle. To the left is a gravel road, a microwave relay tower, and the strange culvert-cum-shelter. Straight ahead is the Three Corner Rock Trail from Stebbins Creek. And to the right is the rock summit itself. Concrete steps lead to within 12 feet of the top, but it's easy to clamber the rest of the way to the burned lookout tower's square foundations. Mt. Adams looms above the dark silhouette of the Indian Heaven uplands. Mt. Hood rises above the Eagle Creek canyon. The Columbia River glints beside Dog Mountain and snakes west toward Portland.

Other Hiking Options

Backpackers or day hikers with a shuttle car can continue 9.2 miles down the Three Corner Rock Trail through Stebbins Creek's quiet, forested valley. The well-marked lower trailhead can be reached by driving 7.3 miles west of Rock Creek Pass on gravel Road 2000. But if you're driving to this trailhead from Vancouver it's quicker to take Highway 14, turn left at Washougal on the Washougal River Road for 22 paved miles, and fork to the right on gravel Road 2000 for 3.2 miles.

View from Hamilton Mountain's cliffs. Below: *The Beacon Rock Trail.*

31   **Beacon Rock Park**

Easy (to Beacon Rock)
1.8 miles round-trip
600 feet elevation gain
Open all year
Map: Bridal Veil (Green Trails)

Easy (to Rodney Falls)
2.2 miles round-trip
600 feet elevation gain

Difficult (to Hamilton Mountain)
7.6-mile loop
2000 feet elevation gain

Beacon Rock State Park boasts 2 of the Columbia Gorge's most famous and popular trails: a switchbacking path up Beacon Rock's 848-foot-tall block of basalt, and a longer trail that passes beautiful Rodney Falls before climbing steeply to cliff-edge viewpoints on Hamilton Mountain.

Lewis and Clark named Beacon Rock in 1805 while paddling past its cliffs. In 1915 a man named Henry Biddle bought the rock and arduously constructed a well-graded trail to the top, incorporating 47 switchbacks and dozens of railed catwalk bridges. When the Army Corps of Engineers suggested the monolith be blown up for use as a jetty at the mouth of the Columbia, Biddle's family tried to make the area a state park. At first Washington refused the gift. But that decision quickly changed when *Oregon* offered to accept.

To find the park, take Interstate 205 north across the Columbia River and turn right on Highway 14 for 28.6 miles. If you're driving here from the east, take Interstate 84 to Cascade Locks exit 44, pay 75 cents to cross the Bridge of the Gods, and turn left on Highway 14 for 6.9 miles.

To climb Beacon Rock, park in one of the roadside pullouts on either side of Beacon Rock and walk 50 yards along the highway to the signed trailhead, halfway between the parking areas. Although nearly all of the 0.9-mile route has railings, parents may want to hold small children's hands to make sure they stay on the path. From the top, the view stretches from Crown Point to Bonneville Dam. Kids love to point out Burlington Northern's toy trains chugging by, far below. Tiny powerboats cut white V's in the Columbia's green shallows.

If you'd rather take the Hamilton Mountain Trail, turn off Highway 14 opposite Beacon Rock, drive 0.3 mile up a paved road toward the campground, and then veer to the right into a trailhead parking lot.

The path climbs through a second-growth Douglas fir forest with red thimbleberries, blue Oregon grape, and bracken fern. Soon you pass under a powerline, where a trail from the campground joins on the left. At the 1-mile mark a side trail to the right descends to a poor viewpoint of Hardy Falls. Continue on the main trail a few hundred yards and go left on a side trail that ends at a railed cliff beside Rodney Falls, a fascinating, 50-foot cascade trapped in an enormous rock-walled bowl. Return to the main trail and switchback down to a footbridge below the falls — a good turnaround point for hikers with children.

If you're continuing, switchback uphill, keep left at an unmarked fork (the right-hand path descends to the creek above Hardy Falls), and climb 0.2 mile to a fork marking the start of the loop. Keep right on a steep, switchbacking trail up a cliff-edged ridge with dizzying views across the Columbia Gorge. After 1.8 miles you'll finally reach a T-shaped junction at the summit ridgecrest. The path to the right promptly deadends at Hamilton Mountain's summit, where the view is partly obscured by brush.

To continue the loop, turn around and follow the ridgecrest trail past better viewpoints of Mt. Hood, Mt. Adams, and Table Rock. After 0.9 mile, turn left down an abandoned road. Keep left on the road for 1.0 mile to a meadow at a creek crossing. Here veer left onto a level path through a cool alder forest. After 1.1 mile, this path joins the main trail. Turn right to return to your car.

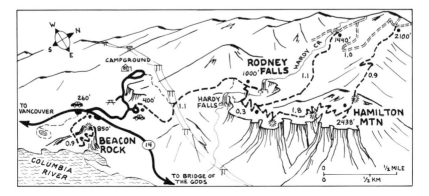

32   Gillette Lake

Easy (to Gillette Lake)
5 miles round-trip
300 feet elevation gain
Open all year
Map: Bonneville Dam (Green Trails)

Moderate (to Greenleaf Overlook)
7.6 miles round-trip
600 feet elevation gain

This convenient stretch of the famous Pacific Crest Trail heads north from Bonneville Dam through a pleasant, nearly level forest to the grassy bank of Gillette Lake. For a slightly longer hike, continue past 2 pretty creeks to a view of the Columbia Gorge at Greenleaf Overlook. Truly hardy hikers can go on to climb landmark Table Mountain — a grueling 15.1-mile round-trip.

The hike's route crosses an enormous landslide that sheared off Table Mountain 700 years ago and dammed the entire Columbia River for days or possibly even months, giving rise to Indian legends of a "Bridge of the Gods" that could be crossed dry-shod. Forest has regrown on the 14-square-mile slide, but the river still swerves toward Oregon here. Watch for other landslide souvenirs along the trail: erratic, house-sized boulders, hummocky terrain, and lakes.

Drive Interstate 84 to Cascade Locks exit 44, pay 75 cents to cross the modern-day Bridge of the Gods, and turn left on Highway 14 for 2 miles to the Bonneville Trailhead on the right. Walk briefly up a gated gravel road to a sign announcing the Tamanous Trail to the PCT. Equestrians share this route, so be sure to step off the trail on the downhill side if you meet horses.

The path climbs through a Douglas fir forest with yellow-blooming Oregon grape in spring, red thimbleberries in summer, and scarlet vine maple leaves in fall. Traverse a low, meadowed ridge with a fine view across the Columbia to

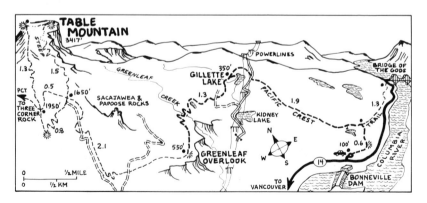

Gillette Lake.   Opposite: Landslide boulders by the Pacific Crest Trail.

Ruckel Ridge (Hike #45) and the canyon of Eagle Creek (Hike #44).

Turn left on the PCT after 0.6 mile and a bit later glimpse a deep, green, brushy-shored lake in the woods to the left. At the 1.7-mile mark the trail briefly skirts a 1990 clearcut. Then the path meets a gravel road, continues on the far side 50 feet to the right, and descends under a powerline. Look on the horizon for Sacajawea and Papoose Rocks, natural rock statues to the left of massive Table Mountain. Then a side trail to the left leads to green Gillette Lake — a pleasant picnic spot, but beware of patches of poison oak brush nearby.

For a better view, hike another 1.3 miles along the PCT to Greenleaf Overlook, a mossy rim at the edge of the ancient landslide. From here you can survey the broken wall of Columbia Gorge cliffs on the Oregon shore.

Other Hiking Options

For a genuine challenge, continue past Greenleaf Overlook for 2.6 miles on the PCT and turn right on a very steep 1.3-mile path to Table Mountain, a pinched plateau with stunning viewpoints on either edge. Be warned that the climb calls for 3500 of elevation gain — most of it in the grueling final mile. And although it's possible to make a loop of this steep pitch, the eastern path to the top requires dangerous scrambling, particularly in wet weather.

33 Grassy Knoll

Easy (to Grassy Knoll)
4.4 miles round-trip
900 feet elevation gain
Open April to December
Maps: Big Huckleberry Mtn., Willard
(Washington, USGS)

Difficult (to Big Huckleberry Mountain)
10.8 miles round-trip
2300 feet elevation gain
Open late May to early November

With wildflower meadows and views of Mt. Adams and Mt. Hood, this ridgecrest path provides an uncrowded alternative to the steep, heavily used Dog Mountain Trail nearby (Hike #34). For a short hike, follow the rolling ridge to a former lookout site at Grassy Knoll. For a longer walk, continue to a taller lookout site atop Big Huckleberry Mountain.

To find the trailhead, drive Interstate 84 to Cascade Locks exit 44, pay 75 cents to cross the Bridge of the Gods, turn right on Highway 14 for 5.9 miles, turn left through Carson on Highway 30 for 4.2 miles, and then turn right on Bear Creek Road. Follow this road — which becomes Road 6808 — for 3.6 paved miles and an additional 7.2 miles of curvy, one-lane gravel to Triangle Pass. Then turn left onto Road 68 for 2.1 miles to where Road 511 joins from the right. Look for the Grassy Knoll Trail sign 50 feet up this side road.

After starting in a small meadow, the path climbs through Douglas fir woods where star-flowered smilacina and vanilla leaf bloom white in May. While some trees are 5 feet thick, winds from the Columbia Gorge keep them short. After a few steep pitches the trail passes a gravel pit and a clearcut, and then levels off along a lovely clifftop rim with views of Mt. Adams across the Big Lava Bed's forested plain. About 300,000 years ago, basalt from the edge of the Indian Heaven high country leveled this 20-square-mile valley, surged down the Little

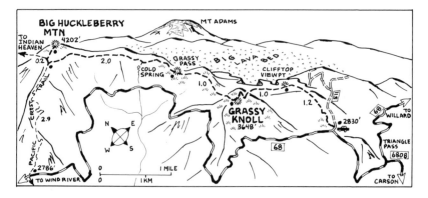

Mt. Adams from clifftop viewpoint.   *Opposite: Mt. Hood from Grassy Knoll.*

White Salmon River, and briefly dammed the Columbia.

Continue up and down through increasing meadows for a mile to Grassy Knoll, where sunflower-like balsamroot blooms in May. Foundation piers mark the lookout site. Mt. Hood rises above Nick Eaton Ridge and conical Wind Mountain. Unless you're really tired, it's worth it to continue another mile along the rolling ridgecrest through meadows of beargrass, lupine, and blue huckleberries to the first-rate view from Grassy Pass.

Beyond this open saddle the trail traverses 2 miles through the woods to the Pacific Crest Trail. Turn right here — and keep right at junctions in the next few yards — to find the short path up to a panoramic view in a berry patch at Big Huckleberry Mountain's summit.

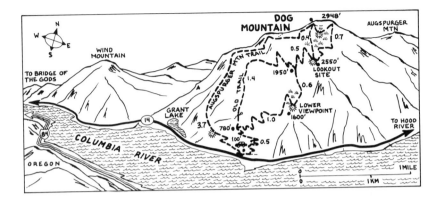

34   Dog Mountain

Moderate (to lower viewpoint)
3 miles round-trip
1500 feet elevation gain
Open all year
Map: Trails of the Col. Gorge (USFS)

Difficult (to summit)
7-mile loop
2900 feet elevation gain

The most spectacular wildflower meadows of the entire Columbia Gorge drape the alp-like slopes of Dog Mountain. In May and June these hills are alive with the colors of Indian paintbrush and lupine. Even flowerless seasons provide breathtaking views of the Columbia Gorge. Such beauty has made the steep, difficult climb to the top very popular. Fortunately the original, precipitous trail has been supplemented with longer, less steep alternative paths.

From Portland, drive Interstate 84 east to the Cascade Locks exit (#44), take the Bridge of the Gods across the river (paying a 75-cent toll on the way), and turn right onto Washington Highway 14. Follow this highway 12 miles to a large parking lot on the left with a wooden sign for the Dog Mountain Trail.

In fact, 2 trails leave this parking area. The older Dog Mountain Trail at the far right end of the lot begins along an ancient road but after 100 yards turns sharply left and begins a relentless, switchbacking climb. Because this path has no views for the first 1.5 miles, most hikers save it as a return route for a loop.

Instead start near the middle of the parking area pullot on the new Augspurger Mountain Trail. This longer, better graded path starts out traversing open woods with views down the Columbia Gorge to Wind Mountain. Beware of lush, three-leaved poison oak along these lower slopes of Dog Mountain. Also notice early summer wildflowers: baby blue eyes, lupine, yellow desert parsley, and purple cluster lilies on onion-like stalks.

After 2 miles the trail ducks into a denser Douglas fir forest brightened in spring by big three-petaled trilliums and tiny six- or seven-petaled starflowers. If you're wearing down, this might be a good place to turn back.

But if your legs are up to the challenge, continue onward to Dog Mountain's grand, windswept summit meadows. In early summer, sunflower-like balsam-root and red Indian paintbrush spangle this steep, airy aerie. There's a flavorful assortment of shy blooms, too: chocolate lilies and wild strawberries. A panorama of the Columbia Gorge's chasm sweeps from Hood River to Cascade Locks. Below Mt. Hood, look for Starvation Creek Falls and sometimes-snowy Mt. Defiance.

After absorbing the view, hike across the summit meadow to its far upper end, where the return loop trail enters the woods. Then keep left at all junctions for the prettiest and least steep route back to your car.

Other Hiking Options

A planned 3.8-mile extension to the Augspurger Mountain Trail will fork to the left off the current trail below the summit of Dog Mountain and lead north to Augspurger Mountain, a 3667-foot peak with meadows and views of its own. Long-range plans propose an additional 4-mile extension north to the Grassy Knoll Trail (Hike #33), allowing backpackers to hike 16.7 miles from Dog Mountain to the Pacific Crest Trail.

The Columbia Gorge and Wind Mountain from the trail.   *Opposite: Cluster lily.*

35 Catherine Creek

Easy (to rock arch)
2.4 miles round-trip
400 feet elevation gain
Open all year
Map: Lyle (USGS)

Easy (to Indian pits)
1 mile round-trip
400 feet elevation gain

The first of these 2 easy hikes leads through Catherine Creek's park-like valley of oaks and meadows to a natural rock arch with a view of the Columbia Gorge from The Dalles to Hood River. The second, shorter walk explores a nearby hillside where mysterious pits in a rockslide are believed to honor the spirits of Indian dead.

Take Interstate 84 to the Hood River Bridge exit (#64) and pay the $1 toll to cross the river. Then turn right onto Washington Highway 14 for 5.8 miles. Just before milepost 71 turn left at a sign for Rowland Lake. Follow a paved county road 0.8 mile around the lake and up a hill. When you see a green barn on the right, look for a wire gate on the left; this is the trailhead to the Indian pits. To find the Catherine Creek trailhead, continue 0.4 mile along the county road and park on the left by a wire gate with rock-filled wood-box gate posts and a small enigmatic sign, "MR 109/3+."

By 1998, expect a new parking area and trail network here. Until then, the hike through Catherine Creek's canyon starts by following the abandoned road past the wire gate. The road is faint for 200 yards as it crosses a barren bedrock flat, but then it angles left to lusher terrain along the creek. After 0.3 mile go right at a fork and cross the creek. Next the route passes an old corral and stable at the foot of the rock arch — actually a splinter of rimrock on the canyon wall.

The valley floor has shrubby clumps of both poison oak and real oak, so pay

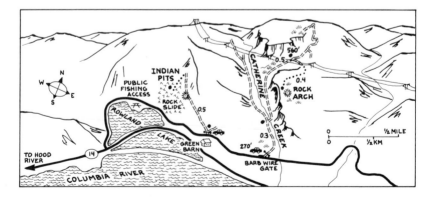

Catherine Creek's rock arch.   Opposite: View of Columbia Gorge from the Indian pits.

attention to the difference: the lobed leaves of poison oak are always in clusters of three while real oak has single leaves. At times poison oak can also be identified by white berries or shiny leaves.

Continue on the old road through an upper meadow where blue lupine blooms in May. Just after passing under a set of powerlines, the road faintly forks. Go to the right, passing back under the powerlines on a faint trail that climbs 100 yards up to a grassy tableland. From there head cross-country to the southwest toward the distant white cone of Mt. Hood. After 0.2 mile, reach the top edge of the canyon rim and follow it downhill toward the arch. Do not climb on the arch or approach too closely, as the sparse vegetation here is fragile.

If you'd like to visit the Indian pits after hiking through Catherine Creek's valley, return to your car and drive 0.4 mile back to the inconspicuous wire gate. Parking is limited here. Walk up the steepish road to the left for 0.3 mile to a viewpoint across a huge lava rockslide to Rowland Lake. Notice the odd walls and pits in the rockslide. To inspect them, continue 100 yards to the end of the road and rock-hop down the rocky slope. The 5- to 15-foot-wide pits are sometimes clustered in groups of 20 or more within meandering rock walls.

Northwest Indians often built small rock-rimmed meditation sites in places where spirits were thought to be powerful — often on mountain peaks. Young men would fast in such locations in the hopes of receiving a spirit vision to guide their adult life. Are the pits here vision quest sites? Perhaps, since they overlook the Columbia River's Memaloose Island. *Memaloose* means "dead" in the language of the Chinook Indians who once lived here, and the island was an important burial site and spiritual center for that powerful rivergoing tribe.

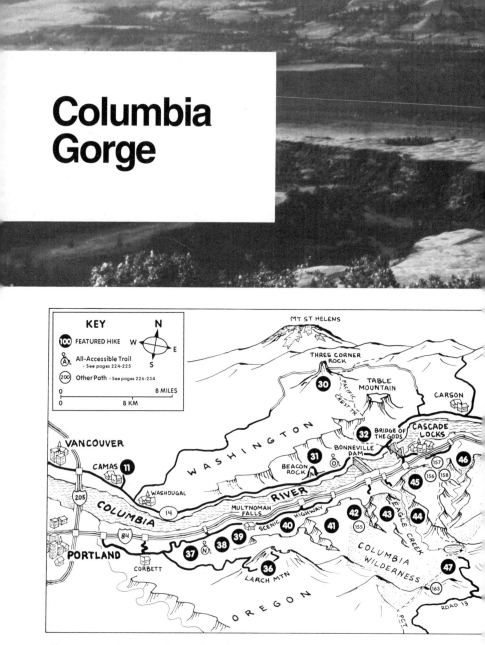

Columbia
Gorge

KEY

N
W **E**
S

100 FEATURED HIKE

A All-Accessible Trail
- See pages 224-225

200 Other Path - See pages 226-234

0   8 MILES
0   8 KM

MT ST HELENS

THREE CORNER
ROCK

30

PACIFIC CREST TR

TABLE
MOUNTAIN

CARSON

32 BRIDGE OF
THE GODS

CASCADE
LOCKS

W A S H I N G T O N

31

BONNEVILLE
DAM

BEACON
ROCK

VANCOUVER

CAMAS **11**

WASHOUGAL

205

C O L U M B I A

R I V E R

46

157

156 158

45

MULTNOMAH
FALLS

SCENIC HIGHWAY

40

42

43

EAGLE CREEK

44

84

37

A **N**

38

39

41

155

C O L U M B I A
WILDERNESS

PORTLAND

CORBETT

36

LARCH MTN

47

163

ROAD 13

O R E G O N

PCT

Above: Rowena Plateau and Mt. Adams from McCall Point (Hike #51).

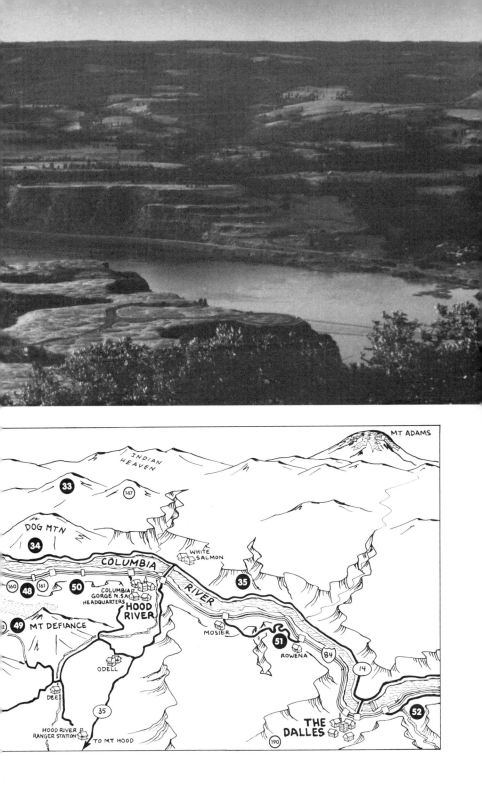

Moderate
6-mile loop
1300 feet elevation gain
Open May through November
Map: Trails of the Columbia Gorge (USFS)

The panoramic viewpoint atop this 4055-foot volcano at the west end of the Columbia Gorge is justly famous. Mount Hood looms across the Bull Run Valley while 4 other snowpeaks mark the horizon. But the charms of Larch Mountain's crater are less well known. A moderate 6-mile loop explores a huge old-growth forest, a meadow of marsh marigolds, and a mossy creek hidden in the throat of the old volcano.

Larch Mountain had a much smaller crater when it stopped erupting some 4 million years ago. During the Ice Age, however, a glacier scoured the peak into an enormous bowl, breached the mountain's north flank, and exposed Sherrard Point — the volcano's central lava plug. When the ice melted, a lake was left that gradually silted in to become a marshy meadow. Trees around the meadow grew to giant size, protected from fire and windstorms by the crater's wall.

Rather than start this loop from the crowded parking area at the summit — which would mean ending the hike with an uphill trudge — it's more fun to start at a secret trailhead near the crater's base. To find the trailhead, take Interstate 84 to Corbett exit 22, drive steeply up a mile to Corbett, turn left on the old Columbia River Highway for 1.9 miles, and then fork to the right on the paved Larch Mountain Road for nearly 12 miles. Half a mile after milepost 11 the Larch Mountain Road makes a sweeping switchback to the right. At the end of the curve's guardrail, turn left onto an unmarked dirt road. If your car has

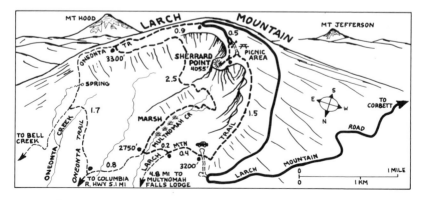

Mount Hood from Sherrard Point.   *Opposite: Avalanche lilies*

low clearance, park here. Otherwise drive 0.3 mile up to the marked trail crossing at the start of a gravel parking area.

Take the downhill trail for 0.4 mile, turn right onto the Multnomah Creek Way Trail, and continue down to a 40-foot bridge over Multnomah Creek amid red cedar, skunk cabbage, and salmonberries. Turn right and follow the creek upstream past a marshy meadow with a view ahead to Sherrard Point's crag. The trail climbs through an ancient grove of hemlock trees.

When you reach a ridgecrest junction, turn right on the Oneonta Trail and climb the ridge. In May this trail is lined with a stunning display of white lilies — both large-leaved trilliums and droopy-headed avalanche lilies. After 0.9 mile the trail ends at the Larch Mountain Road. Walk up the road 0.3 mile to its end and keep right on a paved path to Sherrard Point's railed viewing platform.

To continue the loop, walk back from Sherrard Point but keep right at all junctions. You'll cross a road turnaround, skirt a picnic area, and descend a forested ridge to your car.

Other Hiking Options

To experience the Columbia Gorge from top to bottom, hike from Larch Mountain's 4055-foot summit to the old Columbia River Highway, virtually at sea level. If you can arrange a car shuttle it's a 6.7-mile one-way romp down to the Multnomah Falls Lodge (see Hike #39) and it's 8 miles one way to the Oneonta Trailhead (see Hike #40). Without a shuttle you'll have to start at the bottom — a long, difficult climb.

Upper Latourell Falls.   *Opposite: Columnar basalt at Lower Latourell Falls.*

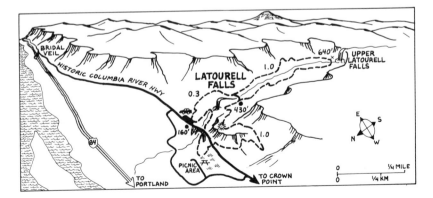

37   Latourell Falls

Easy
2.3-mile loop
600 feet elevation gain
Open all year
Map: Bridal Veil (Green Trails)

Closest to Portland of the Columbia Gorge's great waterfalls, Lower Latourell Falls plunges 249 feet over the lip of an eroded lava flow. An easy 2.3-mile loop trail climbs to the top of the falls, continues to a secluded, 100-foot upper falls, and returns by way of a picnic area.

From Portland take Interstate 84 to the Bridal Veil exit (#28), turn right on the historic Columbia River Highway, and drive 2.8 miles to the Latourell Falls parking area on the left. If you're coming from Hood River, take exit 35 and follow the old highway 10 miles.

Start on the broad paved path leading *uphill* to the left from the lot. Pavement ends just beyond a first viewpoint. The trail climbs through bigleaf maple woods lush with greenery: delicate black-stalked maidenhair fern, little white-starred candyflowers, stinging nettles, and waterleaf, a low-growing but handsome plant with sharply lobed, foot-wide leaves.

Just after a viewpoint at the top of the falls, the trail forks. To the right is Latourell Creek and a scenic footbridge overhung in early summer with edible salmonberries, resembling orange raspberries. If you'd like to shorten the loop hike to a mere 1.3 miles, continue straight across this bridge. Otherwise backtrack to the junction and head upstream on the other fork of the trail. In late spring look here for 2 closely related pink wildflowers: bleeding hearts (with arching fronds) and corydalis (with tall stalks of pink hoods).

After half a mile the trail crosses a bridge at the splash pool of Upper Latourell Falls, a spiraling cascade that arches over a shallow cavern. Follow the loop trail another half mile back downstream, go straight to bypass the lower bridge, and switchback up to a nice viewpoint of the Columbia River. To the west note Rooster Rock, a long splinter of lava that broke off from Crown Point's cliffs only a few thousand years ago and landed upright in the river mud.

Next the loop trail descends to the highway. Cross the road and take the stone steps down to the grassy picnic area. In the middle of the lawn turn right on a paved path that ducks under the 100-foot arch of the highway bridge and emerges at spectacular Lower Latourell Falls. The strangely splayed hexagonal pillars in the falls' cliffy face resulted when the once-molten basalt lava slowly cooled, shrank, and fractured into columns perpendicular to the underlying surface. The loop trail then continues up to your car.

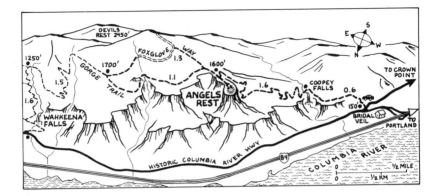

38   Angels Rest

Moderate
4.4 miles round-trip
1500 feet elevation gain
Open all year
Map: Trails of the Columbia Gorge (USFS)

Angels Rest juts like a balcony above the western Columbia Gorge. The trail to this rocky bluff was overswept by a 1991 wildfire, so it traverses an interesting mosaic of forest types. Most of the woods were untouched, while in many areas only the underbrush burned, clearing the forest floor for wildflowers. On a few ridges the trees themselves burned, opening new viewpoints. The changes demonstrate the natural role of fire in Douglas fir forests.

While the viewpoint at Angels Rest makes an excellent goal by itself, it's also tempting to extend the hike by exploring the adjacent plateau. One option is to visit a creekside picnic site by adding an easy 2.4-mile loop. Or better yet, arrange a short car shuttle and continue to beautiful Wahkeena Falls for a 6.4-mile, moderate one-way hike.

From Portland, take Interstate 84 to Bridal Veil exit 28 and park at the junction with the old Columbia River Highway. The Angels Rest Trail begins beside a concrete milepost at the intersection. If you're driving here from the east, take exit 35 and follow the old highway 7.3 miles.

The trail starts out uphill through a fern-filled forest where large white trilliums bloom in early spring. After half a mile you'll get a glimpse of 100-foot Coopey Falls. Then the trail climbs past an upper, 30-foot cascade and crosses

Coopey Creek on a scenic footbridge. By late spring larkspur crowds the woods here with chest-high stalks of blue flowers.

Beyond Coopey Creek the path climbs in earnest, switchbacking up a ridge and traversing a rockslide. Beware of poison oak growing from beneath the trailside rocks. Finally the trail reaches a windy crest with an unmarked junction. Turn left to Angel Rest's miniature mesa, with views of the Columbia River on 3 sides. Look for Crown Point's observatory to the west.

If you'd like to continue on the additional 2.4-mile loop, walk back along the ridgecrest past the first junction until you reach a fork in the trail. Keep right, following the sign for Foxglove Way, and ramble onwards through woods carpeted with star-flowered smilacina in May. When the trail joins a dirt road, turn left. The road becomes a trail and then joins the Gorge Trail. Turn left here for 0.4 mile to a lovely campsite and picnic table in a glen with a creek. A side trail to the right leads to a 20-foot cascade. To complete the loop cross the creek and continue 0.7 mile back to Angels Rest.

If you've arranged a car shuttle to Wahkeena Falls, skip the side trip up Foxglove Way. From Angels Rest simply keep left at every junction and you'll pass the creekside picnic site, Wahkeena Spring, and Fairy Falls en route to the Wahkeena Falls trailhead described in Hike #39.

Angels Rest.   Opposite: Wild iris.

39 Multnomah and Wahkeena Falls

Moderate
5-mile loop
1700 feet elevation gain
Open all year
Map: Trails of the Columbia Gorge (USFS)

Multnomah Falls is not only Oregon's tallest waterfall, it's also the most visited tourist site in the state. No guidebook is needed to direct still more cars to the huge parking lots near the historic lodge, nor to send more hikers jostling up the 1.1-mile path to the top of the 542-foot falls. A delightful, crowd-free alternative is to start at neighboring Wahkeena Falls, sneak up on Multnomah Falls via the view-packed Perdition Trail, and return on a loop past 7 other grand cascades. Unfortunately, this alternate route has been hard hit by natural disasters. Forest fire damage closed the Perdition Trail from 1991 to 1995. Flood damage closed it again in 1996, along with the first mile of the Wahkeena Trail above Wahkeena Falls. With better luck, both routes should reopen in 1997.

If the trail's open, drive here from Portland by taking Interstate 84 to Bridal Veil exit 28. Turn left on the old Columbia River Highway for 2.6 miles to the Wahkeena Falls Picnic Ground pullout on the right. If you're coming from the east, take exit 35 and follow the old highway half a mile past Multnomah Falls.

From the parking area, start at the footbridge and head to the right. The paved trail climbs 0.2 mile to an elegant stone footbridge below Wahkeena Falls, a 242-foot triple cascade in a sculpted chute. Continue on an unpaved path to a junction and turn left onto the Perdition Trail.

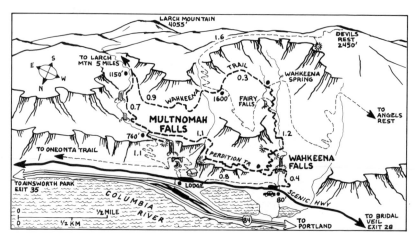

Wahkeena Falls. Opposite: Trail sign at Multnomah Creek.

After 1.1 mile the Perdition Trail reaches Multnomah Creek and joins the Larch Mountain Trail. Before turning right here to continue the 5-mile loop, make a quick detour to the left, crossing the creek and dodging tourists on a paved trail for 0.3 mile to the dizzying view from the platform atop Multnomah Falls. Then return and continue on the quieter path upstream.

The Larch Mountain Trail above Multnomah Falls climbs past 6 more waterfalls between 10 and 100 feet tall. After 0.7 mile, turn right onto the Wahkeena Trail. Climb steadily through woods for 0.9 mile to a saddle with a trail junction. Stick to the Wahkeena Trail. You'll descend to Wahkeena Creek and follow this tumbling, mossy stream 1.6 miles to your car, passing lacy, fan-shaped, 20-foot Fairy Falls along the way.

Other Hiking Options

Hikers who arrange a car shuttle can walk 6.4 miles one way from Wahkeena Falls to the Angels Rest trailhead (see Hike #38), a beautiful, moderate hike.

Devils Rest is a more challenging goal from Wahkeena Falls, requiring a 7-mile round trip and 2400 feet of elevation gain. Although the summit of this forested knoll has no views, a side trail 0.2 before the top leads to a Gorge overlook. Ascend the Wahkeena Trail 1.9 miles until it levels off, and then take the marked Devils Rest Trail to the right.

An even tougher climb is the 13.4-mile round trip from Multnomah Falls to the panoramic view atop 4055-foot Larch Mountain (see Hike #36).

40 Oneonta and Horsetail Falls

Easy
2.7-mile loop
400 feet elevation gain
Open all year
Map: Trails of the Columbia Gorge (USFS)

Next door to busy Multnomah Falls but usually overlooked by tourists, this delightful trail explores a cavern *behind* Ponytail Falls and then loops around Oneonta Gorge, a mossy chasm so narrow that Oneonta Creek fills it wall to wall. What's more, an optional 1.8-mile side trip leads to breathtaking Triple Falls, where 3 plumes of water plunge 120 feet at once.

Take the Ainsworth Park exit (#35) of Interstate 84 and follow the old scenic highway 1.5 miles to the large Horsetail Falls Trailhead parking area. The trail starts beside 176-foot Horsetail Falls and climbs along a mossy slope of little licorice ferns. In late spring tiny white candyflowers and pink geraniums crowd the path.

After 0.2 mile turn right on the Gorge Trail, which soon ducks behind 80-foot Ponytail Falls (also called Upper Horsetail Falls). The lava flow that created this falls' stony lip also buried a layer of soft soil. The falls have washed out the underlying soil, creating the cavern.

Beyond the falls 0.4 mile take a right-hand fork for a quick viewpoint loop out to a cliff edge high above the highway. The view extends up the Columbia to Beacon Rock, but keep children away from the unfenced edge. Then continue on the main trail another 0.4 mile, switchback down to a dramatic metal footbridge above 60-foot Oneonta Falls, and climb to a junction with the Oneonta Trail.

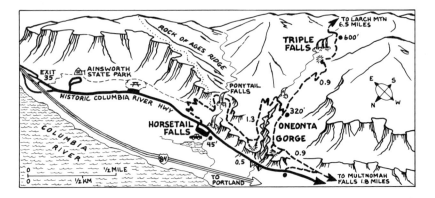

Ponytail Falls.   Opposite: Starflower.

Turn left here if you'd like to take the optional side trip up to Triple Falls and the perfect spot for lunch: a footbridge in a scenic creekside glen at the top of the falls. If you're hiking with children, however, you'd best skip Triple Falls and simply turn right to continue the loop, following the Oneonta Trail 0.9 mile down to the highway.

To complete the loop, walk along the road to the mouth of slot-like Oneonta Gorge. With any luck you'll be able to lounge on the creek's pebble beach here while one of your party runs up the road another third of a mile to fetch the car.

Other Hiking Options

The best way to see the inside of Oneonta Gorge is to put on sneakers and wade knee-deep up the creek from the highway bridge. In late summer when the water's not too deep nor too icy, it's possible to trek half a mile through the 20-foot-wide chasm to an otherwise hidden, 100-foot falls.

Another option is a difficult 9.4-mile loop up Rock of Ages Ridge, gaining 2800 feet. Start as for the main Oneonta-Horsetail loop, but at the ridge end immediately before Ponytail Falls, climb up to the left on an unmaintained user path. The next half mile is a confusion of steep scramble trails. Then follow the view-packed, rocky ridgecrest up to a wooded plateau, turn right on the Horsetail Creek Trail for 3.5 miles, and descend the Oneonta Trail 2.9 miles to the highway.

41   Nesmith Point

Difficult
9.8 miles round-trip
3800 feet elevation gain
Open April through November
Map: Trails of the Columbia Gorge (USFS)

Mountain climbers often use the challenging trail to Nesmith Point as a spring conditioning trip because the goal — the highest point in the cliffs lining the Columbia Gorge — is snow-free by April. But this hike offers other rewards than mere exercise. Expect a variety of wildflowers, the solitude of a high valley's natural amphitheater, and of course a bird's eye view across the Columbia to the snowpeaks of Washington.

Nesmith Point's promontory was unnamed until 1915, when the Portland Mazamas suggested it memorialize James Nesmith, a burly Oregon Trail pioneer whose wagon raft was driven ashore near here by high winds in 1843, and who was forced to wait out the storm reading *The Merry Wives of Windsor*.

If you're coming from Portland on Interstate 84, take exit 35 for Ainsworth Park, turn left toward Dodson for just 200 feet, and turn sharply right onto Frontage Road. (If you miss the Frontage Road turnoff you'll end up back on the freeway.) Then follow Frontage Road 2.1 miles to a big paved pullout on the right — the Yeon Park trailhead for Nesmith Point. If you're driving here from Hood River, take Warrendale exit 37, duck left under the freeway, and turn left for half a mile to the trailhead.

Just after the trailhead the path forks. Keep right, climbing through a lowland forest brightened in summer by chest-high, orange tiger lilies. In 0.9 mile meet the Gorge Trail and turn left. The path climbs relentlessly for the next 2.4 miles, switchbacking up a steep, narrow valley with occasional views out to Beacon Rock and Mt. Adams. Finally climb past huge old-growth cedars in a natural amphitheater at the canyon's head. Then, at a sunny ridgecrest, the forest abruptly shifts to high-elevation fare: small Douglas fir, beargrass, and huckleberries.

After reaching the ridgecrest, climb more gradually along a tilted plateau for 1.3 miles to an abandoned dirt road that leads up to the summit, once the site of a fire lookout tower. Unfortunately trees have grown up, leaving only a view west down the Columbia River to Portland's haze and Silver Star Mountain (Hike #15), the tall brown hump on the horizon. But don't despair; a better viewpoint is nearby. Continue past the old lookout's foundation pier and down into the woods 200 yards. You'll pass the lookout's abandoned outhouse, descend through a forest carpeted with May-blooming trilliums, and emerge at a cliff edge with an aerial view of Beacon Rock's riverside monolith, snowy Mt.

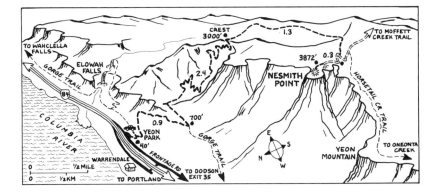

Adams, and flat-topped Mt. St. Helens.

Other Hiking Options

By arranging a short car shuttle you can descend on a less steep but longer path that leads to the Oneonta Trailhead described in Hike #40. From Nesmith Point walk down the dirt road 0.4 mile, turn right on the Horsetail Creek Trail for 5.6 miles, and then turn right on the Oneonta Trail for 2.9 miles to the highway. The hike's total length is 13.8 miles.

View from Nesmith Point.   Opposite: Edible yellow salmonberry.

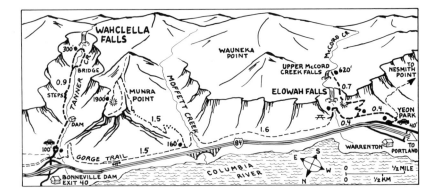

42   Wahclella and Elowah Falls

Easy (to Wahclella Falls)
1.8 miles round-trip
300 feet elevation gain
Open all year
Map: Trails of the Columbia Gorge (USFS)

Easy (to Elowah Falls)
3 miles round-trip
600 feet elevation gain

Two of the Columbia Gorge's best waterfalls are hidden in canyons at the end of short trails. The 0.9-mile path to thundering Wahclella Falls loops through a charming, canyon-end grotto. Just down the road, a 0.8-mile trail to airy, 289-foot Elowah Falls features a side path that climbs past a Gorge viewpoint to an additional 100-foot falls. For a quick afternoon stroll, choose just one of the hikes. For a longer walk, try both.

To start the Wahclella Falls hike, drive Interstate 84 to Bonneville Dam exit 40, turn to the south (away from the dam), and keep right for 100 yards to a turnaround and parking area. The trail begins on an old gated road alongside bouldery, maple-shaded Tanner Creek. The old road ends at a small water intake dam for the Bonneville fish hatchery. Continue on a trail into the ever-narrowing canyon, passing a side creek's 60-foot fan-shaped falls.

When the trail forks after 0.7 mile, turn right across a plank footbridge. The loop to the base of Wahclella Falls winds past house-sized boulders left from a 1973 landslide and then ducks under a 20-foot cavern. The falls itself is two-tiered, with a plunge in an upper slot followed by a 60-foot horsetail into a wave-tossed pool. Listen here for the *zeet-zeet* of water ouzels, remarkable robin-sized birds that bob on streamside rocks and then dive into the creek, flapping their wings underwater so they can run along the streambed eating insect larvae.

To drive on to Elowah Falls trailhead after finishing the Wahclella Falls hike, take the freeway 3 miles west to Warrendale exit 37, duck left under the freeway, and turn left for half a mile to a big paved parking pullout on the right. If you're driving to Elowah Falls directly from Portland, however, you'll have to use a different route because the Warrendale freeway exit is only accessible from the east. In this case, take exit 35 for Ainsworth Park, turn left toward Dodson for just 200 feet, and then turn sharply right onto Frontage Road for 2.1 miles.

From the Elowah Falls trailhead, keep left on the level main trail 0.8 mile to an enormous cliff-rimmed amphitheater at the base of the falls, a gauzy ribbon so tall that breezes waft it about. The 7 layers of basalt visible in the cliffs are evidence of the many lava flows that surged down the Columbia Gorge in the past 15 million years only to be cut back by the river.

Then backtrack 0.4 mile from Elowah Falls, turn left at a fork, and switchback up to a dramatic, railed ledge blasted out of sheer cliffs. The aerial view here extends from Elowah Falls across the Columbia to Beacon Rock and Hamilton Mountain (Hike #31). Continue to trail's end at a creekside glen above Upper McCord Creek Falls' twin 60-foot fans.

Other Hiking Options

A nearly level 3.1-mile stretch of the Gorge Trail through the woods beside the freeway makes it possible to connect the Wahclella Falls and Elowah Falls trails in a single one-way hike — if you can arrange a short car shuttle. To find the Gorge Trail from the Wahclella Falls parking area, walk 200 feet back toward the freeway and turn left at an orange gate, crossing Tanner Creek on an abandoned concrete bridge of the old Columbia River Highway.

Wahclella Falls.   Opposite: Hamilton Mountain from upper Elowah Falls Trail.

43   Wauna Point

Easy (to Wauna Viewpoint)
3.6 miles round-trip
950 feet elevation gain
Open all year
Map: Trails of the Columbia Gorge (USFS)

Moderate (to Wauna Point)
6.2 miles round-trip
2200 feet elevation gain

Difficult (to Dublin Lake)
10.5-mile loop
3200 feet elevation gain
Open April through November

Several hikes explore rugged Wauna Ridge, which overlooks Bonneville Dam right in the middle of the Columbia Gorge. The first option crosses Eagle Creek on a suspension bridge and switchbacks up to a small, panoramic bluff named Wauna Viewpoint. Two other, more challenging alternatives begin nearby at the Tanner Butte Trailhead. From this trailhead you can either climb 3.1 miles to Wauna Point (a larger, higher bluff with an even better view), or you can continue on a 10.5-mile loop to Dublin Lake, a quiet mountain lake.

To try the short climb to Wauna Viewpoint, start at the Eagle Creek Picnic Area. From Portland, take Interstate 84 to Eagle Creek exit 41, turn right, and keep along the creek 0.3 mile to the suspension footbridge at the start of the trail. If you're coming from Hood River, you'll have to take the Bonneville Dam exit (#40), turn around, and get back on the freeway eastbound in order to reach the Eagle Creek exit.

Hike across Eagle Creek's 200-foot footbridge and keep right on the Gorge Trail, climbing through an old-growth Douglas fir forest with yellow monkey-flowers and orange tiger lilies. After 0.9 mile, turn left on the Wauna Viewpoint Trail and switchback through woods partly burned by a 1991 fire. The knoll at trail's end, beside a powerline, features red Indian paintbrush and a view extending from the pools of the Eagle Creek Hatchery to the Bridge of the Gods and Mt. Adams. There is no direct route from Wauna Viewpoint to Wauna Point.

To take the more difficult Wauna Point and Dublin Lake hikes, drive I-5 to Bonneville Dam exit 40, turn briefly south away from the dam, fork left onto Road 777, follow this gravel road 2.3 miles, and park at a message board on the left beside a creek. Hike up the Tanner Butte Trail past 4 lacy, 20-foot waterfalls in a mossy glen of alder, bleeding hearts, and the red-spurred blooms of columbine. The path twice crosses under huge, crackling powerlines and then climbs steadily through Douglas fir woods carpeted in spring with delicate star-flowered smilacina.

After 2.3 steep miles the path forks, with the Tanner Butte Trail continuing to the right. If you're headed down to Wauna Point, however, keep left past a "Trail Not Maintained" sign for 0.3 mile to another junction. Turn left again on a steep, narrow downhill path that switchbacks under a cliff and scrambles half a mile

Cascade Locks from Wauna Viewpoint.   Opposite: Dublin Lake.

down a precarious, rocky ridgecrest to Wauna Point, a knife-edge promontory overhanging the Gorge. The dizzying view extends across the river to the lakes on Table Mountain's 700-year-old landslide (see Hike #31) and Mt. Adams.

If Dublin Lake's your goal, you might want to bypass the rugged, 1.6-mile side trip down to Wauna Point. Instead keep right on the Tanner Butte Trail, which climbs steadily up a long, tilted plateau into a high-elevation forest of fir and beargrass. Continue straight past the Tanner Cutoff Trail junction 150 yards and turn left on the steep trail down to Dublin Lake. The lake has a nice woodsy setting, with campsites in an old-growth forest knoll on the right.

To continue the loop, return to the Tanner Cutoff Trail junction and take this steep, switchbacking trail 2.3 miles down a ridge to a creek-laced alder forest. Turn right on the Tanner Creek Trail briefly to a gravel powerline access road. Follow this relatively tedious road to the right 2.4 miles to a locked gate. Unless you've left a shuttle car here, you'll walk down the road another half mile to the Tanner Butte Trailhead.

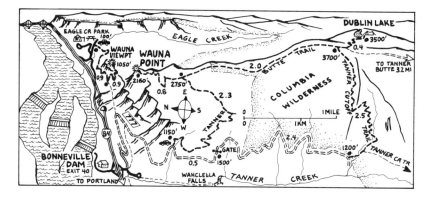

44   Eagle Creek

Easy (to Punchbowl Falls)
4.2 miles round-trip
400 feet elevation gain
Open all year
Map: Trails of the Columbia Gorge (USFS)

Moderate (to High Bridge)
6.6 miles round-trip
600 feet elevation gain

Difficult (to Tunnel Falls)
12 miles round-trip
1200 feet elevation gain

Built in the 1910s to accompany the opening of the Columbia River Highway, the Eagle Creek Trail is one of Oregon's most spectacular paths, passing half a dozen major waterfalls. The trail is also something of an engineering marvel. To maintain an easy grade through this rugged canyon, the builders blasted ledges out of sheer cliffs, bridged a colossal gorge, and even chipped a tunnel through solid rock behind 120-foot Tunnel Falls.

Today the trail is so popular the parking lot fills by 10am on sunny weekends, leaving latecomers to park half a mile away. Although this is a great place to backpack, tenting along the first 7.5 miles is only allowed within 4 designated camp areas, where competition for weekend space is keen. Campfires are strongly discouraged. An additional caution to parents: trailside cliffs make this no place for unsupervised or hard-to-manage children.

If you're coming from the Portland area, take Interstate 84 to Eagle Creek exit 41, turn right, and keep right along the creek for a mile to the road's end. Because the Eagle Creek exit is only accessible from the west, travelers from Hood River will have to take Bonneville Dam exit 40 and double back on the freeway for a mile. Leave nothing of value in your car as break-ins are a problem here.

The trail starts along the creek but soon climbs well above it along a slope of cedars and mossy maples. Look for yellow monkeyflowers and curving fronds

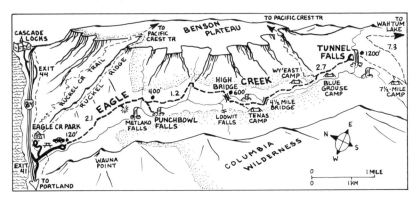

Punchbowl Falls.   *Opposite: Cable handrail on Eagle Creek Trail.*

of maidenhair fern overhanging the path. After 0.8 mile the trail traverses a cliff with cables as handrails. At the 1.5-mile mark several short side trails to the right lead down to a viewpoint of 100-foot Metlako Falls in the distance.

Continue on the main trail 0.3 mile to a ridge-end junction with the Lower Punchbowl Trail, a 0.2-mile side trail down to a broad, 15-foot falls with a bedrock bank suitable for sunbathing. Hike upstream to a gravel beach to peer ahead to picturesque, 30-foot Punchbowl Falls in a huge, mossy rock bowl.

If you're game for a longer hike, return to the Eagle Creek Trail and continue 1.2 miles to High Bridge, a metal footbridge across a dizzying, slot-like chasm. Here the creek has exposed a long crack in the earth — the fault along which this valley formed. For a nice lunch spot, continue 0.4 mile to Tenas Campground (on the right) and Skooknichuck Falls (on the left). For a still longer hike continue a couple miles further, duck behind Tunnel Falls, and 200 yards later gain a view ahead to the valley's last great, unnamed waterfall.

Other Hiking Options

Backpackers or very strong day hikers can make a 16.6-mile loop trip via the Benson Plateau. Take the Eagle Creek Trail 5 miles, turn left on the signed Eagle-Benson Trail, climb 2500 feet in 3 steep miles to a campsite at the Pacific Crest Trail, follow the PCT left 1.4 miles, turn left on the Ruckel Creek Trail for 5.8 miles (see Hike #45), and turn left on the Gorge Trail back to Eagle Creek.

Another classic backpacking trip is the 2- to 3-day loop to Wahtum Lake. For this 26.8-mile tour, hike the Eagle Creek Trail 13.3 miles to Wahtum Lake (see Hike #47), veer left on the PCT for 6.3 miles to the Benson Plateau, and then turn left to descend the Ruckel Creek Trail.

The Ruckel Ridge Trail. Below: Tiger lily.

45   Ruckel Creek

Difficult
9.6 miles round-trip or loop
3700 feet elevation gain
Open April through November
Map: Trails of the Columbia Gorge (USFS)

The challenging Ruckel Creek Trail climbs nearly 4000 feet to the forested Benson Plateau, passing Indian-dug pits, a clifftop viewpoint, and meadowed slopes dotted with late spring wildflowers. Despite the name, the path approaches Ruckel Creek only twice. Adventurers can turn the hike into a loop by starting out up the Ruckel Ridge Trail, a rough, unmaintained path along a rocky crest with numerous viewpoints.

From Portland, take Interstate 84 to Eagle Creek exit 41, turn right, and park by the restroom at the Eagle Creek Park entrance. Because the Eagle Creek exit is only accessible from the west, drivers coming from Hood River will have to take Bonneville Dam exit 40, duck left through an underpass, and get back on the freeway eastbound for a mile.

From the parking area at the park's entrance, walk up the paved road toward the campground 150 yards to a sign marking the Gorge Trail on the left. Follow this path 0.2 mile up beside the campground to a fork signed for Buck Point. Decide here if you want to tackle the loop up rugged Ruckel Ridge or if you'll skip the loop and take the better-maintained Ruckel Creek Trail both ways.

If you opt for the less difficult Ruckel Creek route, keep left on the Gorge Trail for 0.4 mile until the path crosses Ruckel Creek on a picturesque concrete bridge — a remnant of the old Columbia River Highway. Turn right here on a creekside path that switchbacks steeply uphill, heads under a powerline, and 0.3 mile later crosses a strangely hummocky, moss-covered rockslide. The pits here were dug at least 1000 years ago, evidently as vision quest sites for young Indian men.

Next the path switchbacks up for a grueling mile to a viewpoint atop a sheer 500-foot cliff overlooking the Bridge of the Gods, Table Mountain, and Mt. Adams. The trail's next 1.5 miles are relatively level, through grassy slopes of purple cluster lilies and red Indian paintbrush. Finally climb very steeply again to the Benson Plateau. After just 150 yards through this level forest the trail forks. Turn right past a "Trail Not Maintained" sign for another 150 yards to splashing Ruckel Creek — a perfect lunch spot and turnaround point.

If you want to convert the hike into a loop, you'd best start out differently. Back at the junction beside the Eagle Creek Campground you'll want to turn right, cut through the campground to site #5, and hike up to the right past a big sign for the Buck Point Trail. This path climbs 0.6 mile to Buck Point, a viewpoint beneath a powerline. Continue down to the right past a "Trail Not Maintained" sign to a rockslide. Scramble straight up this slide, following cairns and watching for loose rocks. Traverse left around the base of a cliff and then climb steeply to a viewpoint on the ridgecrest. From here on the unofficial Ruckel Ridge Trail is clear enough, although you'll have to step over a few logs and occasionally use your hands as you clamber up and down along the narrow crest for another 3 miles. When you finally gain the level Benson Plateau, follow cairns and blazes 0.3 mile left to the Ruckel Creek crossing described above. Shortly afterwards, turn left on the Ruckel Creek Trail to complete the loop.

Other Hiking Options

A 16.6-mile loop suitable for backpacking connects the Ruckel Creek Trail with the Eagle Creek Trail (see Hike #44).

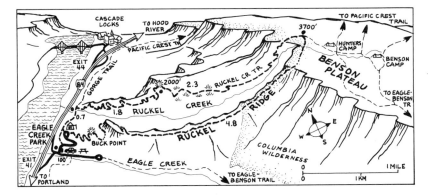

46   Herman Creek

Easy (to Herman Creek bridge)
2 miles round-trip
500 feet elevation gain
Open all year
Map: Trails of the Columbia Gorge (USFS)

Moderate (to forks of Herman Creek)
8.4 miles round-trip
1700 feet elevation gain

Difficult (to Indian Point)
8-mile loop
2600 feet elevation gain

Herman Creek's huge canyon and neighboring Nick Eaton Ridge offer hiking options for nearly everyone. There's an easy walk to a bridge over the alder-shaded creek. There's a moderate hike to the confluence of the creek's forks deep in the wilderness. And finally, there's a more difficult loop that climbs to the viewpoint atop Indian Point's rock pinnacle and returns down the steep wildflower meadows of Nick Eaton Ridge.

From Portland, take Interstate 84 to Cascade Locks exit 44 and drive straight through town 2 miles. Just when you reach the on-ramp for the freeway east, go straight onto a paved road marked "To Oxbow Fish Hatchery." Follow this road 2 miles, turn right at Herman Campground, and drive up through the campground to the trailhead parking loop at the far end. If you're driving from Hood River it's quicker to take Herman Creek exit 47 and head toward the Oxbow Hatchery for 0.6 mile to the trailhead turnoff.

The trail begins in a cool forest of Douglas fir and bigleaf maple. Look for white inside-out flowers and bold orange tiger lilies in summer. Keep left at an unmarked fork near the start, switchback up across a powerline access road fringed with poison oak, and then climb another 0.4 mile to a well-signed fork.

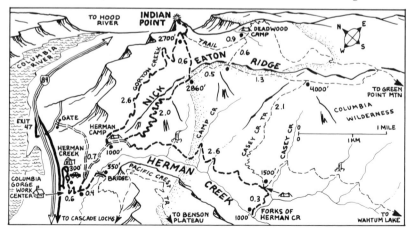

Indian Point.   Opposite: Herman Creek bridge.

If you're interested in the easy hike option, veer right onto the Herman Creek Bridge Trail and descend slightly for 0.4 mile to the 75-foot metal span, where you can relax beside the rushing stream's bouldery banks. If you're aiming for a longer hike, however, keep left at the fork and continue up the Herman Creek Trail. The path soon joins an old dirt road and follows it uphill to the right for 0.6 mile to Herman Camp, a primitive tentsite.

For the moderate hike option, continue straight past Herman Camp. The road soon becomes a trail again and contours through old-growth woods with Herman Creek audible far below. Cross several side creeks, one with a 100-foot waterfall, and finally meet the Casey Creek Trail. Turn right here and descend steeply 0.3 mile to a mossy bower where 2 creeks join.

If you'd prefer the difficult loop hike to Indian Point, turn left when you reach Herman Camp and take the signed Gorton Creek Trail. This path climbs steadily for 2.6 miles before switchbacking up to a junction on a ridge end. To continue the loop you'll turn uphill to the right here on the Ridge Cutoff Trail, but first continue straight 50 yards on the Gorton Creek Trail to find a small, unmarked side path to the left that leads 0.1 mile down Indian Point's ridge to a view from Hood River to Mt. St. Helens. The final 30-foot scramble up an exposed rock pinnacle requires the use of your hands. Turn back here if you're uncertain.

To complete the loop return to the Ridge Cutoff Trail, follow it 0.6 mile, and take the Nick Eaton Trail down a steep ridgecrest through rock gardens of summer blooms: purple penstemon, blue lupine, red Indian paintbrush, and lavender plectritis. Views include the tip of Mt. Hood and Bonneville Dam.

Other Hiking Options

For a weekend backpacking trip try the 26.4-mile loop to Wahtum Lake. Hike 11.2 miles up the Herman Creek Trail and turn left on the Pacific Crest Trail 1.6 miles to the lake (see Hike #47). Then turn around and take the PCT 12.1 miles north across the Benson Plateau to the Herman Creek Bridge Trail.

47   Wahtum Lake

Easy (to Chinidere Mountain)
4.1-mile loop
1100 feet elevation gain
Open June to mid-November
Map: Trails of the Columbia Gorge (USFS)

The loop around this scenic lake climbs on the Pacific Crest Trail past patches of huckleberries and wildflowers to Chinidere Mountain, arguably the best viewpoint in the Columbia Wilderness.

Drive Interstate 84 to West Hood River exit 62, head into Hood River 1.1 mile, turn right on 13th Street, and follow signs for Odell for 3.4 zigzagging miles. After crossing the Hood River Bridge take a right-hand fork past Tucker Park for 6.3 miles. Then fork to the right again toward Dee, cross the river, and turn left on the road to Lost Lake. After 4.9 miles veer right at a "Wahtum Lake" pointer, follow 1-lane paved Road 13 for 4.3 miles, and finally veer right again onto Road 1310 for 6 miles to a pass with primitive Wahtum Lake Campground.

Park by the message board and take the "Wahtum Express Trail" down 252 steps to the lake. Turn right on the Pacific Crest Trail and climb gradually away from the shore through a hemlock forest dotted with blue huckleberries in August. Earlier in summer expect wildflowers: low, 4-petaled white bunchberry, big trilliums, bleeding hearts, mint, and columbine. The rarest bloom of all is cutleaf bugbane, which grows here and at Lost Lake (Hike #63), but nowhere else on earth. Look for its salmonberry-like leaves and 5-foot plumes of tiny white starbursts.

After 1.6 miles the PCT forks. Head uphill to the right past a "Chinidere Mountain" sign on a steepish 0.4-mile switchbacking path to the former lookout

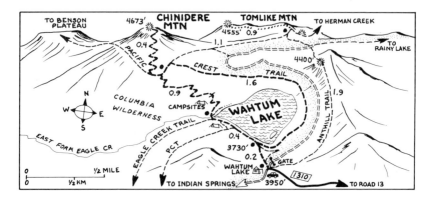

Chinidere Mountain from Wahtum Lake.   Opposite: Cutleaf bugbane.

site's bare summit amid alpine wildflowers: blue gentian, red Indian paint-brush, and purple aster. The 360-degree view includes the entire route of your hike, as well as snowpeaks from Jefferson to Rainier. Mt. St. Helens rises above the broad Benson Plateau, while Mt. Adams looms above Tomlike Mountain's barren ridge. *Chinidere* was the last reigning chief of the Wasco Indians, and his son was named *Tomlike*. Appropriately, *Wahtum* is an Indian word for lake.

To finish the loop, return to the PCT, head left for 100 feet, and turn right on a continuation of the Chinidere Mountain Trail. This path switchbacks 0.9 mile down past several campsites, crosses Wahtum Lake's log-jammed outlet creek, and joins the Eagle Creek Trail. Turn left past some more campsites, join the PCT, pass a nice bathing beach, and then turn right to climb back to your car.

Other Hiking Options

For a slightly wilder 6.6-mile loop, visit Tomlike Mountain instead. Descend to Wahtum Lake, turn right on the PCT for 1.5 miles and turn right on the Herman Creek Trail for 1.1 mile to a junction with the Anthill Trail. Continue straight 300 feet to a switchback at a ridge end. Leave the trail at this corner and bushwhack left, straight out the ridgecrest. The first few hundred yards are a tangle of small trees, but then it's easy walking along the open rock crest 0.9 mile to the summit. To complete the loop, return via the Anthill Trail, which has no anthills but does have a nice viewpoint of Wahtum Lake.

Backpackers often stop at Wahtum Lake on 2- or 3-day loop trips via Eagle Creek (see Hike #44) or Herman Creek (see Hike #46). Camping is banned on the fragile lakeshore, but nice sites have been designated nearby.

48   Mount Defiance North

Easy (to Hole-in-the-Wall Falls)
2.5-mile loop
600 feet elevation gain
Open all year
Map: Trails of the Columbia Gorge (USFS)

Difficult (to summit)
11.8-mile loop
4800 feet elevation gain
Open mid-June through October

One of the most physically demanding paths in Oregon, the Mount Defiance Trail gains nearly 5000 feet of elevation on its way to the highest point in the Columbia Gorge. Ironically, the trail begins with an easy option — a short loop that visits waterfalls, viewpoints, and creek valleys at the mountain's base.

Take Interstate 84 east of Cascade Locks 10 miles to the Starvation Creek Rest Area exit near milepost 54. Since this exit is only accessible from the west, travelers from Hood River will have to turn around at Wyeth exit 51 and return 3 miles. While at the rest area, be sure to take the 100-yard paved path past the restrooms to the base of 186-foot Starvation Creek Falls. The falls earned their name when 2 trains were trapped near here in an 1884 blizzard. Stranded passengers were offered $3 a day to dig out the track while waiting for skiers to arrive with food from Hood River.

To find the Mount Defiance Trail, walk back toward the freeway, follow its noisy shoulder west. The trail veers into the woods, passes mostly-hidden Cabin Creek Falls, and after 0.8 mile crosses a footbridge below Hole-in-the-Wall Falls, which plummets 100 feet from a tunnel. This oddity was created in 1938 when the Oregon Highway Department, upset that Warren Creek Falls wetted the old Columbia River Highway, diverted the creek through a cliff.

In another 0.1 mile reach a junction with the Starvation Ridge Trail. Turn left if you'd like to take the easy loop. This path climbs to a crossing of Warren Creek and then switchbacks up over a grassy ridge to a cliff overlooking the parking area, the river, and Dog Mountain (Hike #34). Continue aross Cabin Creek and soon veer left on the Starvation Cutoff Trail to return to your car.

If you'd prefer the difficult loop, follow the Mount Defiance Trail from Hole-in-the-Wall Falls straight 0.2 mile to 20-foot, fan-shaped Lancaster Falls. After another level half mile the trail suddenly launches upward, climbing 3 miles along a densely wooded ridgecrest. Finally reach a junction with the Mitchell Point Trail (route of the return loop). Continue uphill to the right for 0.2 mile, watching carefully for an unmarked side trail to the right. Take this new scenic route across massive rockslides overlooking Bear Lake, and curve left up to the microwave relay towers at the summit.

To return on a slightly shorter loop, walk past the fenced microwave building and a smaller tower to an old wooden trail sign, Take a path downhill that crosses a dirt road twice. When you return to the Mitchell Point Trail junction

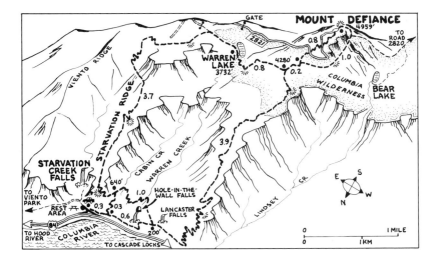

turn right toward Warren Lake. This route crosses an old rockslide with lots of viewpoints as it descends 0.8 mile to the pretty lake, rimmed with rockslides and pines. Though mud-bottomed, Warren Lake is a fine spot to swim or camp.

Beyond the lake the trail continues straight and level for half a mile to an important but unmarked junction where you'll want to turn left onto the Starvation Ridge Trail. If you miss the turnoff, the Mitchell Point Trail ends 50 yards later at a dirt road. The Starvation Ridge Trail, on the other hand, barrels down a wooded ridgecrest for over 3 miles, passing 2 excellent viewpoints. At the bottom turn right on the Starvation Cutoff Trail to return to your car.

The Columbia River from Starvation Ridge.   Opposite: Mt. Hood from Mt. Defiance.

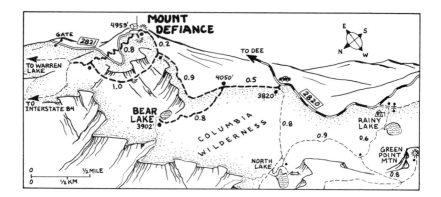

49   Mount Defiance South

Easy (to Bear Lake)
2.6 miles round-trip
400 feet elevation gain
Open June to mid-October
Map: Trails of the Columbia Gorge (USFS)

Moderate (to Mount Defiance)
4.8-mile loop
1500 feet elevation gain

Mt. Defiance was named because it remains defiantly snowclad until June, and not, as hikers might suggest, because the grueling Mount Defiance Trail from Interstate 84 (see Hike #48) is defiantly difficult. If you'd like an easier route to the summit, try starting at this more remote trailhead on the mountain's south side. An 0.8-mile side trail leads to a small campsite at swimmable Bear Lake.

Drive Interstate 84 to West Hood River exit 62, head toward Hood River 1.1 mile, turn right on 13th Street, and follow signs for Odell for 3.4 miles. After crossing the Hood River Bridge take a right-hand fork past Tucker Park for 6.3 miles. Then fork to the right again toward Dee, cross the river, and turn right, following signs for Rainy Lake. Go straight on paved Punchbowl Road for 1.4 miles and continue on washboard gravel Road 2820 for 10 miles to a sign on the right for the Mount Defiance Trail. Park on the shoulder.

Hike 200 feet, turn right at a junction, and climb gradually through a hemlock and fir forest with beargrass and huckleberry bushes. The trail forks after half a mile. To visit Bear Lake, veer left onto a rocky path that descends gradually to the lodgepole pine-rimmed lake, with its view up to Mt. Defiance's thin towers. The shallow water is relatively warm and the shore, lined with flat rocks and a

Rockslide on Mount Defiance.   Opposite: Bear Lake.

few logs, is fine for wading or a quick dip.

To climb the mountain, return to the Mount Defiance Trail and continue uphill 0.9 mile to a junction on an old rockslide. Turn right to reach the summit, with its microwave relay station and its admirable view of Mt. Hood. Walk left past the fenced microwave building to find a short path through the trees to a viewpoint overlooking Bear Lake, the town of Carson, and 3 Washington snowpeaks.

To return on a longer scenic loop, walk past the small radio tower on the far end of the summit to find a wooden sign for the old Mountain Defiance Trail. Take this path down through the woods, cross a dirt road twice, and 400 yards later *watch carefully for a small, unmarked side trail that leads uphill to the left.* Take this path and traverse around the mountain, climbing across view-filled rock-slide slopes. After a mile turn right on the trail back to the car.

50   Wygant Trail

Easy (Chetwoot loop)
5.1-mile loop
800 feet elevation gain
Open all year
Map: Hood River (Green Trails)

Moderate (to upper viewpoint)
6.1-mile loop
1200 feet elevation gain

From the base of Mitchell Point, a landmark of the eastern Columbia Gorge, the Wygant Trail follows a stretch of the old Columbia River Highway, explores the Perham Creek canyon, and climbs to a clifftop viewpoint. Hikers with a bit more energy can continue up the slopes of Wygant Peak to an even more spectacular viewpoint at the 1350-foot level. Wear long pants, as the paths here pass poison oak.

From Cascade Locks take Interstate 84 east 14 miles to Exit 58, the Lausman State Park rest area. Since this rest area is only accessible from the west, travelers from Hood River will have to take Viento Park exit 56 and double back on the freeway 2 miles.

Park at the rest area but don't walk up the obvious, paved path. Instead walk back toward the freeway and take an old gated road that parallels the freeway. The overgrown foundations below this road are the remains of Sonny, an oddly named railroad stop. The place's inhabitants tried to call it Mitchell, but Oregon already had a town by that name. Next they chose Little Boy after a local ranch, but this was rejected as awkward to telegraph. Sonny seemed the next best thing.

At a corner in the road, trail signs direct you onto a path that crosses Mitchell Creek and joins an abandoned section of the old Columbia River Highway for 0.3 mile. In autumn the Douglas fir forest here is bright with red vine maple. Snowberry bushes flaunt white but inedible fruit. In spring look for white sprays

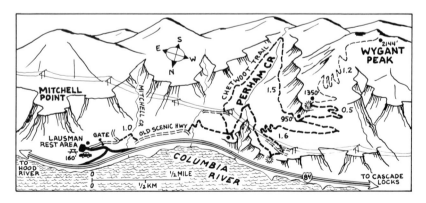

Columbia River and Dog Mountain from upper viewpoint.   Opposite: Trail sign.

of large smilacina and yellow clusters of Oregon grape.

At the 1-mile mark continue straight past a junction with the Chetwoot Trail, the loop's return route. Ignore a side trail to an overgrown viewpoint on the right and continue to a 40-foot log footbridge over rushing, fern-lined Perham Creek.

In another half a mile the trail reaches a viewpoint almost 300 feet directly above the freeway, overlooking 20 miles of the Columbia River. From here the trail ducks straight back into the woods and climbs for over a mile to a junction. The loop route continues straight onto the Chetwoot Trail, but if you have the energy for a worthwhile side trip, turn uphill to the right and climb half a mile in 4 switchbacks to an excellent ridge-end viewpoint across the Gorge to the top of Mt. Adams. Although this trail continues 1.2 miles up Wygant Peak, the route beyond this viewpoint is in disrepair and the overgrown lookout site at the top has no view.

To complete the loop, follow the Chetwoot Trail on a long traverse across Perham Creek's canyon. When you reach a powerline access road, look 50 feet to the right to find the continuation of the path down to the Wygant Trail and the route to the car.

Chetwoot means black bear in Chinook jargon, the old trade language of Northwest Indians. The Chetwoot Trail, built by Portland-area volunteers, was named for a rare sighting of a bear.

51 Tom McCall Preserve

Easy (to plateau ponds)
2.2 miles round-trip
300 feet elevation gain
Open all year
Map: brochure at trailhead

Moderate (to McCall Point)
3.4 miles round-trip
1100 feet elevation gain

This cliff-edged plateau of oak grasslands and wildflowers is one of the most dramatic nature preserves belonging to the Nature Conservancy, a non-profit private organization that quietly purchases ecologically sensitive land. A trail easy enough for children explores several ponds on a lower plateau overlooking the Columbia River, while a steeper path climbs to the breathtaking mountain viewpoint atop McCall Point.

Spring is the best time to visit this dry eastern end of the Columbia Gorge, when flowers dot the slopes. Avoid the heat of July and August. And remember to wear long pants if you're taking the upper trail, as it passes poison oak.

Take Interstate 84 east from Hood River to Mosier exit 69 and follow "Scenic Loop" signs 6.6 miles to the Rowena Crest Viewpoint parking area. If you're coming from The Dalles, take Rowena exit 76 and follow a winding section of the historic Columbia River Highway up to the viewpoint. Because this is a nature preserve, dogs, horses, and bicycles are not allowed. Camping and flower picking are also banned. Hikers must stay on designated trails.

The easy path to the lower plateau starts at a stile and signboard on the opposite side of the highway from the viewpoint's entrance road. From March through May the grasslands here bloom with sunflower-like balsamroot, purple vetch, blue bachelor buttons, and white yarrow. Ten-inch-long ground squirrels zip about the fields from February to June but hibernate the other 7 months.

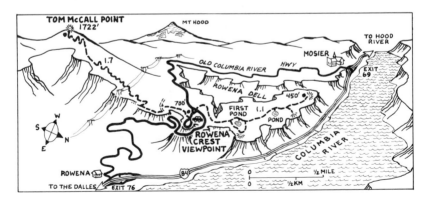

Columbia River from edge of plateau.   Opposite: Mt. Hood from McCall Point.

Where the path crosses a narrow neck leading to the plateau notice the old stone wall that once fenced sheep.

After 0.3 mile take a right-hand fork of the trail around a pond full of lilypads and cattails. Listen for the melodious warble of redwing blackbirds. The trail loops past a cliff-edge viewpoint and returns to the main trail. Continue out the plateau past a smaller, poison-oak-fringed pond, and reach trail's end at a cliff with a view across the Columbia to the town of Lyle at the mouth of the Klickitat River. Note the 8 layers of basalt in the opposite cliffs, evidence of the repeated lava floods that deluged the Columbia Basin and created this plateau 10-15 million years ago.

To try the steeper path up McCall Point, return to the parking area and look for a trail sign on the right at the start of the parking loop. This path joins an ancient road and turns left along the rim edge. When the trail forks at a large signboard, switchback up to the right on a steep path. Here the lower-elevation wildflowers are joined by red Indian paintbrush and blue lupine. The trail switchbacks steeply up the ridgecrest through scrub oak (and poison oak) to a summit meadow with glorious views of Mt. Hood, Mt. Adams, and the entire eastern Columbia Gorge. Avoid the temptation to ramble onto the private land beyond the grassy summit.

52   Lower Deschutes River

Easy (to Ferry Springs)
4.2-mile loop
600 feet elevation gain
Open all year
Map: Wishram, Emerson (USGS)

Moderate (to Gordon Canyon)
7.5-mile loop
800 feet elevation gain

The charms of a desert river are many: bright blue skies, the pungent smell of sage, birdsong across glassy water, and the cool grass of an oasis-like riverbank. You'll find it all on a loop hike from the state park at the mouth of the Deschutes River. You'll also pass whitewater rapids, canyon rimrock viewpoints, and a historic wagon road. The trip's prettiest if it's timed to see the wildflowers of spring or the colors of fall. Just avoid the heat of July and August.

Take Interstate 84 east past The Dalles Dam to the Deschutes Park exit (#97). Follow park signs 2 miles until you cross the river, and then turn right. Drive straight through the park to the far end of the overflow parking area.

The trail begins by following the grassy riverbank 0.2 miles to a marked trail junction at an old homestead. Continue straight along the river, listening for the melodious call of the western meadowlark, Oregon's state bird. This is also a good place to spot a long-tailed, black-and-white magpie — or even a bald eagle.

The riverbank is lined with sumac trees whose multi-leafletted boughs turn scarlet in autumn. The rest of the canyon is silvered with sagebrush, some of it 10 feet tall and hundreds of years old. Also look for tumbling mustard — in spring this plant's shoulder-high stalks sprout tiny yellow flowers; in fall its dried skeleton tumbles with the wind to spread seeds.

After 1.2 miles along the river, the path passes an outhouse, a footbridge, and then Moody Rapids, a mild riffle. A few hundred yards later reach a trail junction with a "Volksmarch" symbol on a post. Decide here how long a hike you want to take. If you've brought young children, you may want to cajole them another 0.2 mile along the river to a good sandy beach, let them romp there awhile, and then simply return the way you came.

If you're interested in the 4.2-mile loop hike to Ferry Springs, however, turn left at the junction near Moody Rapids and switchback up away from the river. After a few hundred yards keep right at another junction and continue 0.3 mile along a tableland to a cliff-edge viewpoint overlooking Rattlesnake Rapids. Here the trail reaches a gravel bike path. Cross the bike path, climb over a stile in a fence, and follow the trail uphill through a dry steppe of waving cheatgrass. The path climbs to a sweeping viewpoint, crosses Ferry Springs' mossy creeklet, and descends back toward the river. This downhill stretch is a remnant of the stagecoach road built in the 1860s to connect The Dalles with the Canyon City gold mines. Recross the bike path and 50 yards later turn right at a junction

The Deschutes River and Gordon Canyon.   Opposite: Western fence lizard.

beside a bench. Follow this path 0.9 mile back to your car.

If you'd prefer the 7.5-mile loop to Gordon Canyon, you'll start out the same along the river trail, but go straight at the trail junction near Moody Rapids, keeping along the river 2 more miles. This very scenic portion of the riverbank trail is not maintained, but it's in good shape as far as Rattlesnake Rapids, a whitewater chute that regularly overturns rafts. After that, it's easy to bush-whack another 0.8 mile through the sage along the riverbank. Then traverse an abandoned farm's field, go through a wooden corral gate, and follow a road 150 yards up to the gravel bike path. Briefly turn right on the bike path, cross Gordon Creek, and walk down through a campable meadow to a beach overlooking Colorado Rapids. If you're backpacking, remember that campfires are banned. To return, follow the bike path 1.5 mile back along the cliffs. When you reach the state park boundary post, backtrack 30 feet to find the loop trail heading uphill to Ferry Springs — the prettiest route back to the car.

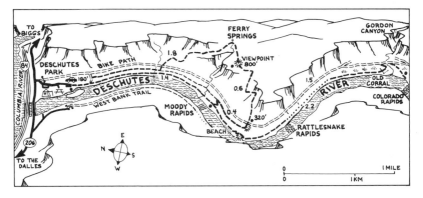

Mount Hood
West

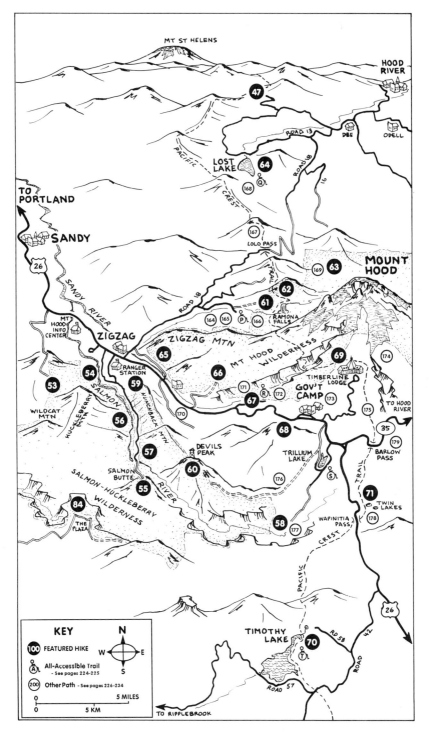

Opposite: Mt. Hood from Lost Lake (Hike #64).

Wildcat Mountain from McIntyre Ridge.   Opposite: Beargrass.

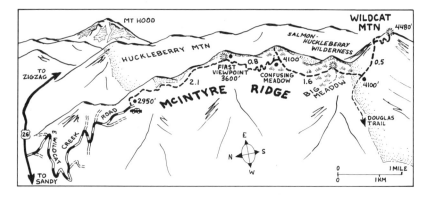

53   Wildcat Mountain

Moderate
10 miles round-trip
1800 feet elevation gain
Open May to mid-November
Map: Salmon-Huckleberry (USFS)

Wildcat Mountain tops one of the westernmost ridges of the Cascades, with views extending from the Willamette Valley to Mt. Hood. The trail to this lookout site is surprisingly uncrowded, although it is less than an hour from Portland. In early summer, rhododendrons bloom in the trailside forest and beargrass plumes brighten the ridgecrest meadows.

Drive 11 miles east of Sandy on Highway 26. Just after the Shamrock Motel turn right onto East Wildcat Creek Road for 4.1 miles. This gravel logging road has many unmarked forks, so always stick to the larger, uphill branch. Once you turn off Highway 26 you'll need to keep left after 0.2 mile, keep left again at 1.5 and 2.1 miles, veer right at 2.8 miles, keep left at 3.1 miles, keep right at 3.4 miles, and veer left at 3.6 miles. Park at road's end beside a sign on the left for the McIntyre Ridge Trail.

The path briefly crosses a clearcut before climbing along McIntyre Ridge's wooded rim. June in these mountain hemlock forests on the edge of the Salmon-Huckleberry Wilderness brings not only pink rhododendrons but also the tiny white blooms of shamrock-leaved oxalis and star-flowered smilacina. After some ups and downs, the path climbs in earnest to the 2.1-mile mark and a viewpoint of Mt. Hood rising above Huckleberry Mountain (Hike #53).

After climbing another 0.8 mile the trail forks in a small but confusing beargrass meadow. Don't take the left fork, which leads to an old overgrown viewpoint. Fork to the right on a faint path for 200 feet, meet a larger trail, and turn right. Study this obscure junction so you can find it when you return.

Beyond the first meadow 0.3 mile the trail enters a much larger and grander field of beargrass extending along the ridgecrest to a small rocky rise with a sweeping view of Mt. Hood, Mt. Jefferson, and Wildcat Mountain ahead. The Coast Range's silhouette stretches south to the tall hump of Marys Peak.

The beargrass in these meadows is not actually grass at all, but rather a disguised lily that blooms on a 2- or 3-year cycle, filling the early summer fields with white plumes only in certain years. Bears eat the starchy roots and Indians once wove with the grass-like leaves.

Continue straight along the ridge another mile, turn left at the junction with the Douglas Trail, and climb 0.4 mile until the path crests. Here take an un-marked side trail uphill to the right 100 yards to a partly overgrown viewpoint at the old lookout site atop Wildcat Mountain.

54   Huckleberry Mountain

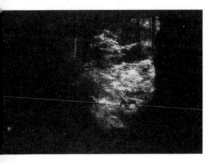

Difficult (via Boulder Ridge)
10.6 miles round-trip
3100 feet elevation gain
Open May to mid-November
Map: Salmon-Huckleberry (USFS)

Difficult (via Bonanza Trail)
11.2 miles round-trip
3000 feet elevation gain

Two equally challenging paths climb to a rocky ridgecrest atop Huckleberry Mountain, where a view of 4 snowpeaks awaits. The popular Boulder Ridge Trail starts at a dramatic footbridge over the Salmon River and climbs past several cliff-edge viewpoints. The Bonanza Trail, on the other hand, starts out along pretty Cheeney Creek and climbs past an explorable old mining tunnel. It's no tougher to sample both routes by hiking up one and down the other, but then you'll need to shuttle a car between trailheads. Better yet, if you stash a bicycle at the Bonanza trailhead (where parking is awkward for cars anyway), you can finish your hike with an easy 4-mile ride back to the big parking lot at the Boulder Ridge trailhead.

To find the Boulder Ridge Trail, drive Highway 26 east from Portland 39 miles and turn right at a large sign for the Wildwood Recreation Site. The gate here is locked at sunset each day and in winter. Keep left for half a mile and park beside the picnic area restrooms. The path starts out by crossing a 300-foot bridge over the chilly, whitewater Salmon River. After a level 0.3 mile through a mossy riverside forest, the path launches upward on its long, switchbacking climb. At the 1.8-mile mark, pass a first glimpse of Mt. Hood and enter the Wilderness. After another steep half mile, a 20-foot path to the left leads to a cliff edge with an impressive view across Wemme and Zigzag Mountain (Hike #64) to Mt. Hood. This viewpoint makes a good turnaround point for a moderate hike. If you're still going strong, continue 2 miles up the wooded ridge and turn right on the Plaza Trail for a mile to the superior view from a rocky crest atop Huckleberry Mountain.

To find the Bonanza Trail, drive Highway 26 a mile east from the Wildwood Recreation Site to the stoplight at Wemme. Turn right on Welches Road for 1.3 miles, keep left at a fork, continue another 0.7 mile to a junction, and go straight past a "One Lane Bridge" sign. Follow this across a bridge, take the second gravel street to the left, and follow East Grove Lane a few hundred yards to a fork. The road straight ahead, closed by a cable, is the start of the trail. But parking is vehemently forbidden here or anywhere else nearby. To avoid being towed you must drive back to a small parking space on the far side of the bridge or to the barely parkable shoulder of Welches Road.

Once you've sorted out the parking problem and hiked back to the trailhead, walk up the steep road 200 yards to a sharp curve and continue straight on a

Mt. Hood from Huckleberry Mountain.   Opposite: Bonanza Mine entrance.

small path. This trail is pleasantly easy for the first 1.6 miles, ambling through dappled alder woods along Cheeney Creek. At the half-mile mark a short side path leads left to a pebbly beach and pool — a good spot to remember for cooling off at the end of your hike. In another mile pass a series of miniature chutes and falls in the creek. Then, after a side path leads left to a campsite, the trail switchbacks steeply up the wooded slope. After climbing 1.2 miles you'll pass the Bonanza Mine's rusting ore-cart rails. The level, 6-foot-tall tunnel beside the trail extends back 100 feet.

To continue, follow the Bonanza Trail another 2.4 steep miles up through Douglas fir woods and turn right on the Plaza Trail along Hunchback Mountain's ridgecrest. After 0.3 mile you'll pass an open saddle with a view, but the best panorama is 0.2 mile beyond.

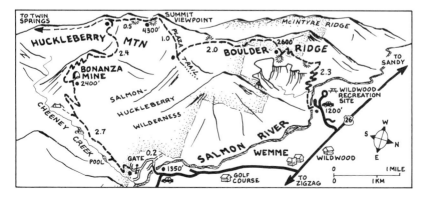

55   Salmon Butte

Difficult
8.6 miles round-trip
2800 feet elevation gain
Open mid-May to mid-November
Map: Salmon-Huckleberry (USFS)

Rhododendrons grow 15 feet tall along the trail to Salmon Butte, a lookout site smack in the midst of the Salmon-Huckleberry Wilderness. Even if you miss the rhodies' flower show in June, consider taking this remarkably well-graded trail for the summit's view across the Salmon River Canyon to Mt. Hood.

Drive Highway 26 to Zigzag (about 42 miles east of Portland) and turn south on the Salmon River Road for 4.9 paved miles and an additional 1.7 gravel miles to a sign for the Salmon Butte Trail. Turn right on a rough dirt road 300 yards to the parking area. The trail begins at a cairn straight ahead.

After briefly crossing a 1972 clearcut, the path dives into an old-growth forest of Douglas fir, red cedar, salal berry bushes, and Oregon grape. At the 1.3-mile mark reach a bare ridge-end with a view ahead to Salmon Butte's green knob and Mack Hall Creek's valley.

Beyond this viewpoint the trail traverses a slope full of colossal rhododendrons. Chosen as Washington's state flower, rhodies cannot withstand a sharp freeze, and so only grow wild along the ocean shore where winters are mild and in the high mountains where snow falls deep enough to insulate them. Although countless colors of rhodies have been bred for city gardens, in the wild these huge, deceptively tropical-looking blooms only come in pink or rarely, white.

At the 3.4-mile mark pass a first viewpoint of Mt. Hood and continue 0.6 mile to a long-abandoned road. Turn right and follow the spiraling road to the

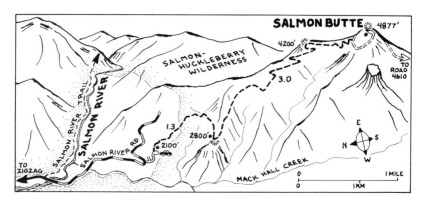

Mt. Hood and Devils Peak from Salmon Butte.   Opposite: Melted glass at lookout site.

summit, where melted glass and rusty nails remain from the lookout tower that burned here. Mt. Hood looms above Devils Peak's green ridge (Hike #59), with snowy Mt. Adams, faint Mt. Rainier, and flat St. Helens to the left. On the southern horizon Mt. Jefferson seems surprisingly close, with all Three Sisters peering over his right shoulder.

The Salmon River.   Opposite: Ten-foot-thick cedar along the path.

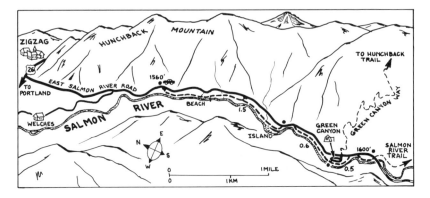

56   Lower Salmon River

Easy
5.2 miles round-trip
100 feet elevation gain
Open all year
Map: Salmon-Huckleberry (USFS)

One of the most accessible old-growth forests in Oregon towers above this portion of the Salmon River. The popular riverside trail here not only passes 10-foot-thick red cedars, it also leads to small sandy beaches with deep green pools suitable for a chilly summer swim. And since a paved road parallels the route, it's easy to arrange a car shuttle so you can hike the 2.4-mile trail one way.

From Portland, take Highway 26 toward Mount Hood for 42 miles. At Zigzag turn right at a sign for the Salmon River Road and follow this paved route 2.7 miles. Two hundred yards beyond the national forest boundary sign, park at a pullout on the right for the Old Salmon River Trail.

The trail promptly descends to the river — a clear, 40-foot-wide mountain stream. In this ancient forest, huge Douglas firs filter sunlight for an understory of vine maple, sword fern, shamrock-shaped sourgrass, and deep green moss. Look for "nursery logs," fallen giants that provide a fertile platform above the brush for rows of seedling trees to catch light and take root.

Many side paths lead to the water's edge from the main, heavily used trail. After 0.5 mile a particularly noticeable cross-path leads to a beach beside a 10-foot-deep pool in the river. Just upstream from this pleasant picnic site the river tumbles over two 4-foot falls.

Continuing on the main trail to the 1.3-mile mark, watch for another worthwhile side trail to the right. This one crosses a bouldery, mostly dry oxbow slough to a forested island with pebbly river beaches.

Just 250 yards after the side trail to the island, the main trail joins the paved road. Walk along the road's shoulder 200 yards until the riverside trail continues. After another half mile you'll pass the campsites of Green Canyon Campground. Stay on the graveled path past the campground and a picnic area. Another 0.2 mile beyond, the trail joins the paved road for 200 yards and then ducks back into the woods for 0.2 mile to the trailhead parking area at the Salmon River Bridge.

Other Hiking Options

If you'd like to extend your hike once you reach the Salmon River Bridge, simply cross the road and continue on the longer, wilder portion of the Salmon River Trail described in Hike #57.

57　Central Salmon River

Easy (to Rolling Riffle Camp)
4.0 miles round-trip
200 feet elevation gain
Open all year
Map: Salmon-Huckleberry (USFS)

Moderate (to canyon viewpoint)
7.2 miles round-trip
900 feet elevation gain

This popular portion of the Salmon River Trail begins with a riverside stroll among huge old-growth trees. After 2 miles, the path leaves the river and climbs to a bluff with a view of the Salmon River's rugged upper canyon, where inaccessible waterfalls roar far below. Backpackers or hardy day hikers can continue on a demanding 15.7-mile loop via the Devils Peak lookout tower.

Start by driving Highway 26 to Zigzag, 42 miles east of Portland. Turn south at a sign for the Salmon River Road and follow this paved route 4.9 miles to a pullout on the left just before a bridge. Start at the "Salmon River Trail" sign on the left and hike upriver through a Douglas fir forest where big white trilliums bloom in spring. After 0.4 mile pass a deep, green river pool with bedrock banks. Beyond this point the forest is even grander, with 8-foot-thick, moss-draped firs.

At the 2-mile mark pass a signed "Toilet Area" on the left and Rolling Riffle Camp on the right. The Forest Service asks backpackers to confine camping in this area to the 10 sites along the riverbank. Space is tight on weekends and campfires are strongly discouraged.

If you're out for an easy day hike, you might want to turn back 0.2 mile further at a footbridge over a side creek, where the big old-growth trees end and the trail leaves the river. If you'd like a longer hike, continue 1.4 miles uphill to a fork in the trail at a "Fragile Area" sign. Veer right for a viewpoint loop across a grassy slope overlooking the Salmon River's huge canyonland. Do not venture

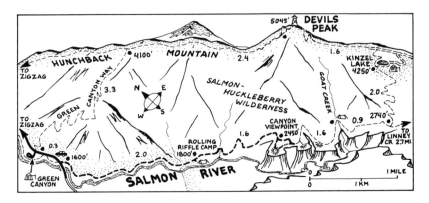

Salmon River Canyon.   Opposite: Fly fishing along the Salmon River Trail.

off the trail, as the steep, pebble-strewn slopes are deceptively slippery. After 300 yards the narrow path reenters the woods and climbs steeply to rejoin the main trail.

The roar in this canyon is caused by a string of waterfalls. Up the Salmon River Trail another 0.2 mile, a side trail to the right leads down to a grassy knoll, from which a rugged scramble path to the right descends 0.3 mile to a partly obscured overlook of aptly named Vanishing Falls, Frustration Falls, and Final Falls. This slippery, unprotected scramble trail has caused at least one fatal accident and is not recommended.

Other Hiking Options

If you'd like to tackle the difficult, 15.7-mile loop via Devils Peak, continue up the Salmon River Trail, passing 4 campsites at Goat Creek, and turn left on the Kinzel Lake Trail. After climbing 2 miles, pass a side trail to the right to the primitive car campground at shallow Kinzel Lake. Continue uphill on a faint, switchbacking trail to dirt Road 2613 and the Hunchback Trailhead to Devils Peak described in Hike #60. Beyond the lookout tower 2.4 miles take the steep Green Canyon Way left 3.3 miles to the road, 0.3 mile from your car.

For a less strenuous backpacking trip, arrange a car shuttle to the upper end of the Salmon River Trail (see Hike #58) and hike up the wilderness river a total of 14.4 miles.

58   Upper Salmon River

Moderate
5.9-mile loop
1200 feet elevation gain
Open mid-May to mid-November
Map: Salmon-Huckleberry (USFS)

Just 4 miles from heavily-used Trillium Lake, this woodsy loop through the upper Salmon River Valley is never crowded. By turns the path passes rhododendrons, huckleberries, and small creeks. Although the trail never gets closer than a stone's throw to the Salmon River itself, a short side trip will take you right down to the rushing whitewater.

Three miles east of Government Camp, turn off Highway 26 at a sign for Trillium Lake. Follow paved Road 2656 for 1.7 miles (passing the Trillium Lake Campground entrance), turn left at a sign for the Salmon River Trailhead, continue 1.8 miles on what is still Road 2656, and then keep straight on gravel Road 309 for 2 miles to a well-marked pullout on the right.

Two trails begin here. Take the one behind the "Salmon River Trail" sign. This path descends steeply to a single-log footbridge over Mud Creek, a clear-pooled, lazy stream that is Trillium Lake's outlet. Then the trail climbs over a hill to mossy little Fir Tree Creek and a trail junction marking the start of the loop.

Take the less-used path uphill to the right. The forest here has grown sparse as Douglas firs redden and die from a budworm infestation. The good news is that the extra light has allowed the rhododendrons and huckleberry bushes to thrive, lining the trail with pink blooms in early summer and blue fruit in late summer.

After another mile meet a larger trail at a T-shaped junction marked only by

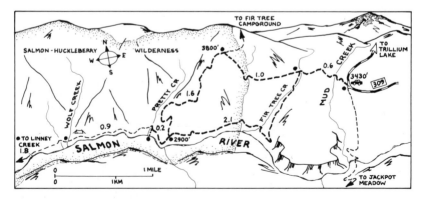

a cairn. Turn left for 1.6 downhill miles to the Salmon River. On the way you'll catch glimpses across the Salmon River Valley to flat-topped High Rock and the distant knob of Salmon Butte (Hike #54). You'll also enter a cooler, greener forest with twinflower, bunchberry, and Oregon grape.

When you reach the Salmon River Trail at the bottom of the hill, a left turn will take you on the loop back toward your car. But before heading back, take a short detour to the right. Just 0.2 mile in this direction the Salmon River Trail crosses a mossy creek overhung with red cedars. Not only is this a nice lunch spot, but it's easy to scramble 100 yards down along the creek to the river itself.

Then return to the loop on the Salmon River Trail, which follows a forested bench upriver for a mile before climbing up toward the trailhead.

Other Hiking Options

For a longer day hike or a backpack trip continue down the Salmon River Trail. An extra mile along the riverbank brings you to a campsite at Wolf Creek. In another 1.8 miles you'll reach a footbridge across the river to campsites at Linney Creek. And if you arrange a car shuttle to Salmon River Road (see Hike #57), you can hike the entire 14.4-mile river trail one way.

Log footbridge over Fir Tree Creek.   Opposite: Twinflower.

59 Hunchback Mountain

Moderate (to rimrock viewpoint)
4.2 miles round-trip
1700 feet elevation gain
Open late April to mid-November
Map: Salmon-Huckleberry (USFS)

Difficult (to Great Pyramid)
9 miles round-trip
2900 feet elevation gain

Handy for a bit of exercise, this trail switchbacks from the Zigzag Ranger Station up the long, wooded ridge known as Hunchback Mountain. After climbing steeply for 2.1 miles, the path passes a cliff-edge viewpoint overlooking the forested valleys of the Salmon-Huckleberry Wilderness. For a better look east to Mt. Hood, continue up and down along the ridgecrest to 3 other viewpoints.

Start at the Zigzag Ranger Station, 42 miles east of Portland on Highway 26. As you drive into the entrance from the highway, veer left into a large parking area. Park near the far end by a sign for the Hunchback Mountain Trail.

After hiking 50 yards you'll cross a side trail, pass a spring house, and head uphill. The first mile, with 8 long switchbacks, is so well graded it's never very steep. Deep moss, lady ferns, sword ferns, and vine maple make the Douglas fir forest here lush and jungly. Traffic noise from the highway slowly fades.

Then the trail suddenly steepens. The second mile, with 10 switchbacks, is a grueling climb. Notice the shamrock-shaped leaves of oxalis covering the forest floor. This April wildflower is also known as sourgrass because its leaves have a tart, refreshing citrus flavor when chewed — in small doses, a good temporary thirst-quencher while climbing.

The rimrock viewpoint at 2.1 miles makes a good goal. From the rim of a 100-foot cliff, views extend across castle-like crags to the green-fluted canyons

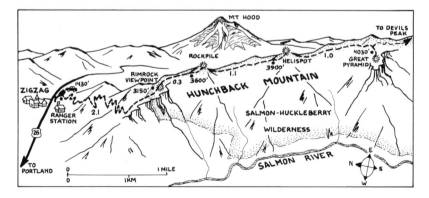

Mt. Hood from Rockpile viewpoint.   *Opposite: Oxalis (sourgrass).*

of the Salmon River. The top half of Mt. Hood protrudes to the east.

After this viewpoint the poorly graded trail roller-coasters along the ridge-crest. Though views are few from the trail itself, 3 short side trails scramble up to panoramas. At the 2.4-mile mark, a "Viewpoint Rockpile" sign directs hikers up 100 steep yards to the right to a rocky crest with a full frontal view of Mt. Hood. After another 1.1 mile along the Hunchback Trail a sign for "Viewpoint Helispot 260" marks a steep 200-yard side trail to a summit with a similar view. And after yet another mile along the Hunchback Trail, a signed side trail leads to Great Pyramid, a narrow rock promontory jutting out above the Salmon River Valley.

Other Hiking Options

The Hunchback Trail continues past Great Pyramid with some steep ups and downs for 3.6 miles to the Devils Peak lookout tower. While this would be a very difficult 16.2-mile round trip from Zigzag, the hike can be shortened by shuttling a car to one of the 3 trailheads nearer to Devils Peak: Green Canyon Campground, the Cool Creek Trailhead, or the Hunchback Trailhead near Kinzel Lake. These routes are described in Hikes #57 and #60.

Devils Peak lookout.   Below: Mt. Hood from the trail.

60   Devils Peak Lookout

Easy (from Road 2613)
2.4 miles round-trip
600 feet elevation gain
Open June to mid-November
Map: Salmon-Huckleberry (USFS)

Difficult (via Cool Creek Trail)
8.2 miles round-trip
3200 feet elevation gain

The unstaffed lookout tower atop Devils Peak, with a view from Mt. Hood to Mt. Jefferson, is maintained by volunteers as a cozy shelter and lunch spot for hikers. Getting there, however, poses a dilemma. The trail from Road 2613 is short, easy, and scenic — but the drive to the trailhead is a nightmare on a seemingly endless dirt road. The other trailhead is easily accessible — but the hike itself is 3 times longer and demands 5 times more climbing.

If you opt for the easy walk (and the hard drive), take Highway 26 to the Trillium Lake turnoff 3 miles east of Government Camp. Follow paved Road 2656 for 1.7 miles — passing the campground entrance — and then keep right on Road 2612 around the lake. After another 1.5 miles turn left onto Road 2613 and follow this narrow, bouldery, rough dirt road for 10 miles to its end at the Hunchback Mountain Trailhead. High-clearance 4-wheel-drive vehicles can navigate these final miles well enough, but passenger cars will find them slow and punishing.

The trail starts beside an abandoned garage and traverses a forest full of pink rhododendrons (in June), beargrass blooms (in July), and ripe blue huckleberries (in August). After 0.4 mile emerge from the woods at a ridgecrest with a stunning view of Mt. Hood to the north. Be sure to peer south over the ridgecrest, too, into the Salmon River's wilderness valley. Next the path switchbacks twice up the side of Devils Peak, passes the steep Cool Creek Trail on the right, and 100 yards later meets a trail on the left to the lookout tower. The tower itself is generally unlocked, with battened windows, a wood stove, and 2 cots. Since the site is no longer used for fire spotting, trees have grown up, limiting the view somewhat.

If you prefer to get here via a more rugged hike (but an easier drive), take Highway 26 to the Still Creek Road turnoff 1.4 miles east of Zigzag. Follow this road 2.6 miles to the end of pavement and continue on good gravel 0.3 mile to the crossing of Cool Creek. Drive slowly another 300 yards, watching for an inconspicuous "Cool Creek Trail" sign on the right. Park near here, beside a short spur road leading down to the picnickable shore of Still Creek.

Despite its name, the Cool Creek Trail never approaches a creek. Instead it launches up a ridge at a grueling grade. After 0.7 mile the path emerges from the woods to a slope with June-blooming rhododendrons and vistas of Mt. Hood. Then the trail climbs again through woods until the 3.5-mile mark, when it reaches a bare ridgecrest with a view extending all the way to Mt. Adams. After another half mile turn right onto the Hunchback Trail for 100 yards to the lookout path.

Other Hiking Options

By arranging a car shuttle, you can descend from Devils Peak on the 8-mile Hunchback Trail to the Zigzag Ranger Station (see Hike #59).

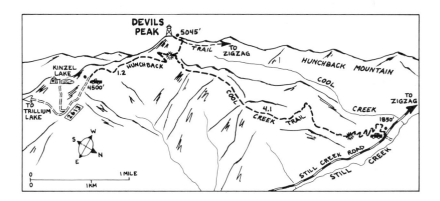

61   Ramona Falls

Easy (to Ramona Falls)
4.5-mile loop
700 feet elevation gain
Open late April through November
Map: Mt. Hood Wilderness (USFS)

Moderate (to Bald Mountain)
10.6-mile loop
Open June to mid-November
1700 feet elevation gain

Difficult (to Yocum Ridge)
15.1 miles round-trip
Open late July through October
3500 feet elevation gain

The easy loop to Ramona Falls' lacy, 120-foot cascade is understandably one of the most popular hikes in the Mount Hood area. The falls fan picturesquely across a stair-stepped cliff of columnar basalt. But Ramona Falls is also on the route of 2 longer, less well-known trips: a loop along the Pacific Crest Trail to a viewpoint on Bald Mountain, and a challenging climb up Yocum Ridge to a breathtaking overlook of Mt. Hood's glaciers.

Note that there are 2 Ramona Falls trailheads. If your car can't handle the rugged dirt road to the upper trailhead, you'll want to take the paved road to the lower trailhead and hike up a pleasant riverside path to the upper trailhead, but this will add 2.4 miles to your walk's round-trip mileage.

Turn north off Highway 26 at Zigzag (42 miles east of Portland) onto East Lolo Pass Road. After 4.9 miles veer right onto paved Road 1825. In 0.7 mile turn right across the Sandy River bridge. Follow Road 1825 another 2 miles, and then fork left onto Road 100 . After a few hundred yards you'll have to choose between the 2 trailheads. Either turn left to the lower trailhead or drive straight 1.4 miles on a miserably rocky road to the upper trailhead.

From the upper trailhead, hike across the Sandy River on a high metal footbridge built to withstand raging winter floods. In another 100 yards reach a trail junction marking the start of the Ramona Falls Loop. Admittedly, it's slightly shorter to the falls if you turn right here, but that route is so dry and desolate it's best to leave it for the return trip. So instead go straight, following the "Bald Mountain Trail 1/2" sign. This path crosses a creek and traverses a lodgepole pine forest to the wild Muddy Fork of the Sandy River. Turn right here on a path that soon follows the mossy bank of Ramona Creek — a delightful woodsy stream that's perfect for children to play in.

At the base of Ramona Falls you'll join the Pacific Crest Trail. To complete the easy loop, turn right and keep right. If you're backpacking, note that camping is banned within 500 feet of the falls. A side path leads to a designated camping area just south of the falls.

If you're interested in a longer hike, turn left at the falls and follow the Pacific Crest Trail up 0.6 mile to a trail junction at the forested crest of Yocum Ridge. To

Mt. Hood and Yocum Ridge from the Muddy Fork.   Opposite: Ramona Falls.

the right is a path switchbacking 4.7 miles up Yocum Ridge to a glorious above-timberline landscape on an alpine shoulder of Mt. Hood, where views extend from Mt. Rainier to Mt. Jefferson.

If you'd prefer the less arduous Bald Mountain loop, continue straight on the PCT as it traverses around Yocum Ridge to Muddy Fork, a milky glacial outwash river. The bridgeless crossing is tricky in June and on summer afternoons, when snowmelt swells this 2-branched torrent. After crossing both branches the PCT climbs steadily to a cliff-edged meadow on Bald Mountain with a sweeping view dominated by Mt. Hood. Half a mile beyond the viewpoint turn sharply left at a 4-way trail junction, following the "Bald Mountain Trail" pointer. This path descends in 7 long switchbacks to a 60-foot bridge over the Muddy Fork. Cross and keep right to return to your car.

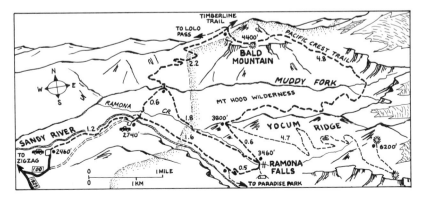

62   McNeil Point

Easy (around Bald Mountain)
2.3-mile loop
400 feet elevation gain
Open June to early November
Map: Mt. Hood Wilderness (USFS)

Moderate (to ponds below McNeil Point)
7 miles round-trip
Open mid-July through October
1500 feet elevation gain

Wildflowers, tumbling brooks, and craggy mountain vistas lend alpine splendor to this ridge on Mt. Hood's northwest shoulder. An easy loop circles Bald Mountain to a picture-postcard view of Mt. Hood. But for real alpine drama, climb the Timberline Trail to a pair of ponds reflecting massive McNeil Point.

Turn north off Highway 26 at the Zigzag store (42 miles east of Portland) onto East Lolo Pass Road. After 4.2 miles veer right onto paved Road 1825. In 0.7 mile go straight onto Road 1828 and follow signs for "Top Spur Trail No. 785" for another 7.1 miles to a pullout on a good gravel road.

The Top Spur Trail starts in a patch of blue huckleberries (ripe in August), and climbs through a forest of hemlock and Douglas fir. Look for bunchberry, carpeting the ground with white blooms in June and red berries in fall.

After 0.5 mile turn right on the Pacific Crest Trail for 60 yards to a big, 4-way trail junction. Continue uphill to the right on the PCT. This route soon emerges from the woods onto the steep, meadowed face of Bald Mountain, with views ahead to Mt. Hood and west to the distant Willamette Valley. After 0.4 mile through these meadows, watch carefully for the unmarked loop trail around Bald Mountain. When the PCT reenters the woods after the second, smaller meadow, continue 100 yards to a fork in a draw, just beyond a campsite on the left. *Take the unmarked left-hand fork* over a ridge 100 yards to an unsigned junction with the Timberline Trail. For the easy loop, turn left here to return to the car. If

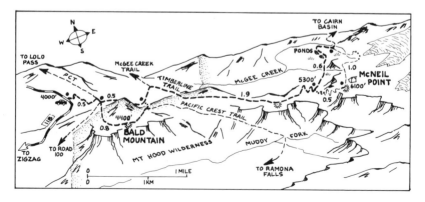

McNeil Point (ridge at right) from Timberline Trail.   *Opposite: Bunchberry.*

you'd like a longer hike, turn right.

Beyond Bald Mountain, the Timberline Trail climbs up a ridgecrest with wind-dwarfed firs, summer-blooming beargrass, and views of Mt. Hood. After 1.9 miles the trail switchbacks 4 times up a steep wildflower meadow and passes an unmarked scramble trail on the right. Keep straight on the Timberline Trail, which now passes a creek and 2 reflecting ponds amidst a dazzling display of early August wildflowers: red Indian paintbrush, blue lupine, and the fuzzy seedheads of old-man-of-the-mountain (western Pasque flower). From the ponds, sharp eyes can spot the McNeil Point shelter high on the ridge above.

If you're backpacking, be sure to camp out of sight in the woods and not on the fragile meadows or shore. Bring a stove, as campfires are banned within 500 feet of the shelter and are discouraged anywhere near timberline.

Other Hiking Options

No marked trails lead to the McNeil Point shelter, and heavy use of this very fragile alpine area may spur the Forest Service to eliminate the 1.5-mile user path that makes a rugged loop possible. To try the loop, continue 0.2 mile past the ponds to an unmarked junction at a creek crossing. Go straight on the path up the creek toward Mt. Hood. This path fades somewhat in 0.3 mile at the base of a snowfield, but climb steeply left to a ridgecrest and then traverse to the right across a rockslide. In a mile the path reaches the 10-foot-square stone shelter, built in the 1930s by the CCC and later named to honor Portland newspaperman Fred McNeil (1893-1958). The extremely steep, final portion of the unofficial loop trail dives 0.5 mile down a rocky ridge-end from the shelter to the Timberline Trail. Only attempt this dangerous section if you're prepared to use your hands and watch for loose rocks.

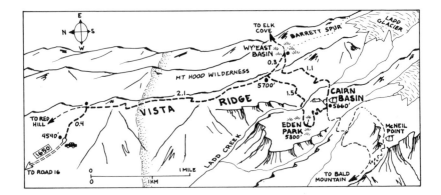

63   Cairn Basin   🏕

Moderate
7.9-mile loop
1700 feet elevation gain
Open mid-July through October
Map: Mt. Hood Wilderness (USFS)

This alpine trail up Vista Ridge not only has views of Mt. Hood's craggy north face, it also loops through 3 wildflower-packed vales: Wy'East Basin, Cairn Basin, and Eden Park.

From Highway 26, turn north at the Zigzag store onto East Lolo Pass Road (Road 18) and follow this paved route 10.5 miles to Lolo Pass. Here turn right onto gravel McGee Creek Road (Road 1810) for 7.7 miles until it rejoins Road 18. Then continue on pavement 3.2 miles and turn right onto Road 16. From here on, signs for "Vista Ridge Trail No. 626" will direct you 9 miles along Roads 16 and 1650 uphill to the trailhead. The final 0.7 mile of Road 1650 is rough but still passable for passenger cars.

The trail begins along an old cat road but soon dives into a lichen-draped forest of hemlock and Douglas fir. After 0.4 mile turn right and ascend a long, forested ridge. Blue huckleberry bushes here mingle with false huckleberry (mock azalea), recognizable by its bigger bell-shaped flowers and larger whorled leaves.

After 2.1 miles, reach a trail junction on a meadowed ridge with views of 4 mountains: Hood, Adams, St. Helens, and Rainier. The alpine wildflowers — best in early August — include red Indian paintbrush, pink heather, blue lupine, and entire hillsides of delicate white avalanche lilies.

Turn left at this junction for 0.3 mile to a basin called Wy'East — after Mt. Hood's legendary Indian name. Turn right in Wy'East Basin's lupine-filled meadow following a sign for Cairn Basin. This path crosses a ridge and switchbacks down to a bridgeless crossing of Ladd Creek. Look up and down this sometimes raging stream for the safest place to cross. On the far shore the path leads into the forested but badly trammeled Cairn Basin area. A 10-foot-square stone shelter stands on the left, while a path to the right leads to a designated camping area.

The main trail is confused here by overuse, but continue on the level through the trees to a trail junction beside a wildflower-lined creeklet. Turn right and switchback down 0.3 mile to Eden Park's meadowy bowl. Just beyond Eden Park, recross bridgeless Ladd Creek as best you can. On the far shore the path scrambles upstream a bit before climbing back to the Vista Ridge Trail and the route back to the car.

Other Hiking Options

The alpine country around Cairn Basin invites exploration. One option is to take the 2.7-mile loop west along the Timberline Trail to McNeil Point (see Hike #61). Another possibility is to climb cross-country from Wy'East Basin up a series of meadows and bluffs to Barrett Spur, an open ridge with breathtaking views of the Coe and Ladd Glaciers. The topmost viewpoint accessible without climbing gear is 1.3 miles from Wy'East Basin and a grueling 2000 feet up.

Avalanche lilies and Mt. Hood from Vista Ridge.   Opposite: Cairn Basin's shelter.

64   Lost Lake

Easy (around the lake)
3.4-mile loop
100 feet elevation gain
Open mid-May through October
Map: Bull Run Lake (USGS)

Moderate (to Lost Lake Butte)
3.8 miles round-trip
1300 feet elevation gain

An old-growth forest circles Lost Lake, the classic setting for picture postcards of Mt. Hood. For an easy loop, try the 3.4-mile lakeshore trail. If this isn't quite enough exercise, climb the neighboring volcanic butte to a former lookout site with a broader panorama.

Lost Lake was known to the Hood River Indians as E-e-kwahl-a-mat-yam-ishkt, or "Heart of the Mountains." When an expedition of white men had trouble finding the legendary lake in 1880 they declared they were not lost; the lake was. Today the lake is quite definitely found. A $3.8 million Forest Service project completed in 1993 restored the overused lakeshore, added a half-mile-long boardwalk through an old-growth cedar grove, and expanded the campground to one of the largest in Northwest Oregon.

To find the lake from Portland, take Highway 26 for 42 miles, turn left at the Zigzag store onto East Lolo Pass Road (Road 18) and follow this paved route 10.5 miles to Lolo Pass. Here turn right onto gravel McGee Creek Road (Road 1810) for 7.7 miles until it rejoins Road 18. Continue on pavement 7 miles and then turn left onto Road 13 for 6 miles to the Lost Lake entry station booth.

To find the lake from Interstate 84, take West Hood River exit 62, drive into town 1.1 mile, turn right on 13th Street, and follow signs for Odell 3.4 miles. After crossing a bridge turn right past Tucker Park for 6.3 miles, fork to the right to Dee, and follow signs 14 miles to Lost Lake. Travelers from Portland will find

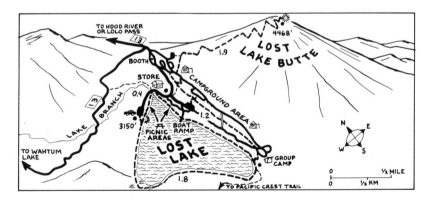

The Lost Lake Old Growth Trail.   Opposite: Mt. Hood from Lost Lake Butte.

this route 10 miles longer than the route via Lolo Pass, but entirely paved.

Drive past the Lost Lake entry booth, follow signs to the rustic general store, and continue right around the lake to a picnic area parking lot at road's end. The lakeshore trail begins at the far end of the parking lot, where the view of Mt. Hood is at its finest. Numbered posts along the trail correspond to numbers in a nature trail booklet available at the store for a quarter.

The broad lakeshore path sets out through a forest of big hemlocks and cedars. Count on seeing striped Townsend's chipmunks, orange-bellied Douglas squirrels, gray jays, and pointy-hooded Stellar's jays, all of which are accustomed to gleaning crumbs from the nearby picnic area. Small white wildflowers dot the forest floor in early summer: queen's cup, bunchberry, and vanilla leaf. After 0.6 mile a boardwalk crosses the lake's marshy inlet creek, where huge-leaved skunk cabbage puts out yellow blooms.

At the 1.8-mile mark, the Huckleberry Trail joins from the right. A hundred yards later veer to the right on the Old Growth Trail. This graveled path switchbacks twice to a campground road. Follow the road 100 feet to find the continuation of the trail — a remarkable half-mile boardwalk through a grove of 8-foot-thick cedars. Decked pullouts have benches and interpretive signs. Beyond the end of boardwalk 0.3 mile turn left, make your way down through the campground, and follow the lakeshore path onward to your car.

Climb Lost Lake Butte either at the end of the lakeshore loop or as a separate trip. The butte's trail begins at the entrance to Campground Loop B and climbs steadily through woods thick with rhododendrons and beargrass. The old lookout tower has been reduced to a pile of boards, but the view is intact: huge Mt. Hood to the south, a glimpse of Lost Lake to the west, Adams and Rainier to the north, and the brown Columbia River Plateau far to the east.

Cliffs near West Zigzag's lookout site.   Opposite: Vine maple.

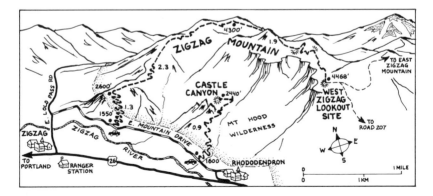

65　West Zigzag Mountain

Easy (to Castle Canyon)
1.8 miles round-trip
800 feet elevation gain
Open all year
Map: Mt. Hood Wilderness (USFS)

Difficult (to lookout site)
11 miles round-trip
Open May through November
3100 feet elevation gain

Forests cloak this steep ridge in the westernmost corner of the Mt. Hood Wilderness, but 2 convenient trails lead to viewpoints above the trees. The first is a short but very steep path to a collection of craggy rock towers. The second is a strenuous conditioning hike — a 3000-foot climb at a steady grade to the clifftop site of a former lookout building.

At the village of Zigzag, turn north off Highway 26 onto East Lolo Pass Road for 0.4 mile. Then turn right onto gravel East Mountain Drive. After 0.7 mile you'll see a sign on the left marking the Zigzag Mountain Trail (the path to the lookout site). If you drive another 0.9 mile down the road you'll reach the signed trailhead for the path to Castle Canyon.

If you're starting up the Castle Canyon Trail, you'll switchback up through a young Douglas fir forest with a smattering of little vine maple trees that turn brilliant red in autumn. The most common bush here is salal, whose tough blue berries were valued by Northwest Indians. Nineteenth-century botanist David Douglas so admired this evergreen shrub that he popularized its use as an ornamental in England's formal gardens.

After half a mile of stiff climbing you'll pass the first of this canyon's mossy rock outcroppings. Just before the trail peters out at the 0.9-mile mark, contour left to a rocky spine among the towers. Footing is hazardous here, so hang onto children. The barren bluff of the West Zigzag lookout site is visible above to the east while Hunchback Mountain (Hike #59) looms across the Zigzag Valley.

If you'd prefer to climb to the better view at the West Zigzag lookout site, start your hike at the Zigzag Mountain Trailhead instead. This path climbs relentlessly for its first 3.6 miles, yet is so well graded it gains over 3000 feet without being unbearably steep. On the way up you'll leave the vine maple/salal zone, pass through a level where pink rhododendrons bloom in June, and finally enter a high-altitude fir forest with beargrass and manzanita.

The final 1.9 miles to the lookout site follow the ridgecrest up and down, sometimes skirting cliffs with views east to Mt. Hood or west down the Sandy River toward Portland. Four concrete piers mark the site of the old fire lookout on a dramatic bluff high above the crags of Castle Canyon and the towns of Rhododendron and Zigzag. Flag Mountain looks like the green back of a crocodile sleeping in the Zigzag Valley below, while the tip of Mt. Jefferson peers over the shoulder of Devils Peak (Hike #59).

66   East Zigzag Mountain

Moderate (to East Zigzag)
7.7-mile loop
1700 feet elevation gain
Open mid-May to mid-November
Map: Mt. Hood Wilderness (USFS)

Difficult (to East and West Zigzag)
11.1-mile loop
2400 feet elevation gain

The meadow atop East Zigzag Mountain offers a full frontal view of Mt. Hood and glimpses of 4 more distant Cascade peaks. From the trailhead in Devil Canyon you can hike to East Zigzag's summit via either of 2 loops: a moderate route or a more difficult loop that extends along a ridgecrest to West Zigzag's lookout site. In either case it's tempting to take the short, nearly level detour to Cast Lake, a nice lunch stop.

To find the trailhead, take Highway 26 to a turnoff 1.5 miles east of Rhododendron and 100 yards west of milepost 47. Turn north onto paved Road 27 for 0.6 mile, then turn left onto gravel Road 207 for 4.5 narrow, winding miles to a parking area at road's end. The final 0.5 mile of this road is very rough and rocky. Passengers cars should proceed with caution.

Start on the Burnt Lake Trail, which for its first 2 miles is actually an ancient road leading to a long-abandoned campground at Devils Meadow. In June expect pink rhododendrons, delicate twinflowers, and tiny white starflowers blooming in the quiet trailside forest. Devils Meadow is a bracken-filled slope with July flowers: purple aster, red paintbrush, yellow goldenrod, and an occasional tiger lily.

Follow "Burnt Lake Trail" signs up from Devils Meadow and straight past a junction with the Devils Tie Trail (the short loop's return route). You'll switchback up through drier woods, gaining views south to Hunchback Mountain

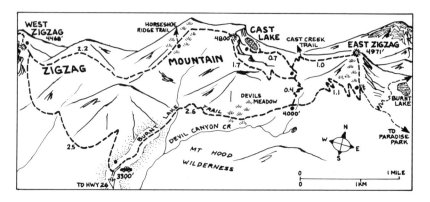

Mt. Hood from trail junction near East Zigzag.   Opposite: Cast Lake.

(Hike #58), Devils Peak (Hike #59), and Mt. Jefferson. Then crest a ridge to a trail junction with a terrific view of Mt. Hood. Notice Burnt Lake below the peak and Paradise Park (Hike #68) on the mountain's right shoulder.

Turn left along the ridgecrest, following the Zigzag Mountain Trail steeply up to the East Zigzag lookout site, where the view widens to include Mt. St. Helens, the distant flats of the Willamette Valley, and the entire route of your hike. Then continue downhill 0.7 mile, turn left at a junction with the Cast Creek Trail, and 300 yards later reach the Cast Lake junction. Unless you're truly exhausted, it's worth it to detour 0.7 mile over a little pass to Cast Lake, a remarkably crawdad-filled pool with a sometimes island and a glimpse of Mt. Hood's tip.

When you continue on the Zigzag Mountain Trail past the Cast Lake turnoff, you'll soon reach a junction with the Devils Tie Trail. For the short 7.7-mile loop, go left on the trail that switchbacks down to Devils Meadow and the path back to the car. For the longer loop via West Zigzag, go uphill to the right.

This next portion of the Zigzag Mountain Trail climbs steeply to a clifftop overlooking Cast Lake, then dips across a forested saddle to the scenic beargrass meadows at the junction of the Horseshoe Ridge Trail. Continue 2.2 viewless miles on the sometimes rocky, brushy Zigzag Mountain Trail to a junction with the West Zigzag Trail that leads back down to your car — but don't go to your car yet! First continue 0.2 mile on the ridgecrest trail to the dramatic clifftop site of West Zigzag's former lookout, now marked by concrete piers.

67　Laurel Hill

Easy (with shuttle)
3.7 miles one-way
900 feet elevation gain
Open March to mid-December
Map: Mt. Hood Wilderness (USFS)

For a walk through history, try the Pioneer Bridle Trail along this low, forested ridge near Government Camp. The route follows a notorious section of the Barlow Trail that was converted to a hiking path by Civilian Conservation Corps workers in 1935. The path also passes a mine shaft and an abandoned portion of the first paved highway around Mt. Hood.

Sam Barlow laid out a wagon road from The Dalles to Sandy in 1845 to spare Oregon Trail pioneers the dangers of rafting the Columbia River. Most travelers ended up cursing Laurel Hill, where Barlow's brushy route plunged so steeply into the Zigzag River Valley that wagons had to be unhitched and winched down backwards. Ironically, the rhododendrons that now delight hikers with pink blooms in early summer only infuriated the pioneers, who typically passed here in bloomless October and mistook the tough-limbed brush for laurel.

Because this hike parallels Highway 26, it's easy to arrange a car shuttle and walk the trail one way. If you don't have a second car to leave at the upper trailhead, why not leave a bicycle there instead? It's a quick 4-mile downhill shoosh along the highway back to the lower trailhead.

To leave a vehicle at the upper trailhead, drive Highway 26 to between mileposts 52 and 53, a mile west of Government Camp. Opposite the western entrance to Mt. Hood Ski Bowl, turn north off the highway onto Road 522 past a "Dead End" sign. Park in 0.2 mile at a gate.

To start your hike at the lower trailhead, drive Highway 26 to between mileposts 48 and 49. Turn north onto Road 2639 at the sign "Mt. Hood Kiwanis Camp," drive a mere 0.1 mile (200 yards) and park on the left shoulder beside a small yellow "Warning Buried Cable" sign. The unmarked trail starts on the opposite side of the road from this sign. After 20 yards on the path, turn left at a trail junction. Expect highway noise along most of the trail, as well as evidence of horse and mountain bike use.

The lichen-draped, second-growth forest here is an odd mixture of trees from the east and west sides of the Cascades, including lodgepole pine, western hemlock, and red cedar. After 0.3 mile switchback up beside the slope where pioneers winched down their wagons. At the top of this hill the trail first becomes recognizable as an ancient roadbed, a marvel of pioneer engineering. At the 1.7-mile mark the roadbed crosses a rockslide where you can often hear the *meep!* of rabbit-like pikas. At the 2.3-mile mark you hike through a tunnel

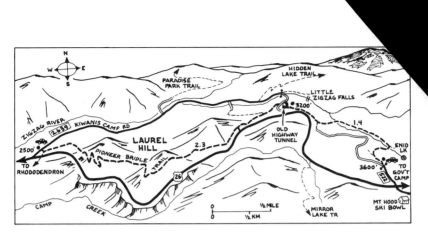

under a long-abandoned stretch of paved highway. This is a portion of the original Mt. Hood Loop, completed about 1921 from Portland up the Columbia Gorge to Hood River and back around Mt. Hood. Touted as a tourist attraction, the paved loop once lured thousands of Model T drivers out of the city.

Beyond the tunnel 0.3 mile you'll briefly follow the Highway 26 guardrail before ducking back into the forest on the quietest and prettiest portion of the trail. To the left, glimpse the whitewater of the Little Zigzag River. At the 3-mile mark, veer left at a large, unmarked trail junction and soon follow a lovely creek. Just after crossing the creek for the second time you'll reach the only boggy part of the trail, a 100-foot stretch that's tough in tennis shoes. Then it's 0.3 mile to the gate and the upper trailhead.

Other Hiking Options

For a worthwhile detour, visit Little Zigzag Falls. From the old highway tunnel follow the abandoned highway down 0.1 mile and turn right on the well-marked 0.2-mile path to the falls.

Trail tunnel beneath abandoned highway.   Opposite: Rhododendron.

Mirror Lake

Easy (to Mirror Lake)
3.2 miles round-trip
700 feet elevation gain
Open mid-May to mid-November
Map: Mt. Hood Wilderness (USFS)

Moderate (to summit viewpoint)
6.4 miles round-trip
1500 feet elevation gain

Avoid this popular hike on summer weekends, when the unmarked parking area is jammed and the trail crowded. But on weekdays or in the off-season, the trip is hard to beat. The relatively easy path starts at a waterfall and climbs to a subalpine lake mirroring Mt. Hood. Hikers with weary soles can stop to reflect by the lake while more energetic hikers chug on up through the wildflowers to an even more spectacular viewpoint atop Tom Dick & Harry Mountain.

Drive Highway 26 to between mileposts 51 and 52, about 2 miles west of Government Camp. Park on the highway's south shoulder by a footbridge and (usually) a cluster of other cars. The footbridge spans Camp Creek just above Yocum Falls, a long, lacy cascade overhung with yellow monkeyflowers. Cross the bridge and enter a deep, cool forest. In early summer expect pink rhododendrons and numerous white woodland wildflowers: 4- or 6-leaved bunchberry, wild lily-of-the-valley, and star-flowered smilacina.

After 0.4 mile traverse a rockslide where you're almost certain to hear the cheeping cry of pikas; with patience, you'll spot one of these little round-eared "rock rabbits." Then switchback up another mile to a trail junction. Keep right around the lakeshore.

Heavy use has brought some restrictions here. Do not enter areas that have been roped off to allow plants to regrow. If you're backpacking, tent well away from the shore; 6 sites are designated.

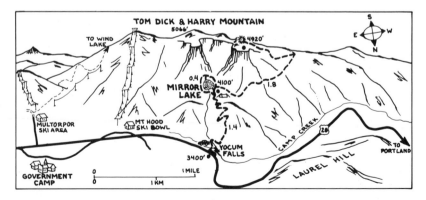

Mt. Hood from Mirror Lake.   Opposite: Mirror Lake from Tom Dick & Harry Mountain.

The first little beach you pass is the best for swimming. Although the lake bottom is muddy, the water warms by late summer. Another 100 yards past the beach the trail forks. Keep left if you'd like to circle the lake (and discover some quieter picnic spots). Turn right if you're headed to the viewpoint atop Tom Dick & Harry Mountain.

The viewpoint path traverses a slope cleared of trees by winter avalanches. In summer the hillside sports alpine wildflowers, masses of huckleberries (ripe in late August), and views of the Zigzag Valley. After climbing 0.8 mile reach a monstrous 6-foot cairn and turn sharply left. The trail grows fainter and rockier on this wooded ridge, and after 0.7 mile ends altogether at a summit rockpile. Continue 100 yards up to a 3-sided rock windbreak atop the shaley summit. Purple penstemons and a shaggy brown marmot live here. Views extend south across the green ridges of the Salmon-Huckleberry Wilderness to Mt. Jefferson, and north across Mirror Lake to Government Camp and Mt. Hood.

Tom Dick & Harry Mountain was named for its 3 distinct summits. The trail ends at the westernmost of the tops; the other 2 are off-limits to protect peregrine falcon habitat.

69   Timberline Lodge Trails

Easy (to Zigzag Canyon)
4.4 miles round-trip
500 feet elevation gain
Open mid-July through October
Map: Mt. Hood Wilderness (USFS)

Moderate (to Silcox Hut)
2.2-mile loop
1100 feet elevation gain

Difficult (to Paradise Park)
12.2-mile loop
2300 feet elevation gain

Mt. Hood's Timberline Lodge began as a Depression-era make-work program, but by the time President Roosevelt dedicated this elegantly rustic hotel in 1937 it had become a grand expression of Northwest art. Surprisingly, few visitors venture very far into the scenic alpine landscape that lured hotel builders here in the first place. Three particularly tempting goals await hikers: the Silcox Hut, Zigzag Canyon, and Paradise Park. To reach the trailhead, drive Highway 26 to Government Camp and follow signs 6 miles up to the huge parking lot.

The Silcox Hut served as upper terminus for Timberline's original Magic Mile ski lift from 1939 to 1962. Reopened as a chalet in 1992, it now offers overnight bunks and a limited cafe in the European alpine tradition. To hike there, walk past the right-hand side of the Timberline Lodge and go uphill 200 yards. Cross a snow gully on the right and promptly turn uphill onto the Mountaineer Trail, a braided path through wind-gnarled firs and August-blooming blue lupine. After 0.6 mile, join a dirt road for the remainder of the climb to the hut. To return on a loop, contour 100 yards across a snowfield from the Silcox Hut to the new Magic Mile chairlift and follow a service road back down to the lodge. Tenderfeet should note the lift is open to non-skiing passengers 10am to 1:30pm from

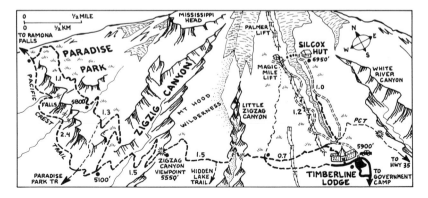

Zigzag Canyon and Mt. Hood.   Opposite: The Silcox Hut.

Memorial Day to Labor Day — for a fee, of course.

For a more wilderness-oriented hike, take the Pacific Crest Trail to Zigzag Canyon or Paradise Park. From the patio behind Timberline Lodge, follow a "Timberline Trail" pointer up a paved path amidst lupine and cushion-shaped clumps of white phlox. Keep uphill until pavement ends and the path ducks left under a chairlift. Now the trail contours through gorgeous wildflower meadows with views south to Mt. Jefferson and the Three Sisters. At the 1-mile mark the path dips into a 200-foot-deep gully to cross the Little Zigzag River on stepping stones (a possible turnaround point for hikers with small children). Then continue another easy 1.2 miles to an overlook of Zigzag Canyon, a 700-foot-deep chasm gouged into Mt. Hood's cindery flank by the glacier-fed Zigzag River.

If you're headed for Paradise Park, continue 1.5 grueling miles as the PCT switchbacks to cross this huge gorge. At a trail junction on the far side, turn right onto the Paradise Loop Trail and climb another mile to meadows stuffed with August wildflowers: beargrass, paintbrush, lupine, and avalanche lilies. If you're backpacking, tent under the trees and *not* in the fragile meadows.

To complete the loop, keep straight on the Paradise Loop Trail until it crosses a big creek and reaches a bare area — the site of a stone shelter smashed by a falling tree in 1994 and painstakingly removed. From the shelter site, head uphill to find a path traversing left below a cliffy bluff. This path leads 1.1 mile through heather fields before descending to the PCT. Then turn left for 2.4 miles to return to Zigzag Canyon and the route back.

Other Hiking Options

For a shorter walk than any of these, follow the PCT east from Timberline Lodge and descend half a mile to an overlook of the White River Canyon.

For a 3- to 5-day backpack, try hiking the entire 37.6-mile Timberline Trail around Mt. Hood. The route starts out along the PCT to Paradise Park.

Timothy Lake

Easy (to Timothy Lake viewpoint)
4.4 miles round-trip
100 feet elevation gain
Open May through November
Maps: Mt Wilson, Timothy L. (Green Trails)

Difficult (around Timothy Lake)
12-mile loop
200 feet elevation gain

This hike starts at sapphire Little Crater Lake and follows the Pacific Crest Trail to the forested shore of Timothy Lake, one of the Cascades' larger and more scenic reservoirs. Hikers interested in a longer loop can continue all the way around Timothy Lake, passing 4 campgrounds, several beaches, and views of Mt. Hood and Mt. Jefferson.

Little Crater Lake may only be 100 feet across, but it's as blue and as geologically unusual as its bigger National Park cousin. For centuries an artesian spring has been welling up in a wildflower meadow 15 miles south of Mt. Hood. The cold, gushing water has gradually worn away an underlying layer of soft siltstone, leaving a 45-foot-deep funnel of astonishingly clear blue water.

Drive Highway 26 to a turnoff 3.4 miles east of Wapinitia Pass (between mileposts 65 and 66). At a sign for Timothy Lake, turn onto paved Skyline Road 42 for 4 miles. Then turn right onto paved Abbott Road 58 for 1.4 miles to Little Crater Campground. Park at the far end of the campground loop by a trail sign.

The short paved path to the lake crosses a meadow with blue gentians and a view of Mt. Hood. Go right around the little lake, cross a fence on a stile, enter an old-growth forest of big Douglas firs, and reach the Pacific Crest Trail. Turn left onto this wide trail for 0.3 mile to a junction marking the start of the Timothy Lake loop. Keep left on the PCT.

After this junction the PCT promptly crosses swift, 50-foot-wide Crater Creek on a scenic footbridge — a possible turnaround point for hikers with small children. For the next mile, occasional springs gush out beside the trail. Several side trails to the right lead into lakeshore meadows dotted with stumps and grazing cows. Beyond Crater Creek 1.6 miles the trail climbs through woods to a "Timothy Lake" sign and your first view across the main body of the lake. This makes a good stopping point, particularly if you bushwhack 100 yards down to a scenic peninsula.

If you'd like to hike all the way around the lake, continue 2 miles on the PCT and turn right on the Timothy Lake Trail. Follow this path across the lake's main inlet (the Oak Grove Fork Clackamas River) and then keep right, sticking to the lakeshore. In the next 3 miles you'll pass a number of car campgrounds, boat ramps, and bathing beaches. Finally reach a planked boom of floating logs, chained end to end across the reservoir's mouth to protect the dam. While this precarious boom is open to hikers, it's safer to cross on the dam.

Timothy Lake and Mt. Hood.   Opposite: Log boom near the dam.

On the far shore, continue on the lakeshore path 1.2 miles before detouring to the right to explore Meditation Point, a peninsula with a boater campground. Then continue 3 miles around the lake to complete the loop.

Other Hiking Options
You can also drive to Timothy Lake from the Clackamas River side. Take Highway 224 east of Estacada 25.6 miles to the bridge at Ripplebrook, turn left onto paved Road 57, and follow signs to Timothy Lake. In this case, it's quicker to start your hike at the dam.

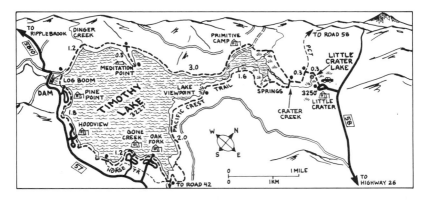

Mount Hood East

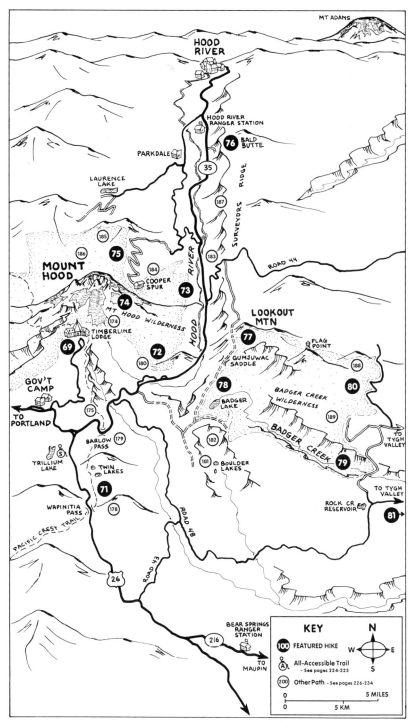

Opposite: Mt. Hood from Gnarl Ridge (Hike #72).

71 Twin Lakes

Easy (around Lower Twin Lake)
5.1 miles round-trip
700 feet elevation gain
Open June to early November
Map: Mt. Hood Wilderness (Geo-Graphics)

Moderate (to Palmateer Point)
9.1-mile loop
1500 feet elevation gain

Children like Lower Twin Lake for lots of reasons. The hike isn't too long, the water's swimmable, the beach has logs for climbing, there's plenty of campsites, and there's a path around the lake for exploring. Adults will appreciate the option of a longer loop hike past less-visited Upper Twin Lake and Palmateer Point, a cliff-edge viewpoint of Mt. Hood and the historic Barlow Creek Valley.

Drive Highway 26 to milepost 62 (east of Government Camp 8 miles), and turn at the Frog Lake Sno-Park. Park at the far left-hand end of this huge lot.

The trail starts beneath a brown skier-symbol sign and promptly meets the Pacific Crest Trail. Turn right onto this wide path and keep straight on it for 1.4 miles, climbing gradually from a mountain hemlock forest into woods dominated by firs. Although a budworm infestation has reddened or killed many of the firs, the extra sunlight has allowed the understory to thrive. Expect ripe huckleberries in late summer and the blooms of rhododendrons and beargrass in early summer.

Turn right at a trail junction, following a pointer for Lower Twin Lake. This path crests a saddle and slowly descends to a junction near the far end of the lake. Turn right for 100 yards to the lakeshore and camping area.

To continue on a longer loop, return to the lake-end trail junction and take the 0.7-mile path to Upper Twin Lake, a shallower pool with a view of Hood's head. Keep right around the shore for 100 yards and then veer to the right onto

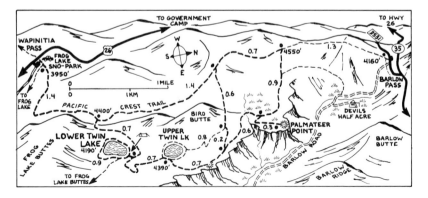

Upper Twin Lake.   Opposite: Blue huckleberries.

Palmateer View Trail #482. A bit narrower and rockier, this path passes the rim of a 100-foot cliff with a full-length view of Mt. Hood.

Continue straight 1.3 miles until the trail crosses a small creek and enters a meadow. A small "Viewpoint" sign here marks the 0.3-mile side trail up to Palmateer Point, overlooking a dramatic, glacially carved valley that served as the route for the 1845 Barlow Road between The Dalles and Sandy. The meadow visible far below (now a primitive campground with an outhouse) was one of the highest campsites used by covered wagon pioneers on Sam Barlow's rugged trail and was named the Devil's Half Acre because of its wintry weather early in autumn.

To complete the loop, return to the main trail and follow it up through the meadow and a lodgepole pine forest to the PCT. Turn left here for 3.5 easy miles back to the car.

Other Hiking Options

With a shuttle car you can hike one-way from Wapinitia Pass to Barlow Pass in just 6.9 miles and still visit both Twin Lakes and Palmateer Point. Drive Highway 35 to Barlow Pass and turn briefly south on Road 3531 to the PCT trailhead parking area.

72   Elk Meadows

Moderate (to Elk Meadows)
6.8 miles round-trip
1200 feet elevation gain
Open late June through October
Map: Mt. Hood Wilderness (USFS)

Difficult (to Gnarl Ridge)
10.2 miles round-trip
2200 feet elevation gain
Open mid-July through October

Two of Mt. Hood's most scenic hiking goals are tucked away on the mountain's southeast flank: a rustic shelter amidst Elk Meadows' wildflowers, and Gnarl Ridge's breathtaking cliff-edge viewpoint with wind-dwarfed pines. Visit either destination, or take a slightly longer loop and visit both.

From Portland, drive Highway 26 past Government Camp, then take Highway 35 toward Hood River for 8 miles to a large brown "Clark Creek Sno-Park" sign. (From Hood River, take Highway 35 for 33 miles to the sno-park.) Drive 0.3 mile along the sno-park's loop road and park on the shoulder beside an "Elk Meadows Trail" sign on the left.

The trail soon follows the lovely bank of rushing, bouldery Clark Creek. The fir forest here is jubilant with blue lupine blooms in July and ripe blue huckleberries in August. After a mile of gradual climbing, meet the heavily worn trail from Hood River Meadows and turn right, crossing Clark Creek on a footbridge. Continue nearly level for 0.6 mile, ignore the Newton Creek Trail on the left, and cross raging Newton Creek on logs.

The path now launches up a wooded ridge in 8 long switchbacks, finally reaching a 4-way trail junction at a saddle. If you want the shortest route to Gnarl Ridge, turn left here and stick to the ridgecrest for 2.5 uphill miles.

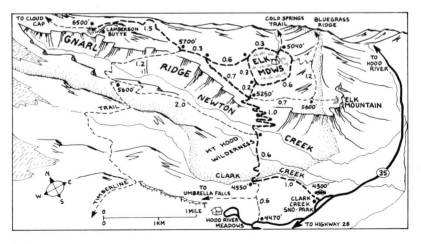

Mt. Hood from Gnarl Ridge.   Opposite: Elk Meadows' shelter.

But if you're headed for Elk Meadows, go straight. In 400 yards turn right on the Elk Meadows Perimeter Trail, a 1.2-mile circuit designed to keep hikers from tramping through the fragile meadows in the middle. If you're backpacking, note that the meadows (and tree islands in the meadows) are off-limits for tents, while the perimeter trail passes several usable campsites in the woods. After 0.6 mile the perimeter trail turns left at a junction beside a creek. Forty yards later reach an unmarked fork. Keep left here to find a 3-sided shelter with a picture-postcard view across the meadows to Mt. Hood.

To return to the car, simply follow the perimeter trail the rest of the way around the meadows. If you still have the energy to climb to Gnarl Ridge, however, hike 0.3 mile from the shelter along the perimeter trail and turn right at a sign, "To Gnarl Ridge." This route climbs 0.9 mile to the Timberline Trail. Follow the "Cloud Cap" pointer to the right and climb 1.5 miles into an alpine landscape where views extend from Mt. Adams to the Three Sisters. Finally pass the remains of a stone shelter on the left and reach a colossal cliff edge overlooking Newton Creek's 800-foot-deep chasm. Cowering whitebark pines form a gnarled mat along the rim. Turn back here — or, if you're feeling sprightly, scramble up Lamberson Butte, a rocky outcrop 400 yards to the south.

Other Hiking Options

If you're heading for Elk Meadows, it's only 1.4 miles further to make a loop via the old lookout site at Elk Mountain. Turn right at the 4-way trail junction just before the meadows, climb 0.7 mile to a spur trail leading to the viewpoint, and return along Bluegrass Ridge.

If you've hiked to Gnarl Ridge, it's only 1.2 miles further to return on a dramatic loop across Newton Creek's canyon. Just stay on the Timberline Trail as it descends to Newton Creek (bridgeless, so use caution). Then climb briefly to the Newton Creek Trail junction and turn left.

Tamanawas Falls.   Below: Golden-mantled ground squirrel.

73   Tamanawas Falls

Easy (direct to falls)
3.8 miles round-trip
500 feet elevation gain
Open late April through November
Map: Mt. Hood Wilderness (USFS)

Moderate (via Polallie Overlook)
5.6-mile loop
900 feet elevation gain

The Northwest Indians believed everyone has a *tamanawas* — a friendly guardian spirit. Tamanawas Falls seems as though it might be Mt. Hood's guardian, an inspiring 100-foot curtain of white water in a green canyon at the mountain's eastern base.

The path to the falls is a delight, with 4 scenic footbridges and lots of access to mossy-banked Cold Spring Creek. There's even a pack of cute golden-mantled ground squirrels at the falls for extra entertainment. Children will enjoy hiking the same trail both directions, but adults may prefer returning on a slightly longer 5.6-mile loop past the Polallie Overlook. And eager hikers can further extend the trip by taking the East Fork Trail another 4.1 miles along a whitewater branch of the Hood River.

Drive Highway 35 around Mt. Hood to the well-marked East Fork Trailhead near milepost 72, about 0.2 mile north of Sherwood Campground. Park by a message board at the north end of the pullout. Although the path is unclear near the parking area, simply walk 200 feet to the East Fork Hood River, a bouldery torrent milky with the silt of Hood's glaciers. Cross on an impressive footbridge and turn right on the East Fork Trail.

The mountain hemlock forest here is carpeted with twinflower, a tiny double-belled white wildflower with shiny little leaves. This delicate flower's Latin name is *Linnaea borealis* because it was a favorite of Linnaeas, the 18th-century Swedish botanist who invented the system of identifying plants with 2 Latin names.

After 0.6 mile on the East Fork Trail turn left and follow a path up Cold Spring Creek 1.3 miles to the base of Tamanawas Falls. The falls spills over the lip of an old lava flow. The same basalt forms the canyon walls and is visible as a cliff of hexagonal columns along the East Fork Hood River.

If you'd like to return on the 5.6-mile loop, hike back 0.4 mile from the falls. Just after the second footbridge turn left and switchback up to a ridgetop trail junction. Turn right (following the Polallie Campground pointer), descend gradually for a mile, and then take a 150-yard detour to the Polallie Overlook. The clifftop view of brushy Polallie Creek is only impressive if you know the creek's history. In 1980 an 80-foot-deep flash flood roared past here, destroying an old growth forest and 6 miles of Highway 35. (To see the flood's origin, a raw canyon headwall 4 miles upstream, take Hike #74 to Cooper Spur.)

To complete the loop, continue 200 yards on the main trail and turn right onto the East Fork Trail.

Other Hiking Options

For a longer riverside hike, park opposite the entrance to Robin Hood Campground (near milepost 68 of Highway 35), walk through the campground, and continue 4.1 miles along the East Fork Hood River to the start of the Tamanawas Falls hike described above. Although this portion of the East Fork Trail is open to mountain bikes and passes a few clearcuts, it offers quiet river vistas and backpacking campsites.

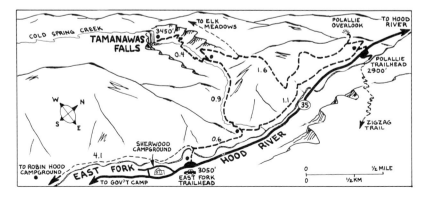

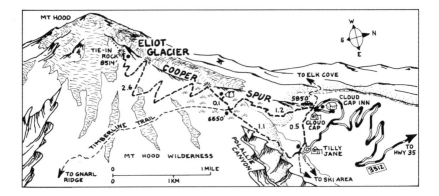

74   Cooper Spur

Moderate (to shelter)
3.0-mile loop
1000 feet elevation gain
Open mid-July to mid-October
Map: Mt. Hood Wilderness (USFS)

Difficult (to Tie-In Rock)
8.2-mile loop
2800 feet elevation gain

The highest hiking trail on Mt. Hood switchbacks up Cooper Spur's cindery shoulder to Tie-In Rock, where mountain climbers traditionally rope up. From this vertiginous perch, peaks from Mt. Rainier to the Three Sisters dot the horizon. The massive Eliot Glacier writhes below, a splintered river of ice. And if the thought of a 2800-foot ascent leaves you winded, Cooper Spur has a much easier hiking option: a 3-mile loop to a historic stone shelter at timberline.

Drive Highway 35 around Mt. Hood to the Cooper Spur Ski Area turnoff between mileposts 73 and 74. Head west on Cooper Spur Road for 3.3 miles to Tilly Jane Junction, turn left onto Road 3512 toward Cloud Cap, and follow signs 10.3 miles up to Cloud Cap Campground in a high saddle. The last 9 miles are on a steep, narrow, winding gravel road.

Park beside a sign on the right for the Timberline Trail and walk across the primitive campground 200 feet to a message board beside a trail junction. Go straight, following the Timberline Trail's "Gnarl Ridge" pointer uphill. In 100 yards keep left as the path forks twice (the unmarked right-hand branches lead to the toe of Eliot Glacier). Continue on the Timberline Trail, which in 0.5 mile climbs into a bouldery gully at the head of Tilly Jane Creek. The only plants able to grow here are alpine partridge foot and sand verbena. Large rock cairns mark the path up through the sand. Then the path climbs through a patch of twisted whitebark pines to a trail crossing in a broad field of blue lupine.

Turn right at this junction, taking the Cooper Spur Trail up 200 yards to a hidden 10-foot-square stone shelter built in the 1930s by the Civilian Conservation Corps. The view here extends from Mt. Adams and the Hood River Valley to the brown scablands of the Columbia River Plateau. Lookout Mountain (Hike #76) tops a green ridge to the east.

If you're interested in the tougher 8.2-mile hike, continue up past the shelter on a remarkably well-graded trail with occasional overlooks of Eliot Glacier. After 2.6 switchbacking miles reach a crest with 4 low stone windbreaks and a rock commemorating a 1910 Japanese climbing party. This makes a good stopping point, or you can continue 500 yards along the ridge to Tie-In Rock, a big boulder. But unless you have climbing equipment *do not* venture onto the deceptively dangerous snowfields beyond.

To complete the loop, hike down from the Cooper Spur shelter and go straight at the Timberline Trail junction, following the pointer toward Tilly Jane Campground. This path descends along the rim of Polallie Canyon, a quarter-mile-wide bowl created in December 1980 when rains launched a colossal landslide and flash flood. After 1.1 mile reach a trail junction near a windowless plank cookhouse built by the American Legion in 1924. Turn left, passing the historic Tilly Jane Guard Station and climbing gradually 0.5 mile to your car.

Mt. Hood from Cooper Spur.   *Opposite: Cooper Spur Shelter and Mt. Adams.*

Mt. Hood from Elk Cove.   Opposite: Western Pasque flower (old man of the mountain).

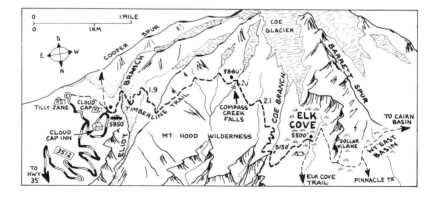

75   Elk Cove

Easy (to Compass Creek Falls)
3.8 miles round-trip
800 feet elevation gain
Open mid-July through October
Map: Mt. Hood Wilderness (USFS)

Moderate (to Elk Cove)
8 miles round-trip
2000 feet elevation gain

The Timberline Trail on Mt. Hood's north slope is a parade of wildflower meadows, mountain viewpoints, and tumbling brooks. By starting at the mile-high Cloud Cap trailhead you needn't climb much to reach these wonders, either. The path contours 1.9 miles to a pretty picnic spot above the 60-foot falls of Compass Creek, a good goal for hikers with children. Beyond that the trail drops sharply to cross a canyon before climbing to Elk Cove, a broad bowl of wildflowers.

Drive Highway 35 around Mt. Hood to the Cooper Spur Ski Area turnoff between mileposts 73 and 74. Head west on Cooper Spur Road for 3.3 miles to Tilly Jane Junction, turn left onto Road 3512 toward Cloud Cap, and follow signs 10.3 miles up to Cloud Cap Campground in a high saddle. The last 9 miles are on a steep, narrow, winding gravel road.

Park beside a sign on the right for the Timberline Trail, walk across the primitive campground 200 feet to a message board beside a trail junction, and turn right. The path sets out through a fir forest where blue lupine bloom in mid-summer and blue huckleberries ripen in late summer. But after 0.2 mile the trail suddenly traverses into the raw, V-shaped canyon of Eliot Branch, a roaring stream whose milky color betrays its glacial origin. The footbridge has a view across the Hood River Valley to Mt. Adams.

Wildflowers decorate the trailside from here on, especially in early August. Near creeks look for yellow and pink monkeyflower. Where snow melted late, expect the dishmop-shaped seed heads of western Pasque flower. In drier areas look for blue lupine, purple daisy-like asters, and red Indian paintbrush.

After 1.5 miles cross the first of Compass Creek's 3 branches. For the easy hike, stop at the third fork, where a 10-foot waterfall below the trail swirls through a rock bowl (and often into a snow cave). To see the much larger waterfall below, continue 200 yards on the trail to a viewpoint.

If you're continuing on to Elk Cove, the Timberline Trail descends gradually for 0.9 mile before switchbacking steeply down to a footbridge across a frothing, 20-foot-wide creek: the Coe Branch. Then the path climbs a wooded ridge to Elk Cove, a cliff-rimmed basin with lupine, paintbrush, and a view of Mt. Hood. Tenting is prohibited in the meadows. If you're backpacking, turn right at the Elk Cove Trail junction for 100 yards to find approved sites among the trees.

Mt. Hood from Bald Butte.   Opposite: Bald Butte from the Oak Ridge Trail.

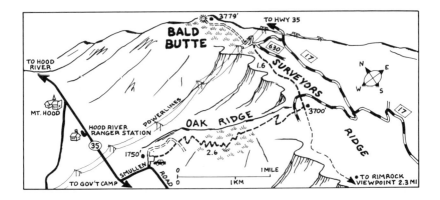

76   **Bald Butte**

Difficult
8.4 miles round-trip
2300 feet elevation gain
Open mid-March through November
Map: Hood River (Green Trails)

When the Hood River orchards blossom beneath snowy Mt. Hood, there's no better way to enjoy the springtime panorama than to climb to the old lookout site in Bald Butte's summit wildflower fields.

From Interstate 84 at Hood River take Exit #64 and follow Highway 35 for 14.8 miles toward Government Camp. Just 1 mile past the Hood River Ranger Station turn left on Smullen Road for 0.3 mile. At the first curve turn left onto an unmarked gravel road for 200 yards to a parking area on the right.

Start at a messageboard announcing the Oak Ridge Trail. The path begins in a partially logged area, crosses a cat road, and enters a dry forest of Douglas fir and long-needled ponderosa pine. The views begin after 0.8 mile, when the path switchbacks up along a ridgecrest grassland of Oregon white oaks and cheery, sunflower-like balsamroot wildflowers. Mt. Hood gleams above the Upper Hood River Valley's crazy quilt of fruit orchards. At the 1.5-mile mark the path crosses a fenceline and ducks into a cooler, higher elevation fir forest with white wildflowers. Look for the large triple leaves of vanilla leaf and the arching fronds of large smilacina.

After climbing 2.5 miles, cross a gravel road on top of Surveyors Ridge and a few yards later turn left onto the Surveyors Ridge Trail. This path follows the broad crest of the 2000-foot fault-block ridge that walls in the Upper Hood River Valley. As you hike north you'll cross a gravel road and a 1975 clearcut before descending slightly to a dirt road in a grassy pass below 4 sets of enormous powerlines.

Continue straight on the dirt road. This jeep track forks to the right underneath the powerlines and winds uphill 0.7 mile to Bald Butte's summit meadows, ablaze with yellow balsamroot in May. From the foundation pier of the old lookout tower the view includes 3 Washington snowpeaks and even the tip of Mt. Jefferson through a pass on Mt. Hood's left flank.

Other Hiking Options

If you turn south along the Surveyors Ridge Trail instead of north you'll reach another former fire lookout site at Rimrock Viewpoint, atop a sheer rock cliff. This goal is 0.7 mile further than Bald Butte and lacks the flowers, but the view is as good and doesn't require hiking a jeep track under powerlines.

77 Lookout Mountain △

Easy (to summit)
2.4 miles round-trip
600 feet elevation gain
Open July through October
Map: Badger Creek Wilderness (USFS)

Moderate (to Oval Lake)
6.2 miles round-trip
1800 feet elevation gain

This summit not only overlooks every Cascade peak from the Three Sisters to Mt. Rainier, it also offers a rare panorama of the Columbia River Plateau and the Badger Creek Wilderness.

Most people climb to Lookout Mountain on a grueling path switchbacking up 3000 feet from Robin Hood Campground via Gumjuwac Saddle. But there's a much easier route, starting at High Prairie's wildflower meadow. And if you take this shortcut you might well have enough energy left to continue along the Divide Trail to seldom-visited Oval Lake and the commanding rock pinnacles at Palisade Point.

Drive Highway 35 around Mt. Hood to the turnoff for Dufur Mill Road 44 (between mileposts 70 and 71, or 2.5 miles north of Robin Hood Campground). Turn east on this paved road for 3.8 miles and then turn right onto gravel High Prairie Road 4410. After another 4.7 miles — always keeping uphill — reach a T-shaped intersection where the gravel road turns to dirt. Turn left on High Prairie Road for 200 yards and park beside a row of posts on the right. The posts block vehicles from the old summit road — now a hiking trail.

As you start up this trail-like road you'll hike through a subalpine meadow with purple asters, fuzzy-leaved yarrow, and a few spire-topped firs. Also look for the foot-long, boat-shaped leaves of false hellebore, an odd plant with a stalk of green flowers and extremely poisonous roots that Indians believed could

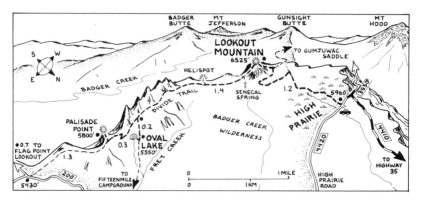

Mt. Hood from Lookout Mountain.   Opposite: Oval Lake.

ward off evil spirits.

Follow the old road up a long switchback to a signed trail junction in a high saddle. Take the Divide Trail left 200 yards to Lookout Mountain's summit.

If you'd like to visit Oval Lake, continue east on the Divide Trail as it descends (at times steeply) along a lovely alpine ridgecrest. After a mile the path descends through hemlock woods to a junction with the Fret Creek Trail. Turn left here for 0.2 mile to Oval Lake, a forest-rimmed pool reflecting several crag-topped bluffs. To continue to the view at Palisade Point, return to the Divide Trail and follow it 0.3 mile east up to a saddle. Beyond the saddle 60 yards take a short scramble trail to Palisade Point, a rock ledge overhanging the Badger Creek Valley. The staffed Flag Point lookout tower is visible 2 miles to the east.

Other Hiking Options

If you'd like a lot more exercise and a little less driving on your way to Lookout Mountain, start at the Gumjuwac Trailhead opposite Robin Hood Campground (on Highway 35 near milepost 68). It's 2.4 steep miles up to Gumjuwac Saddle, where you cross a road and bear left onto the Divide Trail for the final 2.2-mile climb to the summit.

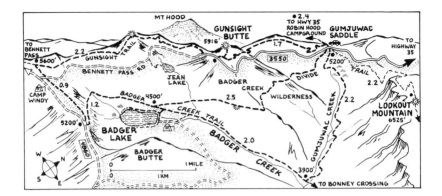

78   Badger Lake   ◭

Moderate (via Badger Creek)
6.7-mile loop
1300 feet elevation gain
Open late June through October
Map: Badger Creek Wilderness (USFS)

Moderate (via Gunsight Butte)
8.5-mile loop
1600 feet elevation gain

    Three different paths lead down to Badger Lake from the Gumjuwac Saddle trailhead, so hikers have a choice of loop options. If you start with a steep descent to Badger Creek you'll amble to the lake through a towering old-growth forest. If, however, you start with a climb along the Gunsight Trail you'll tour the valley rim past viewpoints of Mt. Hood. In either case, it's easiest to return from the lake on the middle of the 3 paths, the well-graded Divide Trail.

    To find the trailhead, drive around Mt. Hood on Highway 35 to the turnoff for Dufur Mill Road 44 (between mileposts 70 and 71, or 2.5 miles north of Robin Hood Campground). Turn east on this paved road for 3.8 miles and then turn right onto gravel High Prairie Road 4410. After another 4.7 uphill miles, turn right onto dirt Bennett Pass Road 3550 for 3.3 bumpy miles. Park by a large sign explaining the origin of the name Gumjuwac Saddle (from Gum Shoe Jack, a rubber-booted shepherd).

    If you've opted for the 6.7-mile loop via Badger Creek, take Gumjuwac Trail #480, immediately to the left of the big Gumjuwac Saddle sign. This path dives down through a meadow. After losing 1300 feet in 2.2 miles turn right on the Badger Creek Trail and climb gradually through a valley-bottom forest of big Douglas firs. In another 2 miles a spur trail to the left leads down to an old earthen dam at Badger Lake.

The dam was built by the Civilian Conservation Corps during World War II as part of an irrigation project. Today both the dam and the CCC's hand-built access road (impassable even for most 4-wheel-drive vehicles) are surrounded by designated Wilderness. Explore the lakeshore on a path to the right. Although this fisherman's trail dead ends in 0.5 mile, it passes several wooded campsites. To complete the Badger Creek loop, return to the Badger Creek Trail, continue 200 yards to a junction with the Divide Trail, turn right, and climb 2.5 miles to your car.

If you'd rather take the 8.5-mile Gunsight Butte loop, start out on the opposite side of the Road 3550 from the big Gumjuwac Saddle sign. Take an unmarked path 30 feet and then fork left, following a small "Gunsight Trail" pointer. This path climbs for 1.5 miles past the wooded summit of Gunsight Butte, joins the dirt Bennett Pass Road for 400 feet, and then continues along the ridgecrest — a series of natural rock gardens where red Indian paintbrush and purple penstemon bloom. Mt. Hood dominates the view, although you can also spot Mt. Adams and Mt. Jefferson.

At the 3.9-mile mark descend to a wooded saddle and turn left onto the Camp Windy Trail. This somewhat rough path crosses Road 3550 and continues 0.8 mile to a pullout beside dirt Road 4860. At the far end of the pullout take the Badger Creek Trail downhill to the left for 1.2 miles to the Divide Trail junction just above Badger Lake. Take a side trip here to explore the lake and then return to the Divide Trail for the 2.5-mile climb to your car.

Other Hiking Options

If you'd prefer a shorter drive but a longer hike, start at the Gumjuwac Trailhead opposite Robin Hood Campground on Highway 35 (near milepost 68). The switchbacking trail up to Gumjuwac Saddle gains 1700 feet in 2.4 miles.

Mt. Hood from Gunsight Butte.   Opposite: Badger Lake from the Divide Trail.

79 Badger Creek

Easy (to creekside boulders)
5.8 miles round-trip
400 feet elevation gain
Open all year
Map: Badger Creek Wilderness (USFS)

Moderate (to Pine Creek)
11.4 miles round-trip
900 feet elevation gain
Open late March to mid-December

Badger Creek winds up from Central Oregon's sagebrush flats to Mt. Hood's forests. In the middle it passes through a strange, mixed zone known as a pine-oak grassland. The hike follows the creek's wilderness canyon through this botanically fascinating middle zone, rich with wildflowers from both the high desert and the mountains.

If you're driving here from the west, take Highway 26 past Mt. Hood. Shortly after milepost 68 turn left onto paved Road 43 at a sign for Wamic. After 6 miles turn right onto paved Road 48 and continue 15.2 miles. Then turn left onto Road 4810, following signs toward Bonney Crossing Campground from here on. After just 0.2 mile, be sure to follow Road 4810's unmarked right-hand turn to avoid ending up at Rock Creek Reservoir. Then take Road 4810 another 1.9 miles, veer right onto paved Road 4811 for 1.2 miles, and turn right onto narrow, roughish gravel Road 2710 for 1.8 miles. Just after passing the entrance to primitive Bonney Crossing Campground, cross a bridge and park on the left by the trailhead sign.

If you're driving here from Highway 197, turn west at Tygh Valley (34 miles south of The Dalles). Follow signs for Wamic, then for Rock Creek Reservoir, and finally for Bonney Crossing Campground.

Trailside wildflowers are best from April to June. In dry grassy areas look for sunflower-like balsamroot, little purple larkspur, erratic-petaled white prairie

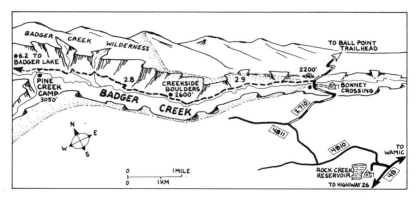

Badger Creek.   Opposite: Ponderosa pine at wilderness boundary.

star, blue lupine, and wild strawberry. In moister conifer woods expect trilliums, twinflower, and smilacina. If you didn't know orchids grow in Oregon, look for the little pink hoods of the rare lady's slipper orchid beside the trail register at the 0.2-mile mark. Hikers with children should remind them not to pick any native plants.

Although the creek is never far away, one of the nicest access points comes after 2.6 miles, when the creek squeezes between a pair of 10-foot boulders, creating a pool and a tiny pebble beach. Hikers with children can turn back here, or perhaps continue 0.3 mile past a scenic cliff to another pair of creekside boulders and a 5-foot waterfall.

Hikers interested in a longer trip can continue another 2.8 miles to an old campsite on a riverbend opposite the cascading confluence of Pine Creek. Here the music of the creeks is particularly sweet, beneath a canopy of ancient red cedar and grand fir. Because this old campsite is too close to the creek and the trail for modern low-impact tenting, backpackers should choose more remote flat spots on the far side of the creek.

Other Hiking Options

Backpackers can continue 6.2 miles past Pine Creek to Badger Lake, where there are several possible side trips and loop options (see Hike #77).

80 Ball Point

Moderate (to helispot)
7.2 miles round-trip
1400 feet elevation gain
Open late March to mid-December
Map: Badger Creek Wilderness (USFS)

In the rain shadow of the Cascades, the Badger Creek Wilderness not only has better weather than nearby Mt. Hood, it's far less crowded. The hike to Ball Point shows just how attractive these eastern foothills can be, with slopes full of early summer wildflowers and with sweeping views from rock pinnacles.

If you're driving here from the west, take Highway 26 past Mt. Hood to a turnoff shortly after milepost 68. Following signs for Wamic, turn left onto paved Road 43 for 6 miles and turn right onto paved Road 48 for 15.2 miles. Then, following signs for Bonney Crossing Campground, turn left onto Road 4810 for 2.1 miles, veer right onto paved Road 4811 for 1.2 miles, and turn right onto Road 2710. Follow this narrow gravel road for 6.7 miles toward Tygh Valley before turning left onto paved Road 27 for 2.1 miles to a pullout and sign on the left for the School Canyon Trail.

If you're driving here from the east, take Highway 197 between Maupin and The Dalles to milepost 33, opposite the Tygh Valley Rodeo Grounds. Turn west onto Shadybrook Road for 1 mile, turn left onto Fairgrounds Road for 1.1 mile, and then turn right onto Badger Creek Road. After 6.4 miles on this gravel road, turn right onto paved Road 27 for 2.1 miles to the School Canyon Trailhead.

The School Canyon Trail begins as an ancient jeep track through a remarkable pine-oak grassland, where gnarled old oaks mingle with stately ponderosa pines amid park-like fields of wildflowers. In May and June expect masses of

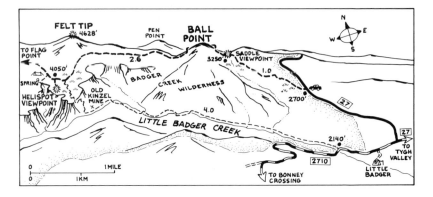

View from helispot.   Opposite: Balsamroot.

red Indian paintbrush, sunflower-like balsamroot, blue lupine, and lobed white prairie star. After 0.8 mile the road becomes a trail that leads up to a saddle viewpoint with a panorama extending to Mt. Jefferson and the Three Sisters. To the east are the Pine Hollow Reservoir and the farmfields of Wamic.

Next the trail ducks into a more conventional Douglas fir forest, bypasses Ball Point, and slowly climbs for a couple miles to a plateau meadow with pinemat manzanita bushes. The Little Badger Trail takes off downhill to the left here, but continue 300 yards to a short side trail to a helispot — an old firefighter landing site surrounded by weird-shaped rock pinnacles. The leftmost set of spires is particularly fun to explore.

If you're backpacking, return to the main trail and continue 100 yards to a campsite on the left. A path down through the campsite leads to a mossy glen with a hidden spring.

Other Hiking Options

By arranging a 3.6-mile car shuttle you can return on the Little Badger Trail, which switchbacks steeply down to the abandoned Kinzel Mine and then follows Little Badger Creek to Road 2710.

Tygh Valley Falls.   Opposite: Turbines in abandoned powerhouse.

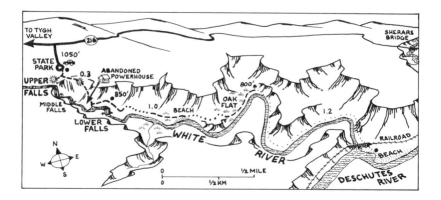

81   Tygh Valley Falls

Easy
0.6 mile round-trip
200 feet elevation loss
Open all year
Map: Maupin (USGS)

This colossal, 3-part waterfall in the desert is hidden at an unassuming park wayside off a small state highway. And although the official trail to the falls is quite short, the attractions are many: riverside sunning rocks, a small sandy beach, and an abandoned hydroelectric power plant full of machinery from the early 1900's. What's more, it's possible to bushwhack another mile or two down the cliff-rimmed canyon toward the confluence with the Deschutes River — although explorers on this lower section must beware of poison oak.

Either before or after the hike, it's fun to drive to nearby Sherars Bridge, a scenic, rocky narrows of the Deschutes where Indians sometimes still dip-net migrating salmon from platforms.

To find the trailhead, take Highway 197 between The Dalles and Maupin. Near milepost 34 in Tygh Valley turn east onto Highway 216 toward Sherars Bridge for 4 miles to the state park entrance road on the right. Park at the picnic area beside a fenced overlook of 80-foot Upper Tygh Valley Falls. Follow a paved path down to the left, cross a plank bridge, and take a steep trail 0.2 mile downhill to the stone ruins of the old powerhouse. Inside are nesting swallows and huge, rusting turbines.

From the beach at the powerhouse you can follow a fainter trail downstream through a stand of pungent, head-high sagebrush. But before setting off, make sure you can recognize the low, triple-leafletted poison oak shrubs lining the path — and be sure to warn any children with you not to touch these plants! A few hundred yards downstream are the broad rock banks of the 20-foot-tall lower falls.

Other Hiking Options

Adventurers can explore the trailless but very beautiful lower portion of this desert canyon. Because poison oak is thick here, wear long pants and plan to wash them after the hike. Shortly after the lower falls, scramble down a rockslide and follow a riverside deer path through a lovely grassland half a mile to a beach. To avoid the cliffs ahead, climb over a low ridge to an oak flat ideal for a secluded backpacking camp. All but the hardiest pathfinders should turn back here, for the final 1.2 miles to the Deschutes River are rough.

Clackamas
Foothills

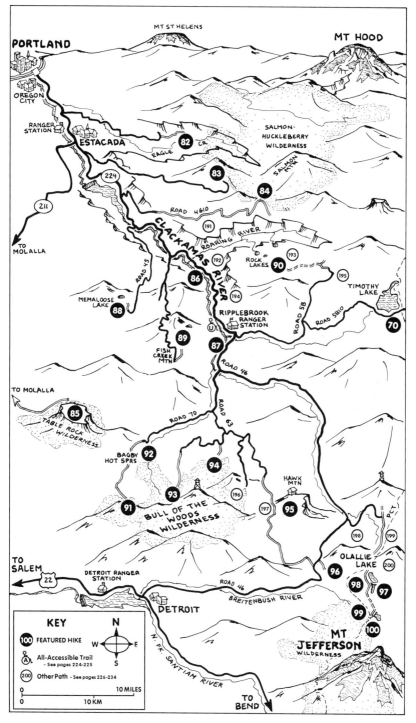

Opposite: Jefferson Park (Hike #100).

The Eagle Creek Trail.   Opposite: Fog shrouds Old Baldy.

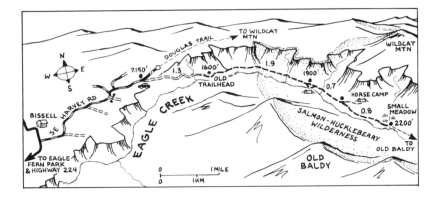

82   Eagle Creek

Moderate
9.4 miles round-trip
1200 feet elevation gain
Open all year
Map: Cherryville (Green Trails)

Not to be confused with the Columbia Gorge's famous Eagle Creek Trail, this little-known path near Estacada follows a rainforest valley into the Salmon-Huckleberry Wilderness. Don't wear tennis shoes to explore these ancient woods, as the path has a few muddy spots even in dry weather.

Drive Highway 224 to milepost 19 (4 miles north of Estacada), take the Eagle Fern Park exit, go straight on Wildcat Mountain Road 2 miles, continue straight on Eagle Fern Park Road 2.4 miles, veer right for 1.7 mile (passing Eagle Fern Park), and then go straight on George Road for 6.3 more paved miles. A total of 11.4 miles from the highway, turn right onto SE Harvey Road, which soon becomes a potholed gravel lane.

Harvey Road has several confusing, unsigned forks, so watch your odometer. Turn left at 0.6 mile, fork to the right at 1.9 and 2.0 miles, and park at the 2.6-mile mark, where an overgrown, unmarked dirt road angles down to the right. The trailhead was once 1.3 miles down this abandoned road, but the track offers no place to turn around and soon becomes impassable.

Hike down the unmarked road, which descends past several clearcuts before finally turning into a trail and leveling out in a grand old-growth forest. Red cedars and bigleaf maples droop huge mossy branches above a green carpet of shamrock-shaped oxalis. Big white trilliums, pink bleeding hearts, yellow wood violets, and crimson salmonberry bloom here in spring.

After 1.9 miles through the big trees, a right-hand fork leads to a creekside campsite — the hike's first access to rushing, boulder-filled Eagle Creek. Continue on the main trail 0.7 miles to another fork. The left-hand, uphill path climbs half a mile to an old horse camp, so keep straight on the river trail. Cross several small side creeks, and after 0.8 mile reach a plank footbridge across a gully in a small meadow of oxalis and yellow violets. Leave the trail here and bushwhack 100 yards right along the gully to a lovely picnic spot at a bend in Eagle Creek — the recommended turnaround point. Suitable campsites are on a wooded flat just downstream.

Adventurers who continue past the little meadow on the Eagle Creek Trail will find that the path grows fainter and brushier for 2 miles, crosses the creek, and scrambles faintly 2.5 miles up a 1800-foot ridge to the Old Baldy Trail described in Hike #82.

83 Old Baldy

Moderate
7.6 miles round-trip
1200 feet cumulative elevation gain
Open June to mid-November
Map: Salmon-Huckleberry (USFS)

Less than an hour's drive from Portland on paved roads, this surprisingly little-used viewpoint trail follows a delightful wooded ridge up and down along the westernmost edge of the Salmon-Huckleberry Wilderness. And although the former lookout site atop Old Baldy is partly overgrown with trees, a newly relocated section of the trail passes a clifftop with an even better vista across the Eagle Creek Valley to 4 Cascade peaks.

Drive south on Highway 224 past Estacada 1.5 miles, turn left on Surface Road for 1.1 mile, and then turn right on Squaw Mountain Road. You'll follow this paved road (which becomes Road 4614) for a total of 14.5 miles, but because of misleading junctions, you'd best watch the odometer. At the 9.8-mile mark be sure *not* to follow an "Old Baldy Trail" sign pointing left. This sign refers to an ancient path obliterated by clearcuts. Instead take the road's right-hand fork, and half a mile later continue straight at another junction. At the 13-mile mark Road 4614 becomes 1-lane. Finally, just 0.2 mile after the road finally starts going downhill, park in a forested saddle at a poorly marked driveway-like pullout on the right. At the end of the 20-foot driveway look for a small wooden sign announcing the Old Baldy Trail.

Follow the trail left through mountain hemlock woods filled with all the proper mid-elevation June flowers: tiny star-flowered smilacina, 4-petaled bunchberry, vanilla leaf, and solitary queen's cup. As the path climbs over the

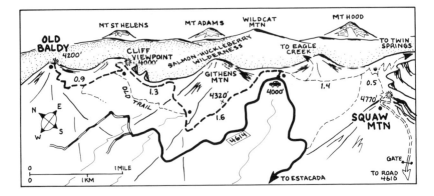

188

Mt. Hood from the Old Baldy Trail.   Opposite: Star-flowered smilacina.

shoulder of Githens Mountain expect rhododendron and beargrass, too.

After 1.6 miles the trail forks in a glen. Ignore the old trail to the left and take the newer, more scenic route up to the right. This path traverses a mile to a forested rim with rounded crags resembling stacks of giant, mossy muffins. When the trail crests beside a stump with a cairn, bushwhack 30 feet to the right to a mossy clifftop viewpoint. Note forested Wildcat Mountain (Hike #52) between the snowy peaks of Mt. Hood and Mt. Adams.

The trail then switchbacks downhill, joins the old trail, traverses half a mile to a junction with a still older abandoned trail, and climbs sharply to the old lookout site with its view across the treetops to Mt. Hood.

Other Hiking Options

For another viewpoint hike from the same trailhead, take the Old Baldy Trail south 1.4 miles and turn right for half a mile to Squaw Mountain, a former lookout site with a 360-degree view. The final few hundred yards of this climb follow a gated road.

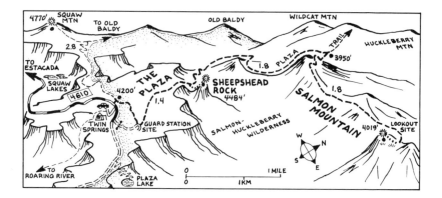

84   Sheepshead Rock

Easy (to Sheepshead Rock)
2.8 miles round-trip
500 feet elevation gain
Open mid-June to early November
Map: Salmon-Huckleberry (USFS)

Difficult (to Salmon Mountain)
10 miles round-trip
1800 feet cumulative elevation gain

In the early 1900s, when the newly created National Forests were threatened by sheepherders and timber thieves, the government built a guard station atop a remote mile-square plateau called The Plaza. By the 1930s wildfire seemed a bigger threat, so rangers strung telephone wires from The Plaza to lookout towers on half a dozen neighboring peaks.

Now that most of The Plaza's forests lie within the protected Salmon-Huckleberry Wilderness, the guard station and lookout towers are gone. The old trails, however, remain.

For an easy sample of these historic paths, hike the Plaza Trail past the original guard station site to Sheepshead Rock, a crag with a view from Mt. Hood to Portland. For a more rugged adventure, continue on an old lookout trail along Salmon Mountain's ridge to an even better viewpoint at one of Northwest Oregon's most remote places.

Drive Highway 224 south of Estacada 6.5 miles. Opposite Promontory Park turn left at a sign for Silver Fox RV Park and veer left onto Road 4610. Stick to this mostly gravel and sometimes rough road for a total of 18.4 miles, following signs for "4610" or "Plaza Trail." Just to be sure, you might watch the odometer and fork to the left at the 7.1-mile mark, turn right at the 8-mile mark, fork to the left at the 17-mile mark, and finally watch for the trailhead sign on the left. Since there is no room to park here, continue a hundred yards to the primitive Twin Springs Campground on the right, and walk back to the trailhead.

Hike up the Plaza Trail 100 feet to a junction and turn right. The sparse mountain hemlock forest here lets in enough sunlight that rhododendrons and huckleberries thrive. Expect big pink blooms in early summer and loads of ripe blue fruit at summer's end. After 0.3 mile the trail briefly joins an abandoned road at the old guard station site and then veers left into the woods again.

After 1.2 miles reach the edge of The Plaza's plateau and start going downhill. Just 100 feet before the first switchback, take an unmarked side path up to the right. This path scrambles up Sheepshead Rock's bare, lumpy crag to the edge of a 100-foot cliff. From here Salmon Mountain's ridge looks like a green arm reaching toward Mt. Hood. To the west, look down the valley of Eagle Creek (Hike #81) to the flats of Portland.

If you're ready for a much more rugged hike, continue down the Plaza Trail 1.8 miles to a signed junction and turn right on the Salmon Mountain Trail. This path clambers up and down along a rhododendron-choked ridgecrest for 1.8 miles, growing steadily fainter and more brushy. Just before reaching a bare knoll the path angles down to the left across a brushy slope and then ends altogether at a saddle. Turn right and bushwhack 200 yards up the open ridgecrest to the old lookout site, with its view of 4 snowpeaks and the entire Salmon-Huckleberry Wilderness.

Looking down from Sheepshead Rock.   Opposite: Salmon Mountain lookout site.

85 Table Rock

Moderate (to Table Rock)
4.6 miles round-trip
1200 feet elevation gain
Open June to mid-November
Map: Bull of the Woods Wilderness (USFS)

Difficult (to Rooster Rock)
7.4 miles round-trip
2300 feet elevation gain

This fortress-shaped plateau, centerpiece of a pocket Wilderness near Molalla, offers a formidable panorama of 10 Cascade snowpeaks and the whole Coast Range. A relatively easy trail ducks below huge columnar basalt cliffs and then switchbacks up the plateau's gentle western slope. Rhododendrons flag the route pink in early summer; gentians dot it with blue in late summer. For a longer hike, continue on a slightly rougher path to Rooster Rock's picturesque crag.

Start by driving to Molalla — either by heading south from Interstate 205 at Oregon City or by heading east from Interstate 5 at Woodburn. From Molalla drive half a mile toward Estacada on Highway 211, turn right onto South Mathias Road for 0.4 mile, turn left on South Feyrer Park Road for 1.6 miles, and then turn right onto South Dickey Prairie Road. Follow this road past several jogs for a total of 5.3 miles to an unsigned junction. Turn right on a bridge across the Molalla River, follow a paved road 12.8 miles to a fork, veer left onto the gravel Middle Fork Road for 2.6 miles, and then turn right at a sign, "Table Rock Trailhead 5.3 Miles." It's actually 5.6 miles and because the trailhead sign on the right is overgrown you might want to watch your odometer. This will also help you avoid a left-hand fork at the 1.8-mile mark and a right-hand fork shortly thereafter.

The trail crosses an old cat road after 100 yards and climbs at a steady grade

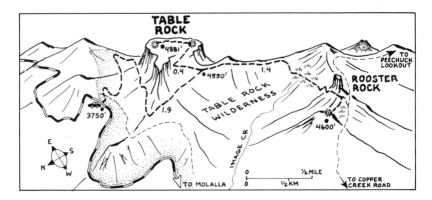

Rooster Rock and Mt. Jefferson.   Opposite: Columnar basalt on Table Rock.

through lichen-draped hemlocks and firs. At the 1-mile mark traverse below Table Rock's dramatic north cliff — a cutaway view of 7 basalt lava flows, 16 to 25 million years old. Here the trail crosses a rockslide where snow patches linger into July. Listen for the peeping cry of the rabbit-like pikas that store dried plants under the boulders for winter.

After 1.9 miles turn left at a junction in a ridgecrest saddle and climb to the summit in 2 long switchbacks. Lined up to the east are every major Cascade peak from Mt. Rainier to the Three Sisters. Beyond the quilt of Willamette Valley farmfields to the west, the Coast Range silhouette stretches from the Tualatin Hills to Marys Peak.

To continue to Rooster Rock, return to the junction in the saddle and go straight, following the rough ridgecrest up and down. The path descends to a meadow of thimbleberries before climbing steeply to an open saddle. Turn right and hike 100 yards up to a rocky knoll with a view across Rooster Rock to the High Cascades.

The Narrows.   Opposite: Candyflower.

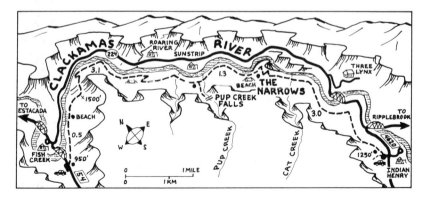

86 Clackamas River Trail

Moderate (with shuttle)
7.8 miles one-way
1300 feet cumulative elevation gain
Open all year
Map: Fish Creek Mtn. (Green Trails)

This all-year trail through the Clackamas River's canyon features hidden beaches, mossy forests, and whitewater viewpoints. A highway unobtrusively follows the river's far shore, making it easy to arrange a car shuttle and hike the 7.8-mile trail one way. If you can't find a second car to shuttle, try a 7.2-mile round-trip hike to Pup Creek Falls, a good picnic spot and turnaround point.

Drive Highway 224 south from Estacada 15 miles. Immediately after passing the Fish Creek Campground, turn right onto Fish Creek Road 54, cross the Clackamas River on a green bridge, and park at a big lot on the right. The signed trailhead is on the opposite of the road. To leave a shuttle car at the upper trailhead you'll have to drive another 7 miles up Highway 224 and go straight (just before a bridge) at a sign for Indian Henry Campground. Follow Road 4620 for 0.6 mile and park on the right, opposite the campground entrance.

Start at the lower trailhead on Fish Creek Road, following a path lined with thousands of April-blooming oxalis. This white wildflower's shamrock-shaped leaves have such a tart flavor they're also called sourgrass. Spring brings trilliums and yellow wood violets to these woods, too. After half a mile the trail passes a lovely stretch of riverbank with mossy bedrock suitable for summer sunbathing and a sandy beach ideal for splashing about.

Beyond the beach the trail spends a mile climbing through the forest to avoid riverside cliffs. Then the path continues gradually up and down along the shore, crossing an occasional powerline clearing. At the 3.6-mile mark (just before crossing 8-foot-wide Pup Creek on a plank), turn right on a 200-yard side trail through an alder grove to a view of Pup Creek Falls.

If you continue on the main trail, you'll reach another side path in 0.9 mile that leads left across a plank to a campsite by a whitewater riffle — the last beach access of the hike. Next the trail climbs a bluff with a view of The Narrows, a 20-foot-wide river gorge. Continue down the far side of the bluff and take a side trail to the left to see this chasm close up. In the final 2.9 miles to Indian Henry Campground, the trail ducks beneath a cliff's overhang, passes a side creek's thin waterfall, and contours through an old-growth forest of 5-foot-thick cedars.

Other Hiking Options

An even more convenient, 5-mile segment of the Clackamas River Trail is scheduled to be built by 1995 between the bridge at Memaloose Road (9 miles south of Estacada) and Armstrong Campground, 14 miles from Estacada.

87 Riverside Trail

Easy (with shuttle)
4 miles one-way
300 feet elevation gain
Open all year
Map: Fish Creek Mtn. (Green Trails)

A classic old-growth forest flanks this popular portion of the Clackamas River near Ripplebrook. Explore it on the Riverside Trail, visiting secluded beaches and clifftop viewpoints. Because paved Road 46 parallels the river, it's easy to arrange a 4-mile car shuttle (or a bicycle shuttle) and hike the path one-way.

From Estacada, take Highway 224 for 26 miles to the bridge at Ripplebrook, fork right onto Road 46, and immediately turn right into Rainbow Campground. Park at a trailhead sign at the far end of the campground loop. In winter when the campground's closed, park at the gate.

The path begins amid big Douglas fir and red cedar with an understory of sword fern and Oregon grape (whose clustered yellow blooms are Oregon's state flower). After 0.2 mile a right-hand spur of the trail dead ends at the gravelly bank of the Oak Grove Fork. Keep left, climbing to the rim of a sunny 400-foot cliff overlooking a broad curve of the Clackamas River.

At the 1-mile mark the trail crosses a footbridge. A few yards later the path forks. The main route follows an inconspicuous "Riverside Trail" pointer left, but first go straight to discover a small sandy beach beside a chilly but swim-mable 50-foot pool, protected from the river's swift current by a large rock.

Then continue on the main trail 0.8 mile, switchbacking up past another viewpoint and down to a footbridge over Tag Creek (with an incorrect sign, "Tar Creek"). Just beyond is another very scenic beach — broad and pebbly, beside

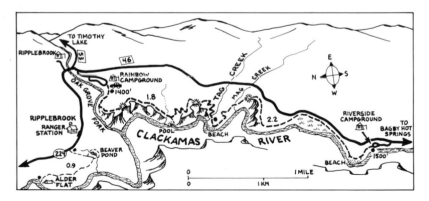

The Clackamas River.   Opposite: Old-growth forest along the Riverside Trail.

the glassy, cliff-backed river.

At the 3-mile mark the trail follows within a stone's throw of Road 46 for a dull half mile before curving out around a pretty river bend to the trailhead at the end of the Riverside Campground loop.

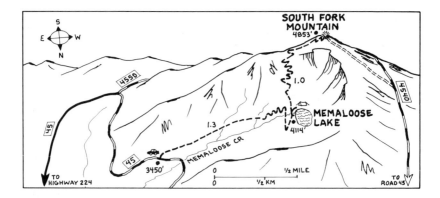

88   Memaloose Lake

Easy (to Memaloose Lake)
2.6 miles round-trip
700 feet elevation gain
Open mid-June to early November
Map: Fish Creek Mtn. (Green Trails)

Moderate (to South Fork Mountain)
4.6 miles round-trip
1400 feet elevation gain

This popular path is only 20 miles from Estacada, yet has the feel of the High Cascades. Hike 1.3 miles through a grand old-growth forest to a mountain lake in the woodsy cirque of a long-vanished glacier. If you like, continue up to the former lookout site atop South Fork Mountain for a view from the Three Sisters to Mt. Rainier.

From Estacada take Highway 224 south 9.3 miles and turn right over a green bridge onto Memaloose Road 45. Drive 11.2 paved miles on this road and then keep right on gravel for another mile to the trailhead sign on the left, just before Memaloose Creek.

The route of the hike lies within a single, isolated square mile of ancient forest, but the valley's steep walls make it seem as though the big woods extend forever. White wildflowers bloom in here in May, and for the rest of summer their delicate green leaves remain to blanket the forest floor. Look for vanilla leaf's 3 large triangular leaves. Oxalis resembles a shamrock, bunchberry has leaves in clusters of 6, and star-flowered smilacina's leaflets resemble arched fronds.

The path crosses a couple of creeklets overhung with elegant lady ferns before switchbacking up to a picnic table at the shallow lake. Turn left when you reach the shore and cross the outlet creek's bed. On your right you'll find a forested flat with several campsites. On your left is a toilet, hidden away from the lake.

And straight ahead is the unmarked path toward South Fork Mountain.

If you're interested in a quick climb, follow this path as it switchbacks up into a higher elevation forest with huckleberries, beargrass, and rhododendrons. The trail crests a ridge and follows it up to the old lookout site. A bit of searching will locate all 4 foundations, inscribed with a 1931 date. To be sure, an ungated dirt road occasionally brings cars to this summit. But this does not diminish the view. To the right of Mt. Jefferson look for pointy 3-Fingered Jack, Broken Top, and all Three Sisters. To the left of Mt. Hood look for Mt. Adams, Mt. Rainier, and Mt. St. Helens.

The trail to Memaloose Lake.   Opposite: Reflection in Memaloose Lake.

89 Fish Creek Mountain ⚠

Moderate
5.8 miles round-trip
1900 feet elevation gain
Open June to early November
Map: Fish Creek Mtn. (Green Trails)

The trail along this tall, rarely visited ridgecrest not only leads to a fine lookout site, but a side path descends to a charming mountain lake backed by a rockslide and the cliffs of Fish Creek Mountain.

Drive Highway 224 south from Estacada 15 miles. Just after Fish Creek Campground, turn right across a green bridge onto paved Fish Creek Road 54. After 1.6 miles fork uphill to the left onto Road 5410 — and a few hundred yards later fork to the right onto Road 5420. Follow this winding road 11.8 miles to the end of pavement. Then turn left and keep left on gravel Road 290 for 1.3 miles to an unmarked, gravel driveway-like parking area on the right. The path starts between this parking pullout and the road.

The trail climbs along a wooded, steep-sided ridgecrest for 1.8 miles. About halfway up you'll pass a level stretch with strange rock outcroppings, anthills, and views back to Mt. Jefferson. Because this high ridge is exposed to so many winter windstorms, expect to step over a few blowdown logs.

When you reach a marked trail junction, head left for 0.4 mile to the summit lookout site, where concrete piers and melted glass remain from the tower that burned here. The view extends south past Mt. Jefferson to all Three Sisters, and northwest to the Portland hills. The best view of Mt. Hood and the community of Ripplebrook, however, is back down the trail a few hundred yards.

After soaking in the view return to the junction, turn left, and switchback 0.7

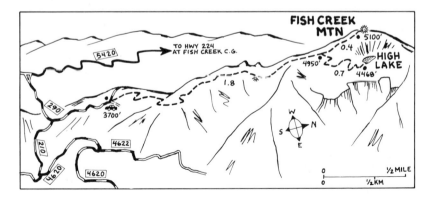

High Lake.   Opposite: Oregon grape.

mile down to a picnic spot at High Lake. Though only 600 feet long, this pretty pool is 20 feet deep and perfectly swimmable. If you continue right around the shore you'll find a campsite with a glimpse of Mt. Hood.

When you return to your car and drive back on gravel Road 290, be sure to keep right at all junctions until you regain paved Road 5420.

90   Rock Lakes

Easy (to Middle Rock Lake)
2 miles round-trip
500 feet elevation loss
Open mid-June to early November
Maps: High Rock, Fish Creek Mtn.
   (Green Trails)

Moderate (to Serene Lake)
7.7-mile loop
1500 feet elevation gain

During the Ice Age, glaciers gouged high, bowl-shaped valleys into the tableland between the Clackamas and Roaring Rivers. Now mountain lakes fill these forested dales. An easy, mile-long trail descends to the Rock Lakes, a collection of 3 pools in the glaciers' footprints. If you continue on a 7.7-mile loop, you'll also get to visit larger Serene Lake, a viewpoint of Mt. Hood, and an old shelter at Cache Meadow.

From Estacada, drive Highway 224 for 26 miles to the bridge at Ripplebrook, fork left onto paved Road 57 (toward Timothy Lake) for 7.4 miles, turn left onto Road 58 for 6.9 miles (following signs to High Rock), turn left onto Abbott Road 4610 for 1.3 paved miles, and then go straight onto dirt Road 240 at a sign for Frazier Fork. Follow this rocky, bumpy, slow road for 4.4 grueling miles, keep left at an unmarked fork beside primitive Frazier Fork Campground, and continue 0.2 mile to road's end at Frazier Turnaround.

Start on the Serene Lake Trail, descending through Douglas fir woods with white wildflowers in early summer: beargrass plumes, bunchberry, and queen's cup. After 0.8 mile turn left for a few hundred yards to a campsite at Middle Rock Lake. If you'd like to do a little exploring, go right at this campsite, cross the lake's outlet creek, follow a faint path to the far end of the lake, and hike up a slope to discover Upper Rock Lake in the Ice Age glacier's rocky cradle. To

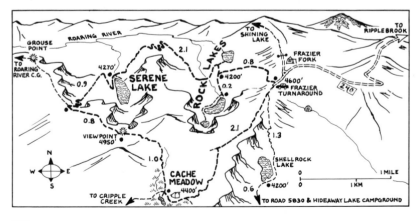

Serene Lake and Mt. Hood.   Opposite: Cache Meadow's shelter.

find the third lake in this valley, return to the main trail, continue downhill 200 yards, and follow a pointer to Lower Rock Lake.

If you're taking the loop hike, continue 2 miles (with some downs and ups) to large, green, very deep Serene Lake. A fork to the left ends at the lake's bouldery east shore, while the main trail continues to a forested campsite on the west side. Here the trail turns uphill and climbs for most of a mile to a trail junction on the edge of a high, forested plateau. Go left. In 0.8 mile you'll traverse a 1-acre clearcut with a super view of Serene Lake, Mt. Hood, and 3 snowpeaks in Washington.

Next the trail descends a mile to a 4-way trail junction at Cache Meadow, with its lakelet and flowers. Turn left for 200 yards to a small log shelter from the early 1930s. The old telephone box, once used by Forest Service employees to report fires, now protects a few emergency rations. To complete the hike, continue past the shelter 300 yards, fork left on trail 517, climb for a mile to an ancient road, and follow it right for a mile to your car.

Other Hiking Options

If you hesitate to take your car on the final 4 miles of bad dirt road to the Frazier Turnaround trailhead, why not start from the paved road near Hideaway Lake instead? This route adds 3.8 miles round-trip distance and 500 feet of elevation gain to your hike, but you pass Shellrock Lake and August huckleberry fields on the way. From Ripplebrook, drive Road 57 for 7.4 miles, turn left onto Road 58 for 3 miles, and turn left onto Road 5830 for 5 miles. You can start the Shellrock Trail either at Hideaway Lake Campground or where the path crosses Road 5830, 0.4 mile past the campground entrance.

91 Whetstone Mountain

Moderate
4.8 miles round-trip
1100 feet elevation gain
Open mid-June to early November
Map: Bull of the Woods Wilderness (USFS)

From Whetstone Mountain's rocky summit, the famous old-growth forests of Opal Creek's valley look like a rumpled green blanket. Eastward the forests roll up into the Bull of the Woods Wilderness, a protected cluster of green peaks. Glinting on the horizon are snowpeaks from Mt. Rainier to the Three Sisters. Though the view is panoramic, the climb to this old lookout site is relatively easy, and the trail passes through great patches of pink rhododendrons in early summer and huge blue huckleberries in August.

Drive Highway 224 from Estacada 26 miles to the bridge at Ripplebrook. Then, following signs for Bagby Hot Springs, keep straight on paved Road 46 for 3.6 miles, turn right onto paved Road 63 for 3.5 miles, and turn right onto paved Road 70. Drive 9 miles on Road 70, and then follow signs for the Whetstone Mountain Trail, turning left onto Road 7030 for 5.6 miles, and turning right onto Road 7020 for 0.7 mile. Just before Road 7020 ends, turn left onto spur Road 028 to a large parking area in a 1980 clearcut.

The trail starts out downhill for 300 yards until it reaches an old-growth fir forest. Along this path are wild huckleberries so large they nearly rival commercial blueberries. If you've come before huckleberry season, admire the white woodland wildflowers instead: 3-petaled trillium, 4- or 6-petaled bunchberry, and 6-petaled queen's cup.

The trail passes between a pond and a rockslide (inhabited by cheeping pikas) at the 0.9-mile mark, and then switchbacks up to a broad, forested ridgetop crowded with rhododendrons. Watch carefully here for an inconspicuous sign and a faint trail joining from the right. Turn right onto this somewhat brushy path and follow it up the ridge. When the path forks at a scrawled signboard after 0.8 mile, go right and switchback up to the summit's bald rock knob.

From the foundation pier of the long-gone lookout tower you can see the entire route of your hike — including your flea-sized car in the clearcut below the snowy tips of Mt. Adams and Mt. Rainier. Sharp eyes can spot the lookout tower atop Bull of the Woods (Hike #92), the tallest wooded peak to the east. Mt. Jefferson rises beside square-topped Battle Ax, while the Three Sisters brood beside square-topped Coffin Mountain to the south. Beyond a stripe of Willamette Valley to the west is the hump of Mary's Peak.

Other Hiking Options

Silver King Lake provides a more challenging goal. From the trail junction at

Mt. Jefferson from Whetstone Mountain.   Opposite: Edible red thimbleberry.

the foot of Whetstone Mountain follow the ridgecrest path 3.3 miles east. At a small meadow in a saddle, fork left onto the Bagby Trail and switchback downhill 0.8 mile. At the foot of a rockslide, watch for a small sign on a tree to the left marking the 0.2-mile side path up to a campsite beside the forest-rimmed lake. The 11.2-mile round-trip has a cumulative elevation gain of 2100 feet.

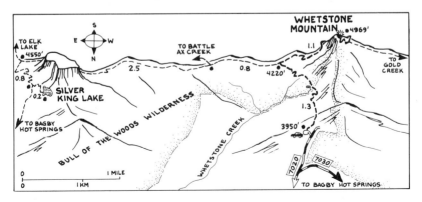

92

Bagby Hot Springs

Easy
3 miles round-trip
200 feet elevation gain
Open all year
Map: Bull of the Woods Wilderness (USFS)

Hollowed-out cedar logs form the bathtubs at this rustic, free hot springs. Even if you don't plan to soak, the trail here is a delight, leading through a towering old-growth forest along a fork of the Collawash River.   Just don't expect solitude. On weekends and all through summer the trail is heavily used and there's a long waiting line at the bath house.

From Estacada, take Highway 224 up the Clackamas River 26 miles to the bridge at Ripplebrook. Then, following signs for Bagby Hot Springs, keep straight on paved Road 46 for 3.6 miles, turn right onto paved Road 63 for 3.5 miles, and turn right onto paved Road 70 for 6 miles to the trailhead parking lot on the left. Leave no valuables in your car, as this area has a history of theft.

The trail crosses a footbridge over Nohorn Creek and launches into a magnificent ancient forest of big Douglas firs and red cedars. In April and May look here for yellow clusters of Oregon grape blossoms and a variety of white blossoms: vanilla leaf, 3-petaled trillium, and bunchberry. In autumn, vine maple leaves become red pinwheels.

At the 1-mile mark pass an overlook of a 10-foot slide falls in the Hot Springs Fork. In another 0.2 mile cross the green-pooled river on a long bridge and climb to a signboard at the hot springs. The log cabin behind the signboard is the original Forest Service guard station. To the left is the bath house, with long benches outside for the waiting line. The old bath house burned in 1979 when

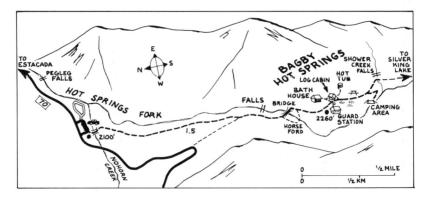

Footbridge over Nohorn Creek.   *Opposite: A cedar tub fills with hot water.*

nighttime bathers carelessly used candles for light. A non-profit group rebuilt the structure to include 5 private rooms and an annex with 4 additional 8-foot tubs.

To fill a tub, lower a wooden lever that diverts scalding water from a trough behind the wall. To adjust the temperature, use one of the plastic buckets to dip cold water from a vat outside. Remember the area's rules: no unleashed dogs, no music, no baths longer than 1 hour, and no soap — it pollutes the creek and harms the tubs. Swimsuits are rare.

If you keep right at the log cabin, you'll follow the Bagby Trail through a meadowed picnic area. After 0.2 mile, a side trail to the right descends to 8 riverside campsites. Shortly thereafter the Bagby Trail passes Shower Creek Falls — a thin, 50-foot cascade.

Other Hiking Options

If you continue up the Bagby Trail through this old-growth valley, you'll enter the Bull of the Woods Wilderness, leave the river, and cross 8 small side creeks. After hiking 6 miles from the hot springs (and gaining 1800 feet), you can take a spur trail to the right, climbing 0.2 mile to a campsite at forest-rimmed Silver King Lake.

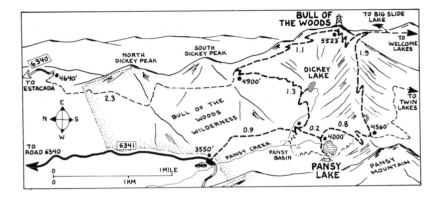

93   Pansy Lake

Easy (to Pansy Lake)
2.4 miles round-trip
500 feet elevation gain
Open mid-May to mid-November
Map: Bull of the Woods Wilderness (USFS)

Moderate (to Bull of the Woods)
7.1-mile loop
2000 feet elevation gain
Open July through October

The romp to this popular mountain lake is easy enough for children, but there's adventure here for hardier hikers as well. A scenic loop continues up to a historic lookout tower in the heart of the Bull of the Woods Wilderness.

This area is part of a 16- to 25-million-year-old volcanic mountain range predating the more famous High Cascade Peaks. Erosion has carved up this older range, exposing quartz veins with ore that attracted prospectors in the late 1800s. One of these early visitors was Robert Bagby, who blazed a trail from Bagby Hot Springs (Hike #91) to a cabin he built by this lake. Because of the color of the copper ore he found here, he named his claim the Pansy Blossom Mine — and the lake became known as Pansy Lake. Some say the name "Bull of the Woods" refers to a big elk bagged by Bagby, but others note the phrase was common in Oregon's ox-logging days as a title for a tough crew boss.

To find the trailhead, take Highway 224 from Estacada for 26 miles to the bridge at Ripplebrook. Keep straight on paved Road 46 for 3.6 miles and then turn right onto Road 63, following this paved road straight for 5.6 miles. At a sign for the Pansy Basin Trail turn right onto Road 6340 for 7.8 miles. Then fork right onto Road 6341 for 3.5 miles. Park at an unmarked pullout on a right-hand curve amidst old-growth forest.

The trail starts at the register box on the left side of the road in a magnificent stand of 5-foot-thick Douglas firs and hemlocks. After climbing gradually for 0.8 mile, cross a charming creek and reach the first of 3 confusing trail junctions. Go left at this first junction (the path straight ahead promptly dives down through Pansy Basin's mini-meadow, following a rough, abandoned route to Pansy Lake). Continue uphill 140 yards, switchbacking to a second, possibly unmarked fork in the trail. This time go straight (the left-hand fork is the return route of the Bull of the Woods loop). Now continue 400 yards to the third confusing junction, almost within sight of Pansy Lake. A right-hand turn here leads around the lakeshore to a camping area.

If after enjoying the lakeshore you'd like to continue on the loop up to the lookout tower, return to the junction beside Pansy Lake and take the other fork, following a pointer toward Twin Lakes. This path climbs above Pansy Lake at a steady grade for 0.8 mile to trail junction at a wooded pass. Turn left and traverse 1.9 miles up a hillside with occasional views of Mt. Jefferson. At a marked junction just before a ridgecrest, turn left and switchback up 0.7 mile to the summit. The 1942-vintage lookout tower is rarely staffed, but the view is panoramic, encompassing every summit from the Three Sisters to Rainier. Below to the east is Big Slide Lake (see Hike #93).

To complete the loop, continue past the lookout on a path descending the ridge to the north. After 1.1 miles *watch carefully for a small signboard on the left* marking a side trail. Turn here, taking this switchbacking path downhill to the left. After 0.8 mile a short spur to the left leads to pretty, brush-rimmed Dickey Lake. Then continue half a mile down to the Pansy Lake Trail and turn right to return to your car.

Other Hiking Options

An easier route to the lookout tower starts near Dickey Peaks. Drive almost to the Pansy Basin Trailhead, but instead keep on Road 6340 to its end, following signs for the Bull of the Woods Trailhead. This 3.4-mile path only gains 900 feet.

Pansy Lake.   Opposite: Bull of the Woods lookout.

94　　Dickey Creek　　

Moderate (to Dickey Creek crossing)
5.8 miles round-trip
900 feet cumulative elevation gain
Open May to early November
Map: Bull of the Woods Wilderness (USFS)

Difficult (to Big Slide Lake)
11 miles round-trip
2300 feet cumulative elevation gain
Open mid-June through October

Of the 3 major valleys cutting into the Bull of the Woods Wilderness from the north, Dickey Creek's is by far the least crowded. For all that, the old-growth forest here is as grand as anything in Bagby Hot Springs' hectic valley (Hike #91) and the mountain lakes are prettier than those in Pansy Creek's oft-visited valley (Hike #92). Why then the isolation? The Dickey Creek Trail begins with a 500-foot downhill scramble — elevation that must later be regained. Accept it as the price of admission to a secret wilderness retreat.

To find the trailhead, drive 26 miles up Highway 224 from Estacada to the bridge at Ripplebrook. Keep straight on paved Road 46 for 3.6 miles and then turn right onto Road 63, following this road straight for 5.6 miles. At a sign for the Dickey Creek Trail turn right onto paved Road 6340. After 7.8 miles turn left onto gravel Road 140 for 1 mile. Then turn right at a T-shaped junction and continue half a mile to the trailhead at road's end.

The trail begins along an abandoned road overgrown with alder. After 0.3 mile, however, the roadbed ends and a rough trail plummets half a mile down into glorious green old-growth woods of 7-foot-thick Douglas firs. Scraggly, flat-needled yew trees and a plush shag carpet of moss add to the grand gloom.

After a few delinquent ups and downs the trail repents, goes straight, and skirts a meadow with a lilypad pond. Although Dickey Creek is audible most of the way, there's no access until the trail finally reaches a small creekside

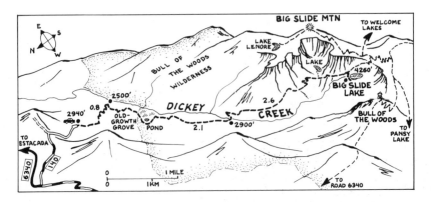

Big Slide Lake.   Opposite: Vanilla leaf.

campsite at the 2.9-mile mark. Here, arching cedar boughs overhang the bouldery stream.

There's no shame in turning back at this lovely lunch spot. But if you've set your sights on Big Slide Lake, hop across the bridgeless creek at this campsite. On the far shore the trail angles up to the left, switches back, and starts a long, hot climb along the valley wall. Rhododendrons overhang the path with pink blooms in early summer. After 2.2 miles the trail crosses the enormous rockslide that gave Big Slide Mountain its name. Listen here for the *meep!* of pikas — the round-eared rabbit-like animals that store tons of dried grass in their rockpile burrows so they can survive the winter without hibernating.

Shortly after the trail leaves the rockslide, a steep side trail to the right leads down to campsites beside Big Slide Lake. Here you can wade to a small island, swim from an underwater rock ledge, or simply watch the plentiful salamanders and small trout laze about in the shallows. Note the Bull of the Woods lookout tower on the ridge above.

Adventurers who love secret places can visit a trailless lake on the return trip. Hike back across the rockslide on the trail. A few hundred yards after reentering the woods, the trail crosses a (sometimes dry) creekbed. Just beyond this ravine bushwhack 200 yards up through a steep forest to a brush-lined lake below Big Slide Mountain's cliffs.

Other Hiking Options

Backpackers (or very hardy day hikers) can continue past Big Slide Lake to either of 2 colossal viewpoints. If you keep left at all trail junctions for 2 miles you'll end up atop 5526-foot Big Slide Mountain, overlooking beautiful Lake Lenore. If you keep right at all junctions you'll reach the lookout tower on 5523-foot Bull of the Woods in 2.2 miles.

95 Hawk Mountain

Moderate
8.4 miles round-trip
1100 feet elevation gain
Open late June through October
Map: Breitenbush (Green Trails)

When fire lookout towers dotted the summits of hundreds of Cascade peaks in the 1940s, only a few staffers had the luxury of sleeping in a separate ground-level building. Even fewer of these rustic cabins remain today. The newly reopened Rho Ridge Trail leads to Hawk Mountain's rare lookout cabin and a stunning, close-up view of Mt. Jefferson.

From Estacada, take Highway 224 up the Clackamas River 26 miles to the bridge at Ripplebrook. Keep straight on paved Road 46 for 3.6 miles and then turn right onto Road 63, following this road straight for 8.7 miles. At a sign for Graham Pass turn left onto paved Road 6350 for 1.2 miles, then fork to the right for 4.5 miles (trading pavement for gravel along the way), and finally fork to the left on what is still Road 6350. Beyond Graham Pass 1.6 miles, park on the right-hand shoulder beside a guardrail closing off spur Road 270. (If you're driving here from the south, turn off Highway 22 at Detroit and follow Breitenbush Road 46 for 17.6 paved miles. A mile past the Breitenbush Lake turnoff turn left onto gravel Road 6350 for 10.6 miles to barricaded Road 270 on your left.)

Walk around the guardrail, hike up Road 270 a few hundred yards, and turn left onto the Rho Ridge Trail. This path crosses Fawn Meadow (sometimes marshy in early summer) before climbing into a lichen-draped mountain hemlock forest with beargrass and huckleberry bushes. After 0.3 mile, the trail skirts a clearcut and crosses the end of a logging road. After another 1.8 miles the trail hits gravel Road 120 in another clearcut. Follow the road left 100 yards to its end, where you'll find a cairn on your right, marking the trail's continuation along the clearcut's edge.

In another 1.3 miles the path follows a sometimes-dry creek up to Round Meadow, where marsh marigolds bloom after the snowmelt. This long, very narrow meadow was not named for its shape, but rather because it is the headwaters for Round Lake, a few miles below.

The trail forks shortly after it curves away from the meadow. Keep left and climb 0.4 mile to the path's second switchback. Stop here a moment to enjoy the hike's best view of Mt. Hood and Sisi Butte. Then continue to Hawk Mountain's summit and the foundations of the long-gone lookout tower. The shiplap-sided cabin is just beyond, in a meadow of white yarrow, red Indian paintbrush, and matted juniper. The door on the porch is sealed and the 7 windows are shuttered

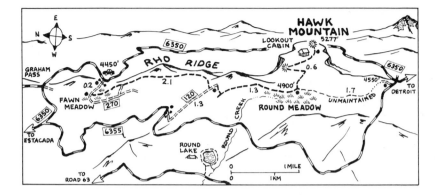

closed, but by carefully bending down one of the shutter nails you can peer in at the crude furnishings. All artifacts are federally protected, right down to the rusty fire extinguisher and old mustard bottle.

The view east includes, from left to right, Olallie Butte, Park Ridge (Hike #100), Mt. Jefferson, Three-Fingered Jack, the Three Sisters, and Mt. Washington.

Hawk Mountain lookout cabin and Mt. Jefferson.   *Opposite: Marsh marigolds.*

96 Red Lake

Easy (to Red Lake)
3.6 miles round-trip
1000 feet elevation gain
Open mid-June to early November
Map: Olallie Butte (USGS)

Moderate (to Potato Butte)
7.4 miles round-trip
1700 feet elevation gain

Of the hundreds of lakes dotting the forested Olallie Lake plateau north of Mt. Jefferson, Red Lake is one of the few to offer a glimpse of the big snowy mountain itself. And once you've climbed to Red Lake, it's not much further to visit 3 other lakes on your way up Potato Butte, an old volcano with a far better view across the plateau to Mt. Jeff. Mosquitoes can be a problem the first half of July.

From the Portland area, take Highway 224 past Estacada 26 miles to the bridge at Ripplebrook and keep straight on Road 46 for another 26.4 paved miles. Then turn left at a large "Red Lake Trail" sign and drive 0.9 mile on gravel Road 380. The trail begins on the left, opposite a sign marking the end of road maintenance.

If you're driving here from Salem or Bend, turn off Highway 22 in Detroit and follow paved Breitenbush Road 46 for 18.2 miles to the signed Red Lake Trail turnoff on the right.

The trail briefly crosses a clearcut before climbing steeply through an old-growth forest of 5-foot-thick mountain hemlocks and Douglas firs. After 0.4 mile the path enters a powerline clearing and joins a dirt road. Turn left on the road for 50 feet and then turn right on a spur road for 200 feet to find the continuation of the trail.

The path reenters the woods and climbs steadily for a mile to a plateau where huckleberries grow among lodgepole pines. At a big and obvious stump, turn

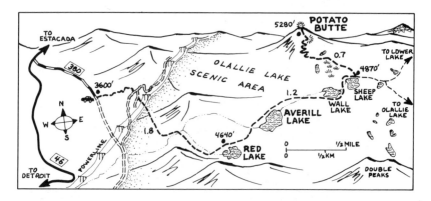

Mt. Jefferson from Potato Butte.   Opposite: Red Lake.

right on a side path to a small beach beside shallow Red Lake. Dragonflies zoom and rough-skinned newts laze in the shallows. Campsites abound.

Having climbed all the way to Red Lake, it's hard not to continue another 1.2 level miles past larger Averill Lake and Wall Lake to Sheep Lake. And once you've reached the far end of Sheep Lake, why not turn left at the "Potato Butte" pointer for a climb to a really good viewpoint? The 0.7-mile trail heads left when it reaches a small meadow and then switchbacks steeply up a slippery cinder slope to the broad summit with its view of Mt. Hood and Olallie Butte. To see Mt. Jefferson, however, you'll have to hike back down the trail 300 yards and bushwhack left 50 feet to a slope of boulders. Atop these rocks is the view you really wanted, including most of the lakes you passed on the hike.

Other Hiking Options

Backpackers or hardy day hikers can explore the Red Lake Trail further east. It's 1.7 miles from Sheep Lake to Top Lake and the route described in Hike #98.

Monon Lake from Olallie Butte.   Opposite: Mt. Jefferson from Olallie Lake.

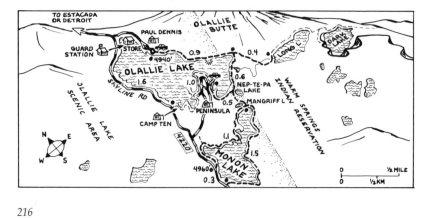

97 Monon Lake

Easy
6.8-mile loop
100 feet elevation gain
Open July to mid-October
Map: Olallie Butte (USGS)

An easy trail loops around the many-bayed shore of Monon Lake, the second largest lake in the Olallie Lake Scenic Area's high, forested plateau. Along the way you'll gain a view of nearby Mt. Jefferson, visit 3 other lakes, and pass bedrock worn smooth by Ice Age glaciers. Mosquitoes can be a problem in July.

From Estacada, take Highway 224 up the Clackamas River 26 miles to the bridge at Ripplebrook and keep straight on paved Road 46 for another 21.5 miles. At the *second* sign for the Olallie Lake Scenic Area turn left onto paved Road 4690. (Travelers from the south can reach this junction by taking Breitenbush Road 46 from Highway 22 at Detroit for 23.1 paved miles.) Drive Road 4690 for 8.1 miles to a stop sign, turn right onto gravel Road 4220 for 7 miles, and turn left at the Peninsula Campground entrance. Follow signs for the boat ramp.

From the boat ramp the trail heads to the right around Olallie Lake's shore with 7215-foot Olallie Butte as a backdrop. The gnarled, subalpine woods along the shore feature blooming heather in July and lots of ripe huckleberries in August. Mile-long Olallie Lake is so pure it's a drinking water source, and as a result, this is the only lake in the area where swimming is banned. Motorboats aren't allowed either, but canoes are common and rowboats can be rented at the rustic store across the lake.

After 0.3 mile turn right at a junction with the Olallie Lake Trail. Hike past 2 small lakes and then turn right at the shore of Monon Lake, where there's a fine view of the top half of Mt. Jefferson. The rounded bedrock of the lakeshore still bears the scratches of the glacial ice that sculpted this lake basin over 6000 years ago.

In 1.1 miles the Monon lakeshore path joins the gravel road and follows it several hundred yards before veering back into the woods. Complete the loop along the more remote east shore of Monon Lake — a good place to find a quiet lunch spot or backpacking campsite.

Other Hiking Options

For a slightly longer hike with better mountain views, start at Paul Dennis Campground. To find this trailhead, follow signs to the Olallie Lake Resort and continue straight to the end of the campground's loop, where the trail starts at a post. The first 0.9 mile around Olallie Lake is a delight, with picture-postcard reflections of Mt. Jefferson. Keep right to join the Monon Lake loop.

Olallie Butte from Top Lake.   *Below: Double Peaks from Olallie Lake.*

98   Top Lake

Easy (to Top Lake)
3.1-mile loop
500 feet elevation gain
Open July to mid-October
Map: Olallie Butte (USGS)

Moderate (to Double Peaks)
5.3-mile loop
1100 feet elevation gain

Half a dozen woodsy lakes and a viewpoint of Mt. Jefferson make this loop on the Pacific Crest Trail fun for children too. Hikers with extra energy can add a short but very steep side trip up Double Peaks for an even better panorama of the lake-dotted Olallie Lake Scenic Area.

If you're driving here from the Portland area, take Highway 224 past Estacada 26 miles to the bridge at Ripplebrook and keep straight on paved Road 46 for another 21.5 miles. At the *second* sign for the Olallie Lake Scenic Area turn left onto paved Road 4690. Drive this road 8.1 miles to a stop sign and turn right onto gravel Road 4220 for 5.1 miles to the junction for the Olallie Lake Resort. Keep right for 0.3 mile to a message board on the right and a small sign for the Red Lake Trail. Park at a pullout on the road's opposite shoulder.

If you're driving here from Salem or Bend, turn off Highway 22 in Detroit, follow Breitenbush Road 46 for 23.1 paved miles, turn right onto Road 4690 for 8.1 miles, and turn right on Road 4220 for 5.4 miles.

The Red Lake Trail ambles through a high-elevation forest of mountain hemlock and lodgepole pine where masses of blue huckleberries ripen in late August. Mosquitoes can be a problem in July. After passing 3 ponds keep right at a possibly unmarked trail junction (the left-hand fork deadends in 0.7 mile at Timber Lake). Soon the path reaches Top Lake, with a pebbly beach and a view ahead to Double Peaks. This is a nice spot to wade, pick berries, or simply watch dragonflies zoom about.

At the far end of Top Lake you'll reach a T-shaped junction. To take the easy loop back, simply turn right and keep right at every junction you find. You'll join the Pacific Crest, pass a rockslide, and descend along a cliff-edged ridge with a view of Mt. Jefferson. Stop here to notice how the clifftop rock has been rounded and scratched by the Ice Age glaciers that buried this whole landscape with moving ice just 6000 years ago. Then continue down the trail to Head Lake, turn right, and walk along the road 0.3 mile to your car.

To take the longer loop to Double Peaks, turn left at the Top Lake junction. This trail switchbacks up to the Pacific Crest Trail, where you turn left for 100 feet to a sign announcing Cigar Lake, a rock-lined, dumbbell-shaped lake. Walk 200 feet past the Cigar Lake sign and leave the PCT, turning right onto a faint side path toward Double Peaks. This path soon forks, but keep left until it starts scrambling steeply up a slope. The path levels off for a few hundred yards along a clifftop rim to the right before a final, very steep ascent between rockslides to Double Peak's ridgecrest. To the right is the first summit, with a view to Mt. Hood and the jumbled peaks of the Bull of the Woods Wilderness. To the left is the taller summit, with an aerial view of the route of your hike.

When you hike back down to Cigar Lake, follow the Pacific Crest Trail to the left for 1.9 miles to continue the loop.

Other Hiking Options

Backpackers or hardy day hikers can explore the Red Lake Trail further west across this forested plateau. It's 1.7 miles from Top Lake to Sheep Lake and the route described in Hike #95. Another option is to hike the PCT south to Breitenbush Lake. It's 2.3 miles from Cigar Lake to the Ruddy Hill junction described in Hike #99.

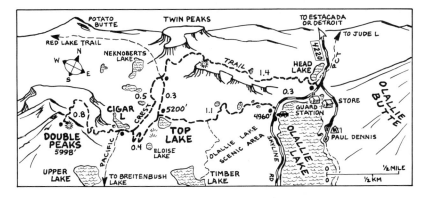

99 Ruddy Hill

Moderate (to Ruddy Hill)
5.3-mile loop
1100 feet elevation gain
Open July to mid-October
Map: Olallie Butte (USGS)

Huckleberries and alpine heather line this easy loop hike along the Pacific Crest Trail from Breitenbush Lake. The loop has views south to Olallie Butte and north to Mt. Jefferson, but for the best view of all, take a short steep detour up Ruddy Hill, a forested cinder cone.

Take Highway 224 south past Estacada for 26 miles to the bridge at Ripplebrook and keep straight on paved Road 46 for another 21.5 miles. At the *second* sign for the Olallie Lake Scenic Area turn left onto paved Road 4690. Drive this road 8.1 miles to a stop sign and turn right onto gravel Road 4220 for 10.5 miles. The final 2 miles of this road are extremely rough, but passable for all but the lowest-clearance passenger cars. Beyond the Breitenbush Lake Campground 0.3 mile turn left to the Pacific Crest Trailhead's huge cinder turnaround.

If you're driving here from Salem or Bend, turn off Highway 22 in Detroit, follow Breitenbush Road 46 for 23.1 paved miles, turn right onto Road 4690 for 8.1 miles, and turn right on Road 4220 for 10.5 miles.

Start at the first message board on your right as you enter the Pacific Crest Trail parking area. After 50 yards turn right on the PCT. Take this trail south across the entrance road and Road 4220, following signs for Upper Lake. The PCT climbs through a sparse subalpine forest loaded with blue huckleberries in August. Pass a pair of charming, heather-shored lakelets and then traverse a cinder slope with views across a high valley to monolithic Pyramid Butte (Hike

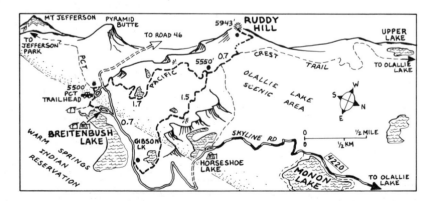

#100), Park Ridge, and Mt. Jefferson.

At the 1.7-mile mark reach a Y-shaped junction. If you'd like to trim the hike to an easy 3.9-mile loop, turn right toward Gibson Lake. Otherwise continue straight on the PCT toward Ruddy Hill. After going straight on the PCT 200 yards ignore the Horseshoe Saddle Trail on the right. In another 300 yards watch carefully for the faint Ruddy Hill path on the left, where the PCT nears the foot of a big, forested hill. This junction may be obscured by fallen trees, but the "Ruddy Hill" sign should be on a log to the left. This side path scrambles steeply up the forested hill and turns left along a ridgecrest to a small heather meadow on Ruddy Hill's cindery summit. The historic wooden box here from the 1930s once held a telephone for rangers to report fires.

To complete the loop, return to the PCT, walk back to the Gibson Lake pointer, and fork to the left. This route climbs to a rim overlooking Horseshoe Lake, Monon Lake (Hike #97), and Olallie Butte. Then descend past Gibson Lake to gravel Road 4220. Turn right along the road 0.4 mile and walk through the Breitenbush Lake Campground to inspect the historic stone shelter there. At the far end of the campground loop you'll find a path that crosses a creek and then forks. Left leads to another shelter; right leads to your car at the PCT trailhead.

Other Hiking Options

For a longer hike or a backpack, continue north on the PCT 1.9 miles past Ruddy Hill to large, cliff-backed Upper Lake. If you plan a car shuttle to the Hike #98 trailhead, you can continue another 2 miles to Olallie Lake.

Olallie Butte from the Horseshoe Lake overlook.   Opposite: Tarn along the PCT.

100 Jefferson Park Ridge

Easy (to Pyramid Butte)
4-mile loop
800 feet elevation gain
Open mid-July to mid-October
Map: Mt. Jefferson Wilderness (USFS)

Moderate (to Park Ridge)
7.4 miles round-trip
1400 feet elevation gain

Difficult (to Jefferson Park)
11.2 miles round-trip
2400 feet elevation gain

Mt. Jefferson fills half the sky from the green alpine meadows and sparkling lakes of Jefferson Park. A heavily-used portion of the Pacific Crest Trail climbs over scenic Park Ridge to this patch of paradise. For a less-demanding trip, consider making your goal the spectacular viewpoint atop Park Ridge. An even easier alternative is a short loop on a meadow-lined section of the old Skyline Trail past Pyramid Butte.

Permits are required to enter the Mt. Jefferson Wilderness. Day hikers can fill out a form at the trailhead, but backpackers must pick up a permit in advance at a ranger station or outdoor store. To avoid crowds, plan this hike for a weekday or for fall.

Take Highway 224 south past Estacada for 26 miles to the bridge at Ripplebrook and keep straight on paved Road 46 for another 21.5 miles. At the *second* sign for the Olallie Lake Scenic Area turn left onto paved Road 4690. Drive this road 8.1 miles to a stop sign and turn right onto gravel Road 4220 for 10.5 miles. The final 2 miles of this road are extremely rough, but passable for all but the lowest-clearance passenger cars. Just beyond Breitenbush Lake turn left to the Pacific Crest Trailhead's cinder turnaround.

If you're driving here from Salem or Bend, turn off Highway 22 in Detroit, follow Breitenbush Road 46 for 23.1 paved miles, turn right onto Road 4690 for

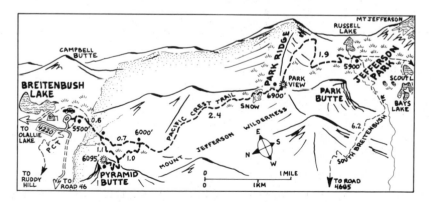

Mt. Jefferson from Park Ridge.   Opposite: Old Skyline Trail sign.

8.1 miles, and turn right on Road 4220 for 10.5 miles.

Start at the first message board on your right as you enter the PCT parking area. After 50 yards turn left and follow the PCT through subalpine woods with lots of lovely openings. Heather and blue lupine bloom here in mid-summer and masses of huckleberries ripen shortly afterwards.

After 0.6 mile the path crosses a footbridge and forks. To the left is the newer, more direct PCT route to Park Ridge and Jefferson Park. If you have the time, or if you're interested in a shorter loop, turn right on the old, unmarked Skyline Trail. This older path meanders past a gushing spring and several meadows to a junction at the base of Pyramid Butte. Here you can either turn right for the steep, switchbacking half-mile climb to a cliff-edge viewpoint atop Pyramid Butte, or you can head left to climb back to the PCT.

If you're continuing up the PCT to Park Ridge you'll gradually climb past timberline. Alpine heather, white partridge foot, purple aster, and red Indian paintbrush give way to a rocky landscape with snowfields. Follow cairns carefully to keep on the trail. Finally reach Park Ridge's windy crest and a breathtaking view ahead to Jefferson Park.

Beyond this point the PCT descends 1.9 miles to the meadows beside swimmable Russell Lake, first and largest of the park's pools. If you're backpacking, tent in the woods away from the fragile meadows. Camping is banned on the peninsulas of Scout and Bays Lakes. Campfires are strongly discouraged and are banned altogether within 100 feet of water or trails.

Other Hiking Options

Two other routes reach Jefferson Park. The less crowded South Breitenbush Trail climbs 2800 feet in 6.2 miles. To find the trailhead, drive paved Road 46 south of Ripplebrook for 33.1 miles (or drive north from Detroit 11.5 miles), and take gravel Road 4685 east for 5 miles. The heavily used Whitewater Trail to Jefferson Park climbs 1800 feet in 5.1 miles. To find it, drive Highway 22 east of Detroit 10.3 miles and turn left on gravel Whitewater Road 2243 to its end.

All-Accessible Trails in Northwest Oregon

People with limited physical abilities need not miss the fun of exploring new trails. Here are 21 paths within a 2-hour drive of Portland accessible to everyone. Most of the trails are paved and several include interpretive signs about natural features or history. Unless otherwise noted, the paths are open year round. For more information, contact the trail's managing agency. For trails in the Portland area, call the Portland Park Bureau's Disabled Citizens Recreation program at (503) 823-4328 (voice or TDD).

PORTLAND AREA (map on page 13)

A. Greenway Park. Paved path along Fanno Cr in Beaverton extends 2.5 mi from Bel-Aire St to N Dakota St, crossing Hall Blvd and Scholls Fy Rd along the way. Side path near Hall Blvd leads to visitable Fanno Farm House, built 1859. Take Hwy 217 to Hall Blvd near Washington Square and go W for 0.4 mi, or take Tri-Met #78 out Hall to the park. Trail access is beside Albertson's parking lot.

B. Trillium Trail. Interpretive nature path loops 0.4 mi through woods of Tryon Cr State Park. Start as for Hike #9 but stay on paved path.

C. George Rogers Park. Paved 0.8-mi path along Willamette R crosses Oswego Cr. Take Hwy 43 (alias Macadam Ave, alias State St) to Lake Oswego, turn down on Ladd, turn R on Furnace to historic iron smelter and footbridge to trail.

D. Powell Butte. Mtn View Trail climbs 0.6 mi to broad, grassy summit with views, where paved path ends. See Hike #10.

E. The Grotto. Gardens, viewpoints, and Catholic statuary line a peaceful 0.9-mi path. Elevator to upper loop has $2 fee. Drive or take Tri-Met #12 out NE Sandy 1 block past 82nd.

F. Burnt Bridge Creek. Greenway bike path extends 1.6 mi through creekside meadows in Vancouver. Drive N on I-5 through Vancouver to 39th St exit, go L on 39th for 1.5 mi, and turn R on Fruit Valley Rd 1.7 mi to parking on R.

G. Champoeg Park. Hike #13 has 3 all-accessible options: take bike path from Visitor Ctr 0.6 mi through meadow to pavilion, or take graveled, 0.4-mi interpretive nature loop from campground, or start at campground and take bike path 1.5 mi E along Willamette R.

H. Willamette Mission Park. Park as for Hike #14. Either take 1.2-mi bike path E through filbert grove to Willamette R and ferry landing, or go W on new, more challenging 3-mi paved loop through riverside woods.

SOUTHWEST WASHINGTON (map on page 43)

I. Coldwater Ridge Visitor Center. Views of Mt St Helens' crater, mudflow, and blast-caused Coldwater Lk from a 0.2-mi paved interpretive loop trail. Take I-5 to Castle Rock (exit 49), drive 46 mi E on Hwy 504. Open Apr-Nov.

J. Trail of 2 Forests. 0.3-mi interpretive loop through lava cast forest in 1900-yr-old basalt flow. Drive as to Hike #19 but park 0.6 mi before Ape Cave.

K. Lava Canyon. Path to waterfalls in mudflow-scoured canyon (see Hike #22). Paved for first 0.5 mi, with boardwalks and interpretive signs. Open May-Nov.

L. Meta Lake. In Mt. St. Helen's blast zone, paved 0.4-mile path from scorched miner's car to lake where aquatic life survived under ice. Open June-Oct.

M. Lewis River Viewpoints. 3 graveled paths lead to waterfall views. Park as for Hike #25 for 0.2-mi trail to massive Lower Lewis R Falls. Then drive 5.5 mi W on Rd 90 to Big Cr Trailhead for 0.7-mi path from 110-ft falls to river overlook. Then drive 3.8 mi further W on Rd 90 to turnoff for 0.2-mi Curly Cr Falls trail.

COLUMBIA GORGE (map on page 87)

N. Latourell and Wahkeena Falls. 2 paved trails to glorious falls. Park as for Hike #35, but take 0.3-mi path *downhill* to Lower Latourell Falls and on to picnic area, where steps block route. Then drive 5.4 mi E to Hike #38 parking area for 0.2-mi trail to stone footbridge beneath Wahkeena Falls.

Lost Lake Old Growth Trail.

O. Four Columbia River Trails. The 3.8-mi paved *Riverfront Tr* traces The Dalles' waterfront; take W exit for The Dalles, go R 1 mi, turn R 0.2 mi on Taylor Rd. The 1.2-mi *Fort Cascades loop* visits site of 1856 Army fort, petroglyph; drive 3.2 mi W of Bridge of the Gods on Hwy 14. The 1.1-mi *Sams-Walker Tr* loops through orchard, forest, wetlands to river; drive 10 mi W of Bonneville Dam on Hwy 14, turn S on Skamania Landing Rd 0.2 mi. Or drive 4 mi farther W on Hwy 14 to the *St. Cloud Tr*, a 0.5-mi loop through homestead orchards with a view of Multnomah Falls.

MOUNT HOOD - WEST (map on page 123)

P. Lost Creek Nature Trail. Barrier-free campground and picnic area features 0.4-mi paved and boardwalk loop to 2 all-accessible fishing piers at beaver pond with Mt Hood view. Drive as to Ramona Falls (Hike #60) but continue on Rd 1825 past jct with Rd 100 for 0.4 mi. Open May-Nov.

Q. Lost Lake Old Growth Trail. Dramatic 1-mi interpretive trail among massive red cedars is half gravel, half boardwalk with decked pullouts. For 2-mi loop, continue on boardwalked lakeshore path, ready in 1994. Drive to Lost Lake (see Hike #63), but keep L at lake to E picnic area parking lot. Open June-Oct.

R. Little Zigzag Falls. 0.3-mi path follows Little Zigzag Cr through woods to falls. Drive 6 mi E of Zigzag on Hwy 26, turn L onto Rd 2639 for 3 mi to its end.

S. Trillium Lake. Picture postcard views of Mt Hood highlight 0.4-mi lakeshore gravel path to fishing pier. All-accessible picnic and camping sites nearby. 3 mi E of Govt Camp turn off Hwy 26, follow signs 1.6 mi to Trillium Lake CG, park at picnic area. Open June-Oct.

T. Little Crater and Timothy Lakes. USFS plans call for all of Hike #69 to be barrier-free. Currently the paved 0.2-mi path to Little Crater L is open, but a cattle fence blocks access to the PCT. The 10.8-mi loop around Timothy L is level, dirt, and all-accessible except a roughish 0.2-mi segment from Oak Fork CG to the PCT. Open May-Nov.

CLACKAMAS FOOTHILLS (map on page 185)

U. Alder Flat Trail. Interpretive 0.5-mi nature trail descends through old-growth forest, circles beaver pond. Drive 25 mi S of Estacada on Hwy 224 and park on R, 500 ft before Ripplebrook Ranger Station.

100 More Hikes in Northwest Oregon

Adventurous hikers can discover plenty of additional trails within a 2-hour drive of the Portland area. The list below covers the most interesting — from urban promenades to rugged wilderness paths. Directions are brief, so be extra careful to bring appropriate maps. Estimated mileages are one-way. Most paths are open only in summer and fall, but symbols beside entries note which hikes are open all year, suitable for kids, or backpackable. For more information, check with the trail's administrative agency. The appropriate ranger district or other offices are abbreviated as follows: (B)–Barlow, (BS)–Bear Springs, (C)–Columbia Gorge National Scenic Area, (D)–Washington Department of Natural Resources, E)–Estacada, (HR)–Hood River, (MA)–Mt Adams, (MS)–Mt St Helens National Monument, (O)–Oregon State Parks, (P)–Portland Park Bureau, (W)–Wind River, (Z)–Zigzag.

PORTLAND AREA (map on page 13)

101. Virginia Lake. Meadowed 2.2-mile loop around marshy lake on Sauvie Island. Expect birds, some cattle. Drive as to Hike #2 but go straight on Sauvie Is Rd 0.5 mile past Reeder Rd turnoff. (O)

102. Holman Park. Convenient 2.6-mi loop in woods S of Forest Park. Turn off Cornell Rd onto 53rd Dr for 0.6 mi. Hike down Birch Tr, turn R onto Wildwood Tr 1.6 mi, turn R to return on Holman Ln. (P)

103. Macleay Trail. Woodsy 5.5-mile loop along Balch Creek joins Wildwood Tr, crosses Cornell Rd, climbs to Pittock Mansion, and returns via Upper Macleay Tr. Gains 800 ft. Drive as to Hike #5 but park beneath Thurman St bridge. (P)

104. Audubon Bird Sanctuary. 3 miles of paths loop through woods at 101-acre Portland Audubon Soc nature ctr, 5151 NW Cornell Rd.

105. Terwilliger Bike Path. Paved 3.5-mi promenade parallels Terwilliger Blvd from Duniway Park (near Hike #7) to Barbur Blvd. (P)

106. Willamette Park. Paved riverside path starts in grassy park, continues 1.5 mi N to River Forum office bldg. Drive SW Macadam to Carolina St, turn W to Willamette Park. (P)

107. Leach Botanical Gardens. Spring blooms line a network of gravel paths in historic 9-acre Portland garden at 6704 SE 122nd. (P)

108. Reed College. Loop 1 mi around narrow, swampy lake on scenic campus. Drive SE 38th St to Steele St, turn W to Reed's North Parking Area, hike down to lake. 1-mi side trip follows lake's outlet cr to SE 28th Ave and famous 7-acre Crystal Sprs Rhododendron Garden. (P)

109. Elk Rock Island. Explore Willamette R peninsula on a 1-mi loop with cottonwoods and herons. Drive McLoughlin Blvd S, take River Rd exit 4 blocks, turn R on Sparrow St to corner of 19th Ave. (P)

110. Mary Young Park. State park on Willamette R has 2.3-mi sawdust path around perimeter amid maples and woodland wildflowers. Drive 2.5 mi S of Lake Oswego on Hwy 43 (alias Macadam Ave). (O)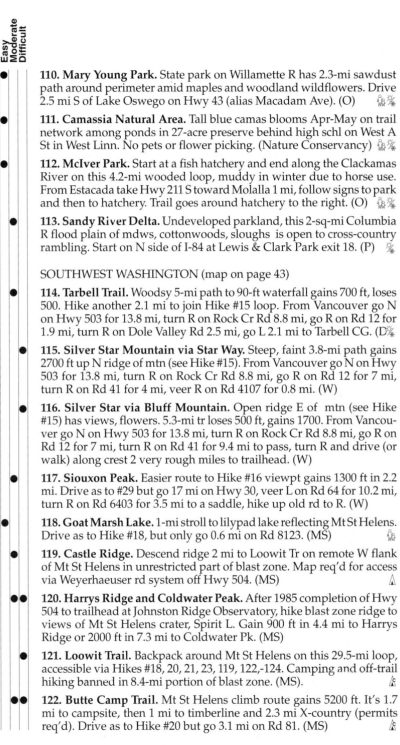

111. Camassia Natural Area. Tall blue camas blooms Apr-May on trail network among ponds in 27-acre preserve behind high schl on West A St in West Linn. No pets or flower picking. (Nature Conservancy)

112. McIver Park. Start at a fish hatchery and end along the Clackamas River on this 4.2-mi wooded loop, muddy in winter due to horse use. From Estacada take Hwy 211 S toward Molalla 1 mi, follow signs to park and then to hatchery. Trail goes around hatchery to the right. (O)

113. Sandy River Delta. Undeveloped parkland, this 2-sq-mi Columbia R flood plain of mdws, cottonwoods, sloughs is open to cross-country rambling. Start on N side of I-84 at Lewis & Clark Park exit 18. (P)

SOUTHWEST WASHINGTON (map on page 43)

114. Tarbell Trail. Woodsy 5-mi path to 90-ft waterfall gains 700 ft, loses 500. Hike another 2.1 mi to join Hike #15 loop. From Vancouver go N on Hwy 503 for 13.8 mi, turn R on Rock Cr Rd 8.8 mi, go R on Rd 12 for 1.9 mi, turn R on Dole Valley Rd 2.5 mi, go L 2.1 mi to Tarbell CG. (D

115. Silver Star Mountain via Star Way. Steep, faint 3.8-mi path gains 2700 ft up N ridge of mtn (see Hike #15). From Vancouver go N on Hwy 503 for 13.8 mi, turn R on Rock Cr Rd 8.8 mi, go R on Rd 12 for 7 mi, turn R on Rd 41 for 4 mi, veer R on Rd 4107 for 0.8 mi. (W)

116. Silver Star via Bluff Mountain. Open ridge E of mtn (see Hike #15) has views, flowers. 5.3-mi tr loses 500 ft, gains 1700. From Vancouver go N on Hwy 503 for 13.8 mi, turn R on Rock Cr Rd 8.8 mi, go R on Rd 12 for 7 mi, turn R on Rd 41 for 9.4 mi to pass, turn R and drive (or walk) along crest 2 very rough miles to trailhead. (W)

117. Siouxon Peak. Easier route to Hike #16 viewpt gains 1300 ft in 2.2 mi. Drive as to #29 but go 17 mi on Hwy 30, veer L on Rd 64 for 10.2 mi, turn R on Rd 6403 for 3.5 mi to a saddle, hike up old rd to R. (W)

118. Goat Marsh Lake. 1-mi stroll to lilypad lake reflecting Mt St Helens. Drive as to Hike #18, but only go 0.6 mi on Rd 8123. (MS)

119. Castle Ridge. Descend ridge 2 mi to Loowit Tr on remote W flank of Mt St Helens in unrestricted part of blast zone. Map req'd for access via Weyerhaeuser rd system off Hwy 504. (MS)

120. Harrys Ridge and Coldwater Peak. After 1985 completion of Hwy 504 to trailhead at Johnston Ridge Observatory, hike blast zone ridge to views of Mt St Helens crater, Spirit L. Gain 900 ft in 4.4 mi to Harrys Ridge or 2000 ft in 7.3 mi to Coldwater Pk. (MS)

121. Loowit Trail. Backpack around Mt St Helens on this 29.5-mi loop, accessible via Hikes #18, 20, 21, 23, 119, 122,-124. Camping and off-trail hiking banned in 8.4-mi portion of blast zone. (MS).

122. Butte Camp Trail. Mt St Helens climb route gains 5200 ft. It's 1.7 mi to campsite, then 1 mi to timberline and 2.3 mi X-country (permits req'd). Drive as to Hike #20 but go 3.1 mi on Rd 81. (MS)

123. Blue Lake Loop. 12.5-mi loop to Mt St Helens timberline follows Toutle, Sheep Canyon (see Hike #18), Loowit, Butte Camp Trails, gains 1700 ft. Drive as to #18 but only go 1.7 mi on Rd 8123. (MS)

124. June Lake. Creekside 1.4-mi path to lk with waterfall joins Loowit Tr. Drive as to Lava Canyon (#21) but go 7.3 mi on Rd 83. (MS)

125. Strawberry Mountain. Gain 1400 ft in 2.5 mi to viewpt of Mt St Helens, blast zone. Drive as to Spirit L (Hike #24), but only go 4.7 mi on Rd 99 to Bear Mdw, hike R on Boundary Tr 0.5 mi, turn R. (MS)

126. Goat Mountain. Follow blast zone rim 5.5 mi to Deadmans L. Gain 1500 ft, lose 800. Drive to #24 but turn R on Rd 26 for 5 mi. (MS)

127. Ghost Lake. From Norway Pass Trailhead (see Hike #24) hike E for 1.5 easy mi on Boundary Tr along blast zone edge to lk. (MS)

128. Badger Peak. Hike pumice-dusted Boundary Tr 4 mi E to Badger L, climb 0.9 to panoramic lookout site. Gain 1900 ft total. Drive as to Spirit L (#24) but only go 21.2 mi on Rd 25, park at Elk Pass. (MS)

129. Craggy Peak. Views await on 4.9-mi path to Boundary Tr jct by this Dark Divide pk. Gain 1700 ft. Drive as to Hike #24, but go 5.4 mi on Rd 25, veer R on Rd 93 for 18.7 mi, turn L on Rd 9327 for 0.3 mi. (MS)

130. Boundary Trail. Backpack 56 mi from Mt St Helens to Mt Adams, following Trail Number One along Dark Divide. Route connects with Hikes #120, 24, 127-129, 132-134, ends at Council Lake. (MS)

131. Lower Lewis River Trail. Quiet 9.5-mi part of river trail passes 1921 Bolt Camp Shelter, old-growth woods. Plan shuttle on Rd 90 between trailheads, 1.1 and 9.1 mi W of Lewis R Falls (#25) trailhead. (MS)

132. Quartz Creek. Steep up-and-down path through old-growth canyon leads 4.5 mi to creekside camp, continues 6 mi to Boundary Tr. Drive to Lewis R Falls (Hike #25), continue 2.7 mi on Rd 90 to bridge. (MS)

133. Quartz Creek Ridge. Well-graded path climbs 1700 ft in 2.8 mi to viewpt, continues 4 mi to Summit Prairie lookout site. Drive 5 mi past Lewis R Falls (#25) on Rd 90, turn L on Rd 9025, keep R for 5.5 mi. (MS)

134. Council Bluff. Hike old rd from Council L to view of Mt Adams, up 900 ft in 1.5 mi. Drive past #25 on Rd 90 for 17 mi, go L on Rd 23. for 3.2 mi, turn L on Rd 2334, keep R to CG. (Randle Ranger Dist)

135. Adams Glacier Meadows. Popular 3.1-mi Killen Cr Tr climbs 1500 ft to vast alpine mdws on N side of Mt Adams. Drive past #25 on Rd 90 17 mi, go L on Rd 23 for 4.7 mi, turn R on Rd 2329 for 5.8 mi. (MA)

136. Lookingglass Lake. Hike up Short Horn Tr 2.8 mi, go L on Round-the-Mtn Tr 2.2 mi, go L for 0.8 mi past Madcat Mdw to lake reflecting Mt Adams. Route gains 1500 ft, loses 600. Drive 6 mi N of Trout Lake on Rd 80, veer R on Rd 8040 for 5.7 mi to Morrison Cr CG. (MA)

137. Gotchen Creek. Stupendous 5.7-mi tr gains 2500 ft beside Aiken Lava Bed to wildflower-packed Bird Cr Mdws at Mt Adams timberline. From town of Trout Lake, drive 5 mi N on Rd 80, turn R on Rd 8020 for 4 mi, go L on Rd 150 for 1 mi to free Snipes Mtn Trailhead. (MA)

Mill Creek Falls (Hike #191).

Easy
Moderate
Difficult

138. Horseshoe Meadow. Follow Pacific Cr Tr up 1400 ft in 4.3 mi to Mt Adams timberline. Take Rd 23 N of Trout Lake 14 mi. (MA)

139. Bird Creek Meadows. Despite bad road and $5 parking fee, the 5-mi loop through alpine wildflowers on Yakima Ind Res portion of Mt Adams draws August crowds. Follow signs from Trout Lake. (MA)

140. Round-the-Mountain Trail. Backpack 3/4 of the way around Mt Adams (rivers, Indian Res block final 1/4.) on 27-mi route from Bird Cr Mdws (see Hike#137) past Hikes #135-6 to Devils Gardens. (MA)

141. Sleeping Beauty Mountain. Landmark lookout site tops 1.4-mi tr gaining 1400 ft. From Trout Lake go W 1 mi, turn R on Rd 88 for 4.8 mi, veer R on Rd 8810 for 6.4 mi, go 0.5 mi R on Rd 040. (MA)

142. Steamboat Mountain. Gain 800 ft in 1.2 mi to cliff-rimmed lookout site. Drive as to Cultus L (#26) but at end of Rd 30 turn *left* on Rd 24 for 3.5 mi, veer L 1 mi on Rd 8854, go L 1.4 mi on Rd 021 to its end. (MA)

143. Sawtooth Mountain. Hike Pacific Cr Tr S through Indian Heaven huckleberry fields, return via craggy pk with view. 5.2-mi loop gains 1200 ft. Drive as to Cultus L (#26) but only go 0.5 mi on Rd 24. (MA)

144. Placid Lake. Popular 0.8-mi stroll to large Indian Heaven lake; continue 0.8 mi to mdws at Chenamus L. Drive N of Carson 32.5 mi on Rd 30, go R at Placid L sign 1.2 mi. (MA)

145. Indian Racetrack via Falls Creek Trail. Rough 2.3-mi tr gains 700 ft to Indian Heaven lakelet, mdw where tribes raced horses until 1928. For view, continue 0.8 up to rd, lookout tower atop Red Mtn. Drive as to Junction L (#27) but go 5 mi on Rd 65 past jct with Rd 60. (MA)

146. Indian Racetrack via PCT. Hike Pacific Cr Tr 3 mi N, turn L 0.5 mi to Indian Racetrack mdw, lakelet. For 7.5-mi loop, turn L to Red Mtn lookout, then descend rugged Rd 6048 to Rd 60 and car. Drive as to Junction L (#27) but only go 2 mi on Rd 60. (MA)

147. Nestor Peak Lookout. Gain 2000 ft in 4.1 mi to tower with view of Mt Hood, Gorge. Cross Hood R toll br, go L 1.5 mi on Hwy 14, go R 2.2 mi along river, go L 2 mi on Hwy 141, turn L 3 mi to Buck Cr Trhd No. 1. Hike Rd N1000 and N1300 for 1.9 mi to end, go L on tr. (DNR)

148. Little Huckleberry Mountain. Berry-lined tr gains 1800 ft in 2.7 mi to panoramic viewpoint. Cross Br of the Gods, go R 15 mi on Hwy 14, turn L for 7.5 mi through Willard, go L on Rd 66 for 12.8 mi. (MA)

149. Weigle Hill. Climb 1600 ft in 2 mi to mid-Gorge viewpoint. Drive as to #27, but only go 1 mi on Rd 65, turn R 0.7 mi to rd's end. (W)

150. Bunker Hill. Tr to wooded knob overlooking Wind R arboretum gains 1400 ft in 1.7 mi. Drive 8.5 mi N of Carson on Rd 30, turn L 1.5 mi to ranger station, then turn R on Rd 43 for 0.6, turn R to PCT. (W)

151. Lower Falls Creek. Follow cr 1.7 mi to base of 250-ft falls. Gain 700 ft. Drive as to Trapper Cr (#29), but continue 0.9 mi further on Rd 30, turn R on Rd 3062, follow signs to Tr 152A. (W)

152. Upper Falls Creek. 2.3-mi path gains 1000 ft to top of falls, doesn't join lower tr. Drive as for #151 but follow signs to Tr 152. (W)

153. Dry Creek Trail. Follow path along large cr through old-growth woods 4 mi. For 13-mi loop, continue up Big Hollow Tr to Observation Pk, gaining 3000 ft. Park as for Trapper Cr (#29). (W)

154. Soda Peaks Lake. Gain 700 ft to craggy Soda Pks, descend 400 ft to lake on 2.2-mi path. Drive 8.5 mi N of Carson on Rd 30, turn L at Stabler 0.5 mi, turn R on Rd 54 for 13 mi to end of pavement. (W)

COLUMBIA GORGE (map on page 87)

155. Munra Point. Great grassy ridge-end viewpoint requires 1800-ft climb on unmaintained scramble trail. Park as for Hike #42, take Gorge Tr 1.5 mi W, turn L 200 yds before Moffett Cr, climb 1.5 mi. (C)

156. Rudolph Spur. Rough 11-mi loop gains 3600 ft. Hike up Ruckel Cr Tr (#45), but as soon as tr reaches Benson Plateau turn L past blazes onto faint, unmaintained tr down Rudolph Spur's ridge. Turn L on PCT, go L on Gorge Tr to complete loop. Adventurers only. (C)

157. Dry Creek Falls. Park at Br of the Gods, hike Pacifc Cr Tr 2 mi S to Dry Cr, go upstream 0.2 mi to 60-ft falls. Then take old rd downstream to complete 4.8-mi loop. Gains 800 ft. (C)

158. PCT to Benson Plateau. Hike to Herman Cr Bridge (see #46), continue 0.9 to Pacific Cr Tr, climb L to wildflowers, views at plateau rim. Gain 3600 ft in 5.6 mi. (C)

159. Wyeth Trail to North Lake. Steep 5.7-mi tr gains 3800 ft to woodsy lake. Continue, keeping R at all jcts, to complete 14.7-mi loop via Green Pt Mtn viewpoint. Take Exit 51 of I-84 to Wyeth CG. (C)

160. Shellrock Mountain. Drive I-84 east 0.8 mi past milepost 52, park on shoulder, scramble up to old Col R Hwy, walk E to find tr up to 1872 wagon rd, walk E to find tr up to viewpt. Gain 1100 ft in 1.3 mi. (C)

161. Starvation Creek to Viento Park. Hikable 1.1-mi section of abandoned Col R Hwy goes E from Starvation Cr Falls (Hike #48). (O)

162. Rainy Lake. Hike past campable lake, keep L at all jcts 1.4 mi to viewpoint atop Green Pt Mtn, gaining 700 ft. Drive as to Mt Defiance S (Hike #49), but continue 1.5 mi on Rd 2820. (C)

163. Indian Mountain. Tr to stunning viewpt of Mt Hood gains 600 ft in 1 mi from Indian Sprs CG. Drive very rough Rd 1310 from Wahtum L (Hike #47) for 3 mi, or hike PCT 3.4 mi from Wahtum L. (C)

MOUNT HOOD - WEST (map on page 123)

164. Horseshoe Ridge. 3-mi climb to views in beargrass mdw gains 1900 ft, joins Zigzag Mtn Tr (see #66). For 11.7-mi loop, return via Cast L Tr (#165). Drive as to Ramona Falls (#61) but turn R off Rd 1825 on Rd 380 past Riley Horse CG for 2.2 mi. (Z)

165. Cast Lake. Ascend ridge 2300 ft in 3.5 mi, keep R for 0.9 mi to lake described in Hike #66. Drive as to Ramona Falls (#61) but turn R off Rd 1825 on Rd 380 past Riley Horse CG for 0.7 mi. (Z)

166. Burnt Lake. Gain 1400 ft in 3 mi to lake with Mt Hood reflection. Continue uphill 1.3 mi to E Zigzag lookout site (see Hike #66). Drive as to Ramona Falls (#61) but at Rd 100 jct keep R for 1.6 mi. (Z)

167. Buck Peak. Pacific Cr Tr follows wooded ridge 7.6 mi N from Lolo Pass to panoramic lookout site. No camping. (Columbia Ranger Dist)

168. Huckleberry Mountain Trail. Park just past the group camp at S end of Lost Lake (see Hike #64), climb 900 ft in 2 mi to Pacific Cr Tr, turn R for 3.5 mi to Buck Pk viewpoint. (HR)

169. Mazama Trail. Delightful path up Cathedral Ridge to timberline mdws on N flank of Mt Hood gains 2200 ft in 3.1 mi, connects with McNeil Point loop (Hike #62) near ponds. Drive as to Cairn Basin (#63) but only go 5.8 mi on Rd 1810, turn R on Rd 1811 for 3 mi. (HR)

170. Flag Mountain. 2.2-mi walk along wooded hill offers views of Mt Hood, gains 900 ft, ends at rd. Drive Hwy 26 to E edge of Rhododendron, turn S on Rd 20 (2620) for 0.8 mi, turn briefly L on Rd 200.

171. Paradise Park Trail. Quieter, steeper route to famous alpine mdws than from Timberline Lodge (#69) gains 3000 ft in 5.8 mi. Drive 4.1 mi E of Rhododendron on Hwy 26, turn L on Rd 2639 for 1.2 mi. (Z)

Mt. Jefferson from Olallie Butte (Hike #200).

Easy
Moderate
Difficult

172. Hidden Lake. Climb 2 mi to small lake with rhodies, continue 3 mi to PCT near Zigzag Canyon (see Hike #69). 2800 ft gain. For 13.2-mi loop, return via Paradise Park Tr (#171). Drive 4.1 mi E of Rhododendron on Hwy 26, turn L on Rd 2639 for 2 mi. (Z)

173. Alpine Ski Trail. Hike 3 mi from Gov't Camp to Timberline Lodge on wildflower-lined, road-like trail gaining 1900 ft. Walk to top of Summit Ski Area's poma lift and head R. (Z)

174. Timberline Trail. Classic 37.6-mi backpack route circles Mt Hood. from Timberline Lodge (#69). Tr connects with Hikes #61-63, 75, 74, 72. Allow 3-5 days. Unbridged crossings of Zigzag, Sandy, Muddy Fork, Eliot Branch, and White Rivers can be dangerous during snowmelt. Water is lower in mornings and after August. (Z, HR)

175. PCT to Timberline Lodge. Start at Barlow Pass on Hwy 35, gain 2000 ft in 5.3 mi amid flowers, views of White R Canyon. (Z)

Easy Moderate Difficult

176. Veda Lake. 1.2-mi tr to lovely 3-acre lake with huckleberries, Mt Hood view, gains 200 ft, loses 400. Drive as to upper trailhead for Devils Pk Hike #60, but only go 3.5 mi on Rd 2613 to Fir Cr CG. (Z)

177. Jackpot Meadows Trail. Park as for Hike #58, descend 1 mi to Salmon R bridge, climb 1.2 mi to Rd 240. Lose 300 ft, gain 800. (Z, BS)

MOUNT HOOD - EAST (map on page 159)

178. Frog Lake Buttes. Hike to Lower Twin L (see #71), but then follow signs 2.2 mi to Cascade crest panorama at Frog L Butte, also accessible by Rd 240. Follow signs for Frog L to complete 6.3-mi loop. (BS)

179. Barlow Butte. 1.8-mi path to wooded knoll begins at PCT trailhead lot just off Hwy 35 at Barlow Pass. Walk S a few yards, veer L across rd, descend 0.4 mi to mdw, turn L, and climb to Mt Hood viewpoint just past butte's overgrown lookout site. Lose 200 ft, gain 1000. (BS)

180. Umbrella Falls. 4.7-mi loop passes 2 falls, gains 600 ft. Take Hwy 35 to Hood R Mdws, drive loop to parking area. Hike Elk Mdw Tr 0.4 mi, go L 2.2 mi to Umbrella Falls, return via Sahalie Falls. (HR)

181. Boulder Lake via Bonney Meadows. Hike downhill (losing 700 ft) for 1.7 mi to cliff-rimmed lake in old-growth forest. Drive Hwy 35 to Bennett Pass, turn S on miserably rocky Rd 3550 for 4.1 mi, turn R on even rougher Rd 4891 for 1.3 mi, turn L to Bonney Mdws CG. (B)

182. Crane Prairie. Visit old growth, scenic mdws, cliff-backed lake on 7.8-mi loop. Park at Bonney Mdws CG as for Hike #181. Hike 1.7 mi to Boulder Lk, then turn left 1 mi (crossing a rd) to Crane Cr Tr, turn L for 1.5 mi to Crane Prairie, go L for 2.4 mi to Rd 4891, go L along rd 1.2 mi to Bonney Mdws CG and car. (B)

183. Zigzag Trail. Switchback up 1200 ft in 1 mi, turn R to Mt Hood viewpt. Park at Polallie Trailhead on Hwy 35 (see Hike #73 map). (HR)

184. Tilly Jane - Polallie Ridge Loop. Hike up 2.6-mi Tilly Jane Ski Tr with Mt Hood views, flowers to 1924 cookhouse at Tilly Jane CG (see Hike #73), turn L to return 2.9 mi via Polallie Ridge Tr. Gain 2000 ft. Drive as to #73, but only go 1.4 mi on Rd 3512 to tr sign on L. (HR)

185. Elk Cove Trail. Ridgecrest route to popular alpine mdws described in Hike #74 is slightly shorter, gaining 1900 ft in 3.5 mi. From Parkdale or Hwy 35, follow signs to Laurence L, turn L on Rd 2840 for 1 mi, turn L on Rd 650 for 1.2 mi. (HR)

186. Pinnacle Trail. Quiet 3.4-mi path to alpine mdws, Timberline Tr on N flank of Mt Hood gains 2200 ft. From Parkdale or Hwy 35, follow signs to Laurence L, turn L on Rd 2840, follow signs to Tr 630. (HR)

187. Surveyors Ridge Trail. Hikable, mostly level 15.4-mi horse/mtn bike path along roaded ridge overlooking Mt Hood includes more than just Bald Butte (Hike #76). To find the southern trailhead, drive Hwy 35 to between mileposts 70 and 71, turn E on Rd 44 for 3.7 mi. (HR)

188. Tygh Creek Trail. Start by creek, climb 1600 ft in 2 mi to wildflowers, views on Pen Point, a knoll in Badger Cr Wilderness. Drive as to Ball Point (Hike #80), but go 1.7 extra mi on Rd 27. (B)

●●|●| **189. Douglas Cabin Trail.** 4-mi tr gains 1200 ft to staffed Flag Pt lookout, view of Badger Cr Wilderness. 9.5-mi loop possible. Drive as to Hike #79, but continue on Rd 2710 an extra 3.8 mi, go L for 3.5 mi. Access rd is gated closed Oct 1 to May 1. (B)

● **190. Mill Creek Falls.** For adventurers only, 2.3-mi path leads up box canyon to stupendous 150-ft falls near The Dalles. Expect poison oak, ticks, rattlesnakes, 8 bridgeless cr crossings. Call The Dalles Watershed at 298-1242 for req'd entry permit, access instructions.

CLACKAMAS FOOTHILLS (map on page 185)

●|● **191. Grouse Point Trail.** Hike to Roaring River on a 1-mi tr that loses 800 ft, then switchback 3.5 mi up a 2800-ft ridge to view at Grouse Pt. Drive as to Hike #84, but after 7.1 mi on Rd 4610, veer R onto Rd 4611 for 6.2 mi to tr on R. (E)

● **192. Dry Ridge.** Steep viewpoint tr from Roaring River CG (on Hwy 224 at milepost 42) switchbacks up 3500 ft in 5.9 mi to Mt Hood view at Grouse Pt's beargrass mdw. Connects with Hikes #90, 191. (E)

● **193. Shining Lake.** Huckleberries, mtn views line 4.8-mi route to brush-rimmed lake. From Frazier Fk CG (see Rock Lks Hike #90), hike gated rd 3.8 mi, descend 600 ft on 1-mi tr to R. (E)　　　　　　　　　　△

●| **194. Cripple Creek Trail.** Convenient, steep path gains 2800 ft in 3.6 mi, crosses 3 logging rds, to Cripple Cr. Continue 1.7 easy mi to Cache Mdw shelter (see Rock Lks Hike #90). Drive 22 mi S of Estacada on Hwy 224 to signed trailhead on L, just after bridge. (E)　　　　　　△

● **195. Anvil Lake.** Level 1.2-mi tr through Blackwolf Mdws to small lake. Drive Hwy 224 through Ripplebrook, turn L on Rd 57 for 7.4 mi, turn L on Rd 58 for 6.2 mi, turn R on Rd 160 for 0.5 mi. (E)　　　　🚶△

●| **196. Welcome Lakes.** 5-mi route gains 2000 ft to small lks in in Bull-of-the-Woods Wilderness. Drive as to Dickey Cr Hike #94 but go straight on Rd 63, follow signs to Elk Lake Tr. (E)　　　　　　△

● **197. Round Lake.** Hike gated rd 0.5 mi through old growth to campground, continue on tr 0.5 mi around lake. Drive as to Hawk Mtn Hike #95, but go straight on Rd 63, follow signs to Round L. (E)　　🚶🚶

● **198. Fish and Si Lakes.** Level 1.2-mi path passes Si L to Fish L in dramatic, forested bowl. Tr continues 1.6 mi across Olallie L Scenic Area to Lower Lake CG. Drive as to Hike #97, but only go 3.4 mi on Rd 4690, turn R on Rd 4691 for 3 mi. (E)　　　　　　🚶🚶

● **199. Russ and Jude Lakes.** Stroll 0.8 mi from Olallie Mdws CG past Brook and Jude Lks to Russ L, view of Olallie Butte. Warm Springs tribal permits req'd for fishing. No camping on Ind Reservation lands. Drive as to Hike #197, but only go 1.4 mi on Rd 4220, veer L to CG. (E)　🚶

● **200. Olallie Butte.** Tr gains 2600 ft in 3.8 mi to views atop NW Oregon's 3rd tallest pk, but final 2.3 mi are on Warm Springs Ind Res, so hiking this part is not encouraged. Drive as to Hike #97, but only go 2.7 mi on Rd 4220, park under 3rd set of powerlines. Tr starts on L of rd. (E)

Index

A

Abraham, Plains of, 56-57, 60-61
Adams Glacier Meadows, 228
Ainsworth State Park, 96
Alder Flat Trail, 196, 225
Alpine Ski Trail, 232
Angels Rest, 92-93
Anthill Trail, 110-111
Anvil Lake, 234
Ape Canyon, 56-57
Ape Cave, 52-53
Audubon Bird Sanctuary, 226
Averill Lake, 214-215

Badger Creek, 176-179
Badger Creek Wilderness, 174-181, 233-234
Badger Lake, 176-177, 179
Badger Peak, 228
Bagby Hot Springs, 206-207
Bald Butte, 172-173
Bald Mountain, 140-143
Ball Point, 180-181
Barlow Butte, 233
Barlow Pass, 162-163, 232
Barlow Trail, 152, 163
Barrett Spur, 144-145, 170
Bays Lake, 222-223
Beacon Rock State Park, 76-77
Bear Lake (Columbia Gorge), 114-115
Bear Lake (Indian Heaven), 66, 68
Benson Plateau, 105, 106-107, 109, 231
Big Hollow Trail, 72-73
Big Huckleberry Mountain, 80-81
Big Slide Lake, 210-211
Bird Creek Meadow, 229
Bird Mountain, 66-67
Blue Lake (Indian Heaven), 68, 70-71
Blue Lake (Mt. St. Helens), 228
Bluegrass Ridge Trail, 164-165
Bluff Mountain Trail, 45, 227
Bonanza Trail, 126-127
Bonney Meadows Campground, 233
Boulder Lakes, 233
Boulder Ridge Trail, 126-127
Boundary Trail, 62-63, 228
Breitenbush Lake, 220-222
Buck Peak, 231
Bull of the Woods lookout, 208-211
Bull of the Woods Wilderness, 204-211, 234
Bunker Hill, 230
Burnt Bridge Creek Greenway, 224

Burnt Lake, 150, 231
Butte Camp, 54, 227

C

Cache Meadow, 202-203
Cairn Basin, 144-145
Camassia Natural Area, 227
Casey Creek Trail, 108-109
Cast Lake, 150-151, 231
Castle Canyon, 148-149
Castle Ridge, 227
Cathedral Ridge, 231
Catherine Creek, 84-85
Champoeg State Park, 38-39, 224
Cheeney Creek, 126-127
Chemeketans, 10
Chetwoot Trail, 116-117
Chinidere Mountain, 110-111
Cigar Lake, 219
Clackamas River, 194-197
Clear Lake, 66, 68
Cloud Cap Campground, 168-171
Cold Springs Trail, 164, 167
Coldwater Peak, 62, 227
Coldwater Ridge Visitor Center, 224
Columbia Wilderness, 102-115, 230-231
Compass Creek Falls, 170-171
Cool Creek Trail, 138-139
Cooper Spur, 168-169
Coopey Falls, 92
Cottonwood, world's largest, 40-41
Council Bluff, 228
Council Crest, 26-27
Craggy Peak, 228
Crane Prairie, 233
Cripple Creek Trail, 202, 234
Crystal Springs Garden, 226
Cultus Lake, 66-67, 69

D

Dark Lake, 216-217
Deadwood Camp, 108
Deep Lake, 66-67
Deschutes River Trail, 120-121
Devils Meadow, 150
Devils Peak lookout, 133, 137, 138-139
Devils Rest, 92, 94-95
Dickey Creek, 210-211
Dickey Lake, 208-209
Divide Trail, 174-177
Dog Mountain, 82-83
Dollar Lake, 170
Double Peaks, 218-219

Douglas Cabin Trail, 234
Douglas Trail, 125, 186
Dry Creek Falls, 230
Dry Creek Trail, 72-73, 230
Dry Ridge, 234
Dryer Creek Meadows, 54-55
Dublin Lake, 102-103

E

Eagle Creek (Clackamas), 186-187

Eagle Creek (Columbia Gorge), 104-105, 107, 111
East Crater Trail, 68-69
East Fork Hood River Trail, 167
East Zigzag Mountain, 150-151
Eden Park, 144-145
Eliot Branch, 170-171
Eliot Glacier, 168-169
Elk Cove, 170-171, 233
Elk Meadows, 164-165
Elk Mountain, 164-165
Elk Rock Island, 226
Elowah Falls, 99, 100-101

F

Fairy Falls, 1, 94-95
Falls Creek, 230
Fanno Creek, 224
Ferry Springs, 120-121
Fir Tree Creek, 134-135
Fish Creek Mountain, 200-201
Fish Lake, 234
Flag Mountain, 231
Flag Point lookout, 174, 234
Forest Park, 18-23
Fort Cascades Trail, 225
Forty-Mile Loop, 18-27, 32, 224, 226
Frazier Fork Campground, 202
Frog Lake Buttes, 162, 233

G

George Rogers Park, 224

Germantown Road, 19
Ghost Lake, 62, 228
Gibson Lake, 220-221
Gifford Peak, 70-71
Gillette Lake, 78-79
Gnarl Ridge, 160, 164-165
Goat Creek, 132-133
Goat Marsh Lake, 227
Goat Mountain, 228
Gordon Canyon, 121
Gorge Trail, 92-103, 106-109
Gorton Creek Trail, 108-109
Gotchen Creek, 228
Government Mineral Springs, 72
Grassy Knoll, 80-81
Green Canyon Way, 130, 132-133
Green Point Mountain, 108, 114, 231
Greenleaf Overlook, 78-79
Greenway Park, 224
Grotto, The, 224
Grouse Point, 202, 234
Gumjuwac Saddle, 174-177
Gunsight Butte, 176-177

H

Hamilton Mountain, 76-77
Hardy Falls, 77
Harmony Falls, 62-63
Harry's Ridge, 62, 227
Hawk Mountain, 212-213
Herman Creek, 108-109
Hickman Cabin, 46
Hidden Lake Trail, 153, 156, 232
Hideaway Lake Campground, 203
High Lake, 200-201
Hole-in-the-Wall Falls, 112-113
Holman Park, 226
Hood River Meadows, 164
Horseshoe Lake, 220-221
Horseshoe Meadow, 229
Horseshoe Ridge (Mt. Hood), 150, 231
Horseshoe Ridge (Siouxon Creek), 46-47
Horsetail Falls, 96-97
Hoyt Arboretum, 24-25
Huckleberries, 44, 66, 69, 70, 110, 134, 139, 144, 155, 162, 191, 199, 204, 212, 214, 217, 219, 220, 223, 229, 230, 233
Huckleberry Mountain (Zigzag), 126-127
Huckleberry Mountain (Lost Lake), 231
Huffman Peak, 46-47
Hunchback Mountain, 132, 136-137, 139

I

Independence Pass Trail, 62-63
Indian Heaven Wilderness, 66-71, 229-230
Indian Henry Campground, 194-195
Indian Mountain, 231

Indian pits, 44-45, 84-85
Indian Point, 108-109
Indian Racetrack, 230

J

Jackpot Meadow, 134, 233
Japanese Garden, 24
Jean Lake, 176
Jefferson Park, 184, 222-223
Jude Lake, 234
Junction Lake, 66, 68-70
June Lake, 228

K

Kinzel Lake, 133, 138-139

L

Lacamas Park, 34-35
Lake Wapiki, 66-67
Lamberson Butte, 164-165
Lancaster Falls, 112-113
Larch Mountain, 88-89, 94-95
Latourell Falls, 90-91, 225
Laurel Hill, 152-153
Lava Canyon, 58-59, 225
Leach Botanical Gardens, 226
Leif Erikson Drive, 18-23
Lemei Lake, 66, 68
Lemei Rock, 66-67
Lenore, Lake, 210-211
Lewis River Trail, 64-65, 225, 228
Linney Creek, 134-135
Little Badger Creek, 180-181
Little Baldy, 45
Little Crater Lake, 158-159, 225
Little Huckleberry Mountain, 230
Little Zigzag Falls, 153, 225
Lolo Pass, 142, 231
Long Lake, 216-217
Lookingglass Lake, 228
Lookout Mountain, 174-175, 176
Loowit Falls (Eagle Creek), 104
Loowit Falls (Mt. St. Helens), 60-61
Loowit Trail, 50-51, 54-57, 60-62, 227
Lost Creek Nature Trail, 225
Lost Lake, 122, 146-147, 225
Lost Lake Butte, 146-147
Lower Falls Creek, 230

M

Macleay Trail, 226
Maple Trail, 20-21
Marquam Nature Park, 12, 26-27
Mary Young Park, 227
Mazamas, 11
McCall Nature Preserve, 86, 118-119
McCord Creek, 100
McGee Creek Trail, 142
McIntyre Ridge, 124-125

McIver State Park, 227
McNeil Point, 142-143, 145
Memaloose Lake, 198-199
Meta Lake, 62, 225
Mill Creek Falls, 229, 234
Mirror Lake, 154-155
Mitchell Point Trail, 112-113
Moffett Creek, 99, 100
Monitor Ridge, 54-55
Monon Lake, 216-217
Mt. Adams Wilderness, 228-229
Mt. Defiance, 112-115
Mt. Hood Wilderness, 140-145, 148-151, 156-157, 164-171, 231-233
Mt. Jefferson Wilderness, 222-223
Mt. Margaret, 62-63
Mt. Mitchell, 48-49
Mt. St. Helens crater, 60-61
Mt. St. Helens summit, 42, 54-55
Mt. St. Helens Volcanic National Monument, 50-63, 227-228
Muddy Fork, 140-141
Muddy River, 56, 58-59
Multnomah Creek, 88-89
Multnomah Falls, 94-95
Munra Point, 100, 230

N

Narrows, The, 194-195
Nesmith Point, 98-99
Nestor Peak lookout, 230
Newton Creek, 164-165
Nick Eaton Ridge, 108-109
North Lake, 114, 231
Norway Pass, 62-63

O

Oak Island, 16-17
Oak Ridge Trail, 172-173
Oaks Bottom Wildlife Refuge, 28-29
Oaks Park amusement park, 28-29
Observation Peak, 72-73
Olallie Butte, 232, 234
Olallie Lake, 216-217, 218-219
Olallie Lake Scenic Area, 214-223
Olallie Meadows Campground, 234
Old Baldy, 186, 188-189
Old Growth Trail, 147, 225
Old-growth forest, 36-37, 51, 56, 65, 72-72, 88-89, 128, 130-132, 146-147, 158, 176, 186-187, 195, 196, 198-199, 206-211, 214, 225, 228, 233, 234
Old Salmon River Trail, 130-131
Oneonta Gorge, 96-97
Oneonta Trail, 88, 96-97
Oval Lake, 174-175
Oxbow Park, 36-37

P

Pacific Crest Trail, 66-71, 74, 78-79, 105, 107, 108-111, 140-142, 156-159, 162-163, 218-223, 225, 228-233
Palisade Point, 174-175
Palmateer Point, 162-163
Pansy Lake, 208-209
Paradise Park, 156-157
Paradise Park Trail, 153, 156-157, 231

Park Ridge, 222-223
Peechuck lookout, 192
Pen Point, 233
Perdition Trail, 94-95
Perham Creek, 116-117
Pinnacle Trail, 170, 233
Pioneer Bridle Trail, 152-153
Pittock Mansion, 24-25, 226
Placid Lake, 229
Plains of Abraham, 56-57, 60-61
Plaza Trail, 126-127, 190-191
Plaza Lake, 190
Polallie Canyon, 168-169
Polallie Ridge Trail, 233
Ponytail Falls, 96-97
Potato Butte, 214-215, 219
Potholes, The, 34-35
Powell Butte, 32-33, 224
Ptarmigan Club, 11
Ptarmigan Trail, 54-55
Punchbowl Falls, 104-105
Pup Creek Falls, 194-195
Pyramid Butte, 222-223

Q

Quartz Creek, 64-65, 228
Quartz Creek Ridge, 228

R

Rainy Lake, 114, 231
Ramona Falls, 140-141
Red Fox Trail, 30

Red Lake Trail, 214-215, 219
Reed College, 226
Rho Ridge Trail, 212-213
Riverside Trail, 196-197
Roaring River, 190, 194, 202, 234
Robin Hood Campground, 167, 175, 177
Rock Creek Falls, 45
Rock Lakes (Indian Heaven), 70-71
Rock Lakes (Clackamas), 202-203
Rock of Ages Ridge, 96-97
Rockingchair Creek, 22-23
Rodney Falls, 76-77
Rogers Park, 224
Rooster Rock, 192-193
Round Lake (Camas), 34
Round Lake (Clackamas), 213, 234
Round-the-Mountain Trail, 229
Rowena Plateau, 86, 118-119
Ruckel Creek, 106-107
Ruckel Ridge, 104, 106-107
Ruddy Hill, 220-221
Rudolph Spur, 230
Russ Lake, 234
Russell Lake, 222-223

S

Sacajawea Rock, 78-79
Sahalie Tyee Lake, 70
Salmon Butte, 128-129
Salmon-Huckleberry Wilderness, 124-139, 186-191, 233
Salmon Mountain, 190-191
Salmon River, 126-127, 130-135
Sandy River, 36-37, 140-141
Sandy River Delta, 227
Sauvie Island, 14-17, 226
Sawtooth Mountain, 229
School Canyon Trail, 180-181
Scout Lake, 222-223
Serene Lake, 202-203
Sheep Canyon, 50-51
Sheep Lake, 214-215
Sheepshead Rock, 190-191
Shellrock Lake, 202-203
Shellrock Mountain, 231
Sherars Bridge, 182-183
Sherrard Point, 88-89
Shining Lake, 202, 234
Shoestring Glacier, 57
Si Lake, 234
Sierra Club, 11
Silcox Hut, 156-157
Silver King Lake, 204-207
Silver Star Mountain, 44-45, 227
Siouxon Creek, 46-47
Siouxon Peak, 46-47, 227

Sister Rocks, 72-73
Sleeping Beauty Mountain, 229
Smith Creek, 58-59
Soda Peaks Lake, 72, 230
South Breitenbush Trail, 222-223
South Fork Mountain, 198-199
Spirit Lake, 62-63
Squaw Mountain, 188-189, 190
St. Helens Lake, 62
Star Way, 227
Starvation Creek Falls, 112-113, 231
Starvation Ridge, 112-113
Steamboat Mountain, 229
Stebbins Creek, 74-75
Strawberry Mountain, 228
Sturgeon Lake, 16
Sturgeon Rock, 45
Surveyors Ridge Trail, 172-173, 233

T

Table Mountain, 78-79
Table Rock, 192-193
Tamanawas Falls, 166-167
Tanner Butte Trail, 102-103
Tanner Creek, 100, 103
Tarbell Trail, 45, 227
Tephra's Pinnacle, 62-63
Terwilliger Bike Path, 226
Thomas Lake, 70-71
Three Corner Rock, 74-75
Tilly Jane Campground, 168-169, 233
Tilly Jane Ski Trail, 233
Timber Lake, 219
Timberline Lodge, 156-157, 232
Timberline Trail, 140-145, 156-157, 164-165, 168-171, 232
Timothy Lake, 158-159, 225
Tom Dick & Harry Mountain, 154-155
Tom McCall Preserve, 86, 118-119
Tombstone Lake, 70
Top Lake, 218-219
Tomlike Mountain, 110-111
Top Spur Trail, 142
Toutle River, South Fork, 50
Trail of Two Forests, 224\
Trails Club, 11
Trapper Creek, 72-73
Trillium Lake, 225
Trillium Trail, 30, 224
Triple Falls, 96-97
Truman Trail, 60-62
Tryon Creek State Park, 30-31
Tunnel Falls, 104-105
Twin Lakes, 162-163
Twin Springs Campground, 190
Tygh Creek Trail, 233

Tygh Valley Falls, 182-183

U

Umbrella Falls, 164, 233
Upper Falls Creek, 230
Upper Lake, 219, 220-221

V

Veda Lake, 233
Vietnam Veteran Memorial, 24
Virginia Lake, 226
Vista Ridge, 144-145

W

Wahclella Falls, 100-101
Wahkeena Falls, 93, 94-95, 225
Wahtum Lake, 105, 109, 110-111
Wapiki Lake, 66-67
Warren Lake, 112-113
Warrior Rock, 14-15
Washington Park, 24-25
Wauna Point, 102-103
Wauna Viewpoint, 102-103
Wauneka Point, 100
Weigle Hill, 230
Welcome Lakes, 208, 210, 234
West Zigzag Mountain, 148-149, 151
Wheatland Ferry, 40-41
Whetstone Mountain, 204-205
White River Canyon, 156-157, 232
White River Falls, 182-183
Whitewater Trail, 223
Wildcat Creek Falls, 46-47
Wildcat Mountain, 124-125
Wildwood Recreation Site, 126-127
Wildwood Trail, 18-25, 226
Willamette Greenway Park, 226
Willamette Mission Park, 40-41, 224
Wind Lake, 154
Wind Mountain, 82-83
Windy Pass, 60-61
Windy Ridge Viewpoint, 60, 62-63
World Forestry Center, 24-25
Wright Meadow, 64
Wy'East Basin, 144-145, 170
Wyeth Trail, 231
Wygant Trail, 116-117

Y

Yacolt Burn, 44
Yeon State Park, 98-101
Yocum Falls, 154
Yocum Ridge, 140-141
Young Park, 227

Z

Zigzag Canyon, 156-157
Zigzag Mountain, 148-151
Zigzag Trail, 167, 233

About the Author

A native of Oregon, William L. Sullivan began hiking at the age of 5 and has been exploring new trails ever since. At 17 he left high school to study at remote Deep Springs College in the California desert, where his duties included milking cows by hand. He went on to earn a B.A. in English from Cornell University and an M.A. in German from the University of Oregon. He and his wife Janell Sorensen bicycled 3000 miles through Europe, studied at Heidelberg University, and built a log cabin by hand on Oregon's Siletz River.

In 1985 Sullivan set out to investigate Oregon's wilderness by backpacking 1,300 miles from the state's westernmost shore at Cape Blanco to Oregon's easternmost point in Hells Canyon. His journal of that adventure, published in 1987 as *Listening for Coyote*, was a finalist for the Oregon Book Award in creative nonfiction. Since then he has authored *Exploring Oregon's Wild Areas* and *100 Hikes in the Central Oregon Cascades*. He and Janell live in Eugene with their children Karen and Ian.